Universalists and Unitarians in America

Universalists and Unitarians in America

A People's History

John A. Buehrens

Skinner House Books
Boston

Printed in the United States

Cover and text design by Suzanne Morgan

print ISBN: 978-1-55896-612-3
eBook ISBN: 978-1-55896-613-0

6 5 4 3 2 1
14 13 12 11

Photo credits:
We gratefully acknowledge permission to reprint the following photographs:
Elizabeth Palmer Peabody, courtesy of Concord Free Public Library, Concord,
Massachusetts; Caroline Dall, courtesy of Massachusetts Historical Society, Bos-
ton; Arlington Street Church Anti-war Rally, courtesy of Arlington Street Church,
Boston; Thomas Whittemore, James Luther Adams, Frederick May Eliot, Quillen
Shinn, and Abner Kneeland, courtesy of Andover-Harvard Theological Library,
Cambridge, Massachusetts.

All Bible passages are quoted from the King James Version.

Library of Congress Cataloging-in-Publication Data

Buehrens, John A., 1947-
  Universalists and Unitarians in America : a people's history / John A. Buehrens.
    p. cm.
  Includes bibliographical references and index.
  ISBN 978-1-55896-612-3 (pbk. : alk. paper)—ISBN 978-1-55896-613-0
(ebook)
  1. Unitarian Universalist Association—History. 2. United States—Church
history. I. Title.
  BX9833.B84 2011
  289.1'73--dc22
                                2010045752

Contents

Introduction   ix

American Independence and the Emergence of Liberal Religion, 1770–1815

The Multiple Origins of Universalism in America   3

Early Unitarianism in America   15

The Age of Jacksonian Democracy, 1815–1848

Universalism in the Second Great Awakening   31

Unitarians and the American Renaissance   45

The Second American Revolution, 1848–1870

Universalism Seeks Unity of the Spirit   67

Unitarians from Reform to Civil War   81

The Last "Gilded Age" of Inequality, 1870–1905

Universalism's Liberal Mission   97

Unitarian Parsonages Move West   109

The Progressive Era, 1905–1935

Unitarian Skepticism and Social Reform   125

Universalism and Modernity   139

Liberal Religion and Humanism, 1935–1960
The Unitarian Renaissance   151
Universalist Humanism and Unitarian
    Universalist Consolidation   167

The Unitarian Universalist Association, 1961–2011
The Marriage During the First Twenty Years   181
The UUA Grows Stronger   195

Further Reading   213
Notes   217
Index   249

Dedicated to the memory of
Rev. Dr. Charles A. Howe (1922–2010),
historian of Universalism and colleague, and
Professor C. Conrad Wright (1919–2011),
historian of Unitarianism and teacher,
and to the work and witness of
Ruth Wilson Sutro,
historian of First Parish in Needham,
Unitarian Universalist,
and to the countless men and women who, like them,
have helped to preserve, recover, and pass on
the stories of human beings devoted to
the living tradition that is
Unitarian Universalism.

Introduction

Religion is people. It may express itself as ideas. It may form in groups and institutions. Leaders may develop. But before everything else, religion is people.

Universalists and Unitarians have a rich history in America. Their numbers have included the known and the unknown, the remembered and the forgotten. Religious groups are often named not by themselves but by their critics—some for their founders, some for distinctive practices, some for their organizational structure. Unitarians and Universalists, however, take their names from *ideas*. No wonder their history is often told as intellectual history.

Universalists did not believe that a loving God would predestine human beings to an eternal hell. They affirmed an inclusive, universal plan of salvation. Unitarians set aside the idea of a Trinity. They affirmed first the unity of God and then the unity of humankind. Many Universalists were unitarian in their theology, but not all. Many Unitarians were universalist in their theology, but not all. Both ideas have roots that predate their emergence in America. Courageous dissenters from early Christian orthodoxy may be associated with them. The use of these terms as applied to groups, however, generally came only after the European Reformation.[1]

Here in America, most early Universalists and Unitarians developed their religious institutions without much imported influence. Their movements were "American originals," arising independently in the era of American independence itself.[2] They arose among people reacting against Puritan Calvinism, although in different social contexts. Both sought more humanistic expressions of Christianity. Over time, both became even more inclusive. Both also produced notable leaders and had a disproportionately large influence on American culture and public life, despite never becoming institutionally large themselves.

Most previous histories have treated American Universalism and Unitarianism separately.[3] They have also tended to emphasize intellectual or institutional history. This short survey deals with both Universalists and Unitarians in parallel development. It emphasizes the lives of people, because "lived religion" in the past can best be approached through biography. It does not ignore intellectual and institutional developments and their leaders. But it pays attention to some Unitarians and Universalists who did not become well known. Since neither group was ever large, but each produced more than its share of American notables, both groups have taken great pride in their most famous members. Yet the history of Universalists and Unitarians in America is more than a list of luminaries. Just as we look up at the sky and often see only the brightest stars, neglecting the patterns formed among those of second and third orders of magnitude, so we have sometimes overlooked some of the most interesting people in our past.

Historians themselves have come to question the "great man" theory of history. Especially in recent decades, feminist historians have done a great deal to recover the stories of women who were often more important in the unfolding of events than dominant narratives suggest. Social historians have done the same with marginalized groups and individuals. Cultural historians and authors of biographical studies have sought new insights into the ways in which contextual factors influenced inner life, and *vice versa*. Many such studies are scattered in books, papers, journals, and monographs read largely by other historians and specialists. Universalists and Unitarians have been extensively re-studied in this way. Not many of their spiritual heirs know this as yet, however. Dominant narratives about our history also need some correction.

Introduction

This book attempts to make creative use of at least some of the new historical studies and biographical resources in order to make them better known to today's Unitarian Universalists. The subtitle is an obvious tribute to the late historian Howard Zinn (1922–2010). His well-known *People's History of the United States* tried to show Americans how to look through some of the self-congratulatory myths about our national history. Aware that history is notoriously written by the winners of its struggles, Zinn called attention to people and dissenting movements that may not have succeeded fully in their time, but that tried, in the words of Dr. Martin Luther King Jr., to help America "live up to the full meaning of its creed." In a similar fashion, it is important for Unitarian Universalists today to go beyond the standard litanies of great men and women affiliated with us through the years. This book's approach may not precisely parallel Zinn's, but popular understanding of our spiritual forebears should at least catch up with current scholarship. And it also seems appropriate to disturb a few of our own myths and stereotypes.

This volume appears in conjunction with the fiftieth anniversary of the consolidation of the Universalist Church of America (UCA) with the American Unitarian Association (AUA) in May, 1961, forming the Unitarian Universalist Association of Congregations (UUA). The occasion raises a rather obvious question: *Why did it take them so long?* We must not arrive at even tentative answers using simplistic stereotypes of the two sides of the now-blended family. The dynamics within and between them deserve to be better understood. Our contemporary struggles to fulfill our promise as a religious movement and to do a better job of influencing the culture around us toward justice need a better understanding of struggles in the past. We have not always been realistic about our own powers. After all, as philosopher George Santayana (whose mother was a Boston Unitarian) once put it: "Those who cannot remember the past are condemned to repeat it."[4]

Many Unitarian Universalists can recite some of the more prominent names among our forebears: Joseph Priestley and

Famous UUs

John Murray, John Adams and Thomas Jefferson, William Ellery Channing and Hosea Ballou, Ralph Waldo Emerson and Theodore Parker, Margaret Fuller and Clara Barton, Susan B. Anthony and Whitney Young. The better-informed can go on beyond the statesmen, writers, clerics, and reformers to list some of our many poets, physicians, scientists, musicians, naturalists, teachers, and organizers. There are new and valuable online resources available to help.[5]

Many of the early stories will seem geographically constricted. American Universalism and Unitarianism both began in New England. Yet an important aim of this volume is to entice readers to become interested in the lives of forebears beyond the famous New Englanders and to investigate their own local origins and history.

Each of the twelve chapters leading up to the consolidation of the two denominations will delve into the lives of Unitarians or Universalists who were not necessarily the most famous of their era, but whose experiences help to illustrate the texture of lived religion in their time or to make connections between important leaders and developments. Here you will meet such people as the Davis brothers of Oxford, Massachusetts, who helped with the first Universalist Convention; Hannah Adams, an impoverished and unmarried Unitarian woman from nearby Medfield, who published the first effort in English at a comprehensive treatment of denominations and religions; Abner Kneeland, the sometime-Universalist who was the last American jailed for blasphemy; Elizabeth Peabody, who bridged between Channing's Unitarianism and the Transcendentalists; Thomas Whittemore, the Universalist minister who was also a banker and railway president; Caroline Healey Dall, reformer, diarist, and sometime wife to a Unitarian missionary to India; the Universalist Washburn brothers of Livermore, Maine, who all became "men of mark"; the women of the Eliot family, ubiquitous in Unitarian leadership, of whom historian Cynthia Grant Tucker wrote in *No Silent Witness*; Owen D. Young, the Universalist who headed General Electric (GE) and the Radio Corporation of America (RCA), yet favored workers' rights;

Clinton Lee Scott, the Universalist humanist whose *Humiliati* disciples worked for consolidation; and Munroe Husbands, the Unitarian layman behind the founding of over five hundred Unitarian fellowships, many of which survive.

The final two chapters take a rather different form from the earlier twelve, discussing the first five decades of consolidated Unitarian Universalism. Any such recent "history"—especially from someone who lived through much of that era as a minister and denominational leader—is inherently a matter of personal perspective. Those chapters include some individual people, places, and personalities active in the formation of the new denomination and in some of its early crises. Yet, as I approach the present era I emphasize my predecessors and successors in the UUA presidency dealing with the broader cultural trends and institutional issues that Unitarians Universalists have encountered in recent decades. Like the celebration of the fiftieth anniversary of the UUA itself, which I have had the honor to chair, the goal of this volume is not self-congratulation, but rather deeper spiritual self-understanding, in order that we as a religious people—who now call ourselves Unitarian Universalists—may continue to contribute generously to the shaping of the larger history in which we participate.

American Independence and the Emergence of Liberal Religion

1770
1815

The Multiple Origins of Universalism in America

The idea of universal salvation, rather than salvation for just the chosen, is an old one. Among Christians, it can be claimed that either Paul or Jesus was "the first Universalist." Paul, who evangelized the Gentiles, spread the good news of God's love in Christ because he believed that it belonged not only to "the chosen people"—to Jews like himself—but to everyone. This may have simply kept faith with a change in the spiritual Master he never knew in the flesh. Jesus, according to the gospels, seems to have begun with a message aimed at his fellow Jews. Along the way he met people considered "other"—sinners, outsiders, like the Syro-Phoenician woman (Mark 7:25–30; Matthew 15:21–28) or the Samaritan woman at the well (John 4). All these he offered a place in the Commonwealth of God.

It is hard for modern readers to understand the deep fear of being excluded from heaven. Under the influence of the Calvinist revivalism of the "Great Awakening" in the eighteenth century, many good people trembled over the idea of being sent to hell and being deprived of communion with God and with their deceased loved ones. When they argued over whether a loving God would send people to an eternal hell, they argued over competing interpretations of the Bible.

American Universalists have long claimed as their founder an Englishman, John Murray (1741–1815)—with a dramatic story of almost biblical character. Here is a short version: In England Murray was an evangelical preacher with a Calvinist theology. He heard of a sect led by one John Relly, whose 1759 book, *Union: or a treatise of consanguinity and affinity between Christ and his church*, said that if all had sinned in Adam, *all* had been saved in Christ— not just the predestined elect. Although Murray initially intended to refute Relly, he instead became convinced of universal salvation and began to preach it himself. Ostracized by fellow evangelicals, he next suffered several personal tragedies. When his only child died, followed by his wife, he was unable to pay their medical bills and went to debtors' prison. Upon release, he vowed never to preach again and left to start a new life in America.

In July 1770, the ship carrying John Murray ran aground at Barnegat Bay, New Jersey, and he went ashore to ask for help. He met Thomas Potter (1689–1777), a local farmer who had a small chapel on his farm at Good Luck Point. Awaiting a minister who would declare a gospel of universal salvation, Potter had built the chapel ten years earlier. When Murray admitted having once preached just such a message, Potter asked him to stay and preach. Murray agreed to do so as long as his ship didn't sail. The wind did not change, and Murray delivered his sermon, renewing his love of preaching. After finally landing in New York, he resumed preaching as an evangelist, though without overemphasizing his universalist convictions.[6]

In 1774, Murray heard of a group in Gloucester, Massachusetts, led by the wealthy merchant Winthrop Sargent, who had also read Relly's *Union*. With them he could speak far more freely. Settling among them, he led Gloucester's relief efforts for the poor during the Revolution, then served as chaplain to General Nathaniel Greene's Rhode Island Brigade in the Continental Army. In 1779 he helped to organize the Independent Christian Church in Gloucester, serving as its pastor. Among the eighty-five charter members, including freed African American Gloster Dalton, was Judith Sargent Stevens, Winthrop Sargent's married daughter. The congregation was soon engaged in a legal battle over being taxed to support the local orthodox parish church and its ministry. Hearing of potential allies among inland Universalists, Murray traveled to Oxford and advised them to incorporate as well.

In 1782 Judith Sargent Stevens anonymously published a Universalist catechism. She also began to write and publish newspaper essays under the pen name "Constantia." She needed to stay constant in the face of two challenges. Her husband, John Stevens, had been ruined financially when the Revolution halted his shipping business. He sailed to the West Indies to avoid his creditors and try to recoup his fortune, but died there in 1786. The second challenge was the legal battle being faced by the Universalists and their minister. At one point John Murray was threatened with prosecution for conducting weddings without being a recognized minister. He found it prudent to return to England. Just before departing, he wrote to Judith Sargent Stevens, proposing marriage. She accepted, Murray returned, and they married.

The legal victory of the Gloucester Universalists in gaining exemption from parish taxes was an important advance toward church-state separation. John Murray's speaking and writing helped to extend the influence of Universalism. Constantia published a pioneering two-part essay, "On the Equality of the Sexes," in the *Massachusetts Magazine* (1790) and began to write and publish poetry. She was raising two daughters adopted during her early marriage, and a third daughter fathered by John Murray. They moved into Boston when John was called to minister to the Universalists in the state's capital. When Boston's ban on theatrical entertainments ended in 1795, Judith became America's first female playwright. Under her new name, Judith Sargent Murray, a book of essays entitled *The Gleaner* appeared, in which a male character declared that

> the idea of the incapability of women is . . . totally inadmissible. . . . To argue against facts is indeed contending with both wind and tide; and, borne down by accumulating examples, conviction of the utility of the present plans will pervade the public mind, and not a dissenting voice will be heard.[7]

She also founded a school for young women on Dorchester's Meetinghouse Hill.

After John Murray's stroke ended his preaching career in 1809, Judith tried to support the two of them, publishing her own work as well as three volumes of his *Letters and Sketches of Sermons*, which sold poorly. Modern readers may be surprised to learn that John Murray was not honored among his contemporary Universalists as a founder. Most recognized that their own version of Universalism was different from that of Relly and Murray. When John died in 1815, Judith moved to Natchez, Mississippi, to live with a married daughter.[8]

When later Universalists revived the dramatic story of John Murray arriving in America and preaching the inclusive gospel of Universalism, they tended to gloss over certain aspects of the story itself: how Thomas Potter had *already* embraced the idea of universal salvation before Murray arrived, and how Murray himself visited Universalist groups in inland New England that he had clearly *not* founded. They also minimized Judith's part in the story and the differences that she had clearly seen between Murray and other Universalists. They ignored that fact that John Murray preached a Trinitarian form of Universalism, with a rather "high" Christology. They emphasized that Revolutionary leaders like General Greene and George Washington retained and even commended Murray as a Continental Army chaplain in spite of his "heresy." By marrying into the merchant class, by helping early Universalists incorporate and win exemption from parish taxes, and by bringing Universalism to the state capital in Boston, Murray had helped Universalism gain acceptance.

All of this later made him Universalism's best candidate for mythic status as early hero and founder. Universalism in America, however, actually had multiple origins and many founders. Lifting up John Murray to singular and legendary status helped later Universalists gloss over growing theological differences among themselves and a truth they later found somewhat uncomfortable: that the earliest Universalists in America were mostly pious, back-country people, largely Baptists. The earliest, but later a minority, were in the Mid-Atlantic region. Thomas Potter was a deeply devout Baptist who was also influenced by Quakers. He may also have known the German "Dunkers" (Baptists) in Pennsylvania, whose pietism emphasized a general atonement rather than a particular predestination of a few to salvation and most others to perdition.[9] The Dunkers' influence had been spread by the work of the early Universalist physician and evangelist Dr. George de Benneville (1703–1793), whose story is even more dramatic than Murray's.[10]

De Benneville was born in London to privileged French Protestant refugees. Queen Anne of England was his godmother. As a youth he was serving as a midshipman in the Royal Navy when "Barbary" pirates overtook the ship off the coast of North Africa. George was so well-treated by his Muslim captors that he described them as "more Christian" than he would have been. He had a vision of himself first in hellfire as "the chief of sinners," but then also as Christ-forgiven, noting "I could not have a doubt but the whole world would be saved by the same power." When he tried to test that proposition by preaching universalism among Roman Catholics in France, he was arrested for spreading heresy and escaped execution only through a last minute reprieve.

De Benneville next lived among radical Protestant pietists in Germany, where he began training as a physician. At one point he became so ill himself that he was assumed to be dead. When he arose from his coffin and from another vision—which called him to preach "the universal and everlasting gospel of boundless, universal love for the entire human race"—de Benneville was again called a public danger and briefly imprisoned.

In 1741 he emigrated with other German pietists to Pennsylvania and arranged for an English translation of *The Everlasting Gospel* (1753) by German universalist minister Paul Siegvolk (George Klein-Nicolai). During the American Revolution he treated the wounded of both sides after the Battle of Germantown (1777), even burying two British soldiers in his own family plot. Ecumenical in spirit, Dr. de Benneville saw

our [universalist] faith [as] essentially the combined faith
of all Christians. As no church is pure in all things, so none
can be found that does not contain some truth. Glorious
truths are found in every church and religion under the
sun. And this glorious chain of truths . . . we believe will
someday unite all of them into one form of love. [11]

In 1781 de Benneville encountered Elhanan Winchester (1751–
1797), a New England-born Baptist revivalist who was then pastor
to Philadelphia's First Baptist Church. Winchester had read both
The Everlasting Gospel and The Restitution of All Things (1761) by
the English universalist Sir George Stonehouse. After encountering
de Benneville, he began preaching "universal restoration," causing
a split in his congregation. Winchester's "Universal Baptists" held
their services in the Hall of the University of Pennsylvania. Among
his hearers there were two other physicians—Dr. John Redman, first
president of Philadelphia's College of Physicians, and Dr. Benjamin
Rush (1745–1813), the best-connected and most famous Universalist of the Revolutionary era.[12] Rush served in the Continental
Congress and signed the Declaration of Independence along with
Jefferson and Adams, both of whom became correspondents and
friends. He was a multi-faceted reformer, concerned about public health, mental illness, prisons, and the abolition of slavery, but
he was not a religious organizer. From 1781 to 1787 Winchester
and de Benneville made evangelical journeys together through the
middle states. John Murray heard of their work and came to Philadelphia to visit them in 1784. When the first Universalist Convention was held in the small hill-country farming village of Oxford,
Massachusetts, in 1785, Winchester served as the moderator.

While a rural village may seem like an odd place for a convention, Universalism had emerged quite spontaneously in hill-
country New England and was already stronger and spreading
faster there than in either the mid-Atlantic states or the towns
and cities of the New England seacoast. The majority of early Universalists were New England hill-country Baptists. The extended

Davis family led the host group of Oxford Universalists. In many ways they were more characteristic of Universalists of the era than either Elhanan Winchester and his Philadelphia flock or John and Judith Sargent Murray's congregation in Gloucester.

During the 1770s, rural New England experienced a good deal of religious revivalism, which became known as the "New Light Stir." Many hill-country towns such as Oxford had parish churches of the congregational Standing Order by which Puritans had sought to purify the Church of England in New England. But this system required college-educated clergy. By the time of the Revolution, the inability of hill-country towns to regularly pay, attract, or retain the required college-educated congregational clergy resulted in lengthy pulpit vacancies and disputes over paying parish taxes for ministerial salaries and meetinghouse upkeep. Laypeople had to wrestle with the scriptures on their own, often persuading one another of radical new interpretations that differed markedly from established Calvinist doctrine about predestination. This was especially true among those who identified neither with the church establishment nor with the village elite.[13]

The Davis brothers of Oxford were a good case in point.[14] Samuel Davis, Jr. (1746–1817), was known throughout the area as a champion wrestler. His brother Elijah Davis (1750–1842) was noted for his memory of scripture, and both had wrestled with its interpretation. Early in the Revolutionary War they received visits from two of their many cousins. Dr. Isaac Davis (1716–1777), of Somers, Connecticut, had written a proto-universalist tract, *What Love Jesus Christ Has for Sinners*. The other cousin was Caleb Rich (1750–1821), who became the leading Universalist evangelist of the New England hill country by the end of the Revolution. Rich had served in the militia at Lexington. When he came to Oxford he hired a substitute to take his place. Three of the Davis brothers married Rich's sisters.

The Davis group in Oxford soon left the parish church, resisted church taxes, and refused to serve in the militia. Other cousins, Ebenezer and Deborah Davis of nearby Charlton, Massachusetts, were pillars of a Baptist church there—until they were expelled for universalism in 1779. The Davis group called themselves "Friends," but they were not Quakers. Other radical sects that also arose during the Revolution—Shakers and Freewill Baptists— spread similarly, through what has been called "clan conversion." Three sons of Benjamin Davis of Oxford all married daughters of Stephen Streeter, whose brother, Adam Streeter, was soon, like Rich, a regional preacher of universal salvation.

In 1784, John Murray, looking for allies in the struggle of his Gloucester Universalists for tax exemption, visited Oxford. Guided by him, the Davis group formed an "Independent Christian Society, commonly called Universalists," on the Gloucester model. The next year, they hosted the first Universalist Convention. Murray attended; Winchester moderated. The bills were paid largely by Ebenezer Davis, who had made his fortune supplying the Continental Army with meat. Of the 130 members of the host congregation, Davis was the surname of thirty-five.

The Universalists tried organizing themselves further at a 1790 meeting in Philadelphia. Few Universalists came from inland New England, however, though the movement was now spreading up the Connecticut River valley into Vermont, New Hampshire, and Maine. Universalists gathered at Oxford again in 1793, with seventy-one congregations represented. Later Universalists often looked back on this occasion as the founding date of the movement, because it produced a New England Universalist Convention with regular meetings and practices.

At the 1794 meeting, also held in Oxford, a young convert of Caleb Rich preached. Hosea Ballou, then twenty-three, was so eloquent that Elhanan Winchester spontaneously and dramatically ordained him to the ministry, right then and there. No bishop was needed, no seminary, presbytery, nor even a covenanted church body—just the baptism of the Holy Spirit, recognized by other ministers of the gospel as a calling to spread the good news. This was characteristic of early Universalism, which embraced some significant differences in doctrine right from the start.

Rich and Ballou were more radical than either John Murray or Elhanan Winchester. Murray, like John Relly, was a Trinitarian who believed that it was Christ who had saved all humanity. Winchester believed that sinners would be given due chastisement after death, but could be ultimately assured of universal restoration. Ballou, on the other hand, like Caleb Rich, believed that sin was punished largely in this life and found it hard to believe that an infinitely good God would require any further punishment in the next. With such differences came a need to express some common affirmations. At the Universalist Convention of 1803, in Winchester, New Hampshire, participants adopted a profession of faith:

Article I. We believe that the Holy Scriptures of the Old and New Testament contain a revelation of the character of God, and of the duty, interest and final destination of mankind.

Article II. We believe that there is one God, whose nature is Love, revealed in one Lord Jesus Christ, by one Holy Spirit of Grace, who will finally restore the whole family of mankind to holiness and happiness.

Article III. We believe that holiness and true happiness are inseparably connected, and that believers ought to be careful to maintain order and practice good works; for these things are good and profitable unto men.

Ballou did not like the statement. He had been influenced by another hill-country radical, Vermont's Ethan Allen, who was not a Bible-believer at all, but rather a rationalist and a deist. Ballou read Allen's *Reason the Only Oracle of Man* (1784) and concluded that Allen was wrong to reject the authority of the Bible, but right that even the Bible should be read using the light of our God-given reason.

In his 1805 *Treatise on Atonement*, Ballou did just that. Often using down-to-earth country stories, he argued not only that sin was punished in this life, not the next, but also that infinite punishment after death was inconsistent with the nature of a loving God. He also rejected the doctrine of the Trinity as illogical and interpreted Jesus as simply *the* definitive human example of how God intends for everyone to achieve oneness with the divine. So Ballou held to a unitarian form of Universalism. As we will see, however, that did not gain him any acceptance among the Harvard-educated clergy of the still-emerging Unitarian movement, even after he became pastor of the Second Universalist Society in Boston in 1817.

By 1815 there were some 125 Universalist congregations. They were mostly in rural New England, but spreading also into upstate New York and out to the Middle West, as New Englanders left for more promising farmland or to become frontier or urban entrepreneurs. Many were ambitious, like Ebenezer Davis. Their faith, a product of the Revolution, was that of strivers and the upwardly mobile. As historian Gordon S. Wood noted, "At the heart of the Revolution lay the assumption that people were not born to be what they might become."[15]

Early Universalists were not so much poor or from the urban working class as they were from "the middling sort" of prosperous farmers, artisans, entrepreneurs, and tradesmen—with a notable number of physicians, as we have seen. So it is a mistake to over-emphasize their contrast with early Unitarians in economic terms. Geography and education were probably more important distinguishing characteristics. Universalism grew up in rural, inland New England. Unitarianism developed more in the seacoast towns, especially Boston, where agitation against British taxation and control of trade began the Revolution. To be sure, Universalists had relatively few wealthy merchant-class families like the one that John Murray married into. Unitarians in the seacoast towns had far more, but their congregations, being more urban, sometimes also included many poor people who were actually far worse off economically than a typical farmer.

Early Universalist clergy were almost entirely self-educated, and not college graduates. Yet they were skilled at debate, either because self-taught people who liked a good argument were drawn to Universalism, or because they acquired these skills while frequently defending their positions against critics. Banding together amid controversy and in rejection of the Standing Order churches (to which early Unitarians still belonged), the Universalists developed the characteristics of a denomination far earlier than the Unitarians did—complete with regional conventions, preaching circuits, tracts to distribute, and an astonishing proliferation of Universalist newspapers and other publications.

Early Universalists were strongly committed to the authority of the Bible, yet they were both liberal and evangelical in spirit. A well-known summary of their message is often attributed to John Murray, but in fact comes from a much later time. In 1950 a Universalist professor of preaching, Alfred Storer Cole, depicted the *zeitgeist* of the Revolutionary era as telling Murray:

> Go out into the highways and by-ways of America, your new country. Give the people, blanketed with a decaying and crumbling Calvinism, something of your new vision. You may possess only a small light but uncover it, let it shine, use it in order to bring more light and understanding to the hearts and minds of men. Give them, not Hell, but hope and courage. Do not push them deeper into their theological despair, but preach the kindness and everlasting love of God.[16]

This was a message heard not just by one, but by many founders of Universalism.

Early Unitarianism in America

It is interesting that American Universalists, as upwardly mobile strivers, in telling their myth of origin often emphasized the English immigrant John Murray, who married well here, and downplayed their deeper origins among back-country Baptists. From the beginning their story tells of the influence of books, travelers, immigrants, and distinguished visitors—yet much of their development was actually at the grass-roots level. American Unitarians, by contrast, have often insisted on describing their own origins in the Revolutionary era as "almost entirely indigenous":[17] no external, foreign help required. Or so they told themselves. Actually, American Unitarianism had two intertwined origins—one native, the other English. Memory of the latter was often actively suppressed for patriotic and ideological reasons.

Indigenous Unitarians, rather than separating from established congregational churches, as the early Universalists did, succeeded in taking over some of the most prominent, usually from within. This occurred particularly in and around Boston. It represented a culmination of a gradual liberalization in New England theology, aided by the semi-democracy of congregational governance—although its actual practice still privileged those members with wealth. Well before the Revolution the prosperous merchant class and their clergy rejected the revivalism of the Great Awakening in the mid-eighteenth century and its echo in the "New Light Stir." Such religious enthusiasm threatened their Enlightenment rationality, their cultural authority, and suggested that perhaps their own wealth might be the result of sinful exploitation rather than their own hard work.

One leader was Charles Chauncey (1705–1787), minister of Boston's First Church. Chauncey's *Seasonable Thoughts on the State of Religion in New England* (1743) represented American religious liberalism's first articulate response to the emotionalism, fear-mongering, and emphasis on individual (rather than social) salvation in evangelical revivalism.[18] Another was Jonathan Mayhew (1720–1766), minister of Boston's West Church, who challenged the pretensions of the British crown to be the "Higher Power" and who, like Chauncey, held an early form of unitarian universalist theology. They were not alone. New England clergy nearer to the seacoast, in touch with the British Enlightenment through both commerce and intellectual exchange, began to soften their Calvinist convictions.

Like Ebenezer Gay (1696–1786), minister of First Parish in Hingham for over sixty years, these ministers no longer preached classic Calvinism. The Dutch Calvinists had summarized that doctrine as Total depravity, Unconditional election, Limited atonement, Irresistible grace, and the Perseverance of the saints—the formula known as TULIP, or the Five Points of Calvinism. Jacobus Arminius, the Dutch opponent of this formula, was the spiritual forebear of Gay, Chauncey, and Mayhew, even if they did not cite him directly. They believed in human free will in the pursuit of redemption. Such "Arminian" or "liberal" clergy were the spiritual leaders of the American Revolution. They refused to defer to the British crown as an authority somehow predestined, nor to bishops, nor to ancient creeds, nor to the British Calvinists' Westminster Confession of 1646.

Yet another liberalizing influence did come from England. Just as the Universalists have told the story of their origins as revolving around an English emigrant, John Murray, while suppressing their indigenous beginnings, so the Unitarians have told a story of indigenous liberalization that is not so much false as it is incomplete.

The proto-Unitarians of America were readers of, and correspondents with, the religious liberals of England. Some of these English liberals were Enlightenment thinkers who stayed within the established churches of Scotland and England. Others were dissenters who rejected the religious establishment. The first openly Unitarian church in England was established in London in 1774. Its minister, Theophilus Lindsey, was a former Anglican vicar. Most English Unitarians had been Presbyterian dissenters, like the minister/scientist Joseph Priestley (1733–1804), who was read by leaders in America even before the Revolution ended. Still another leading English Unitarian minister, William Hazlitt (father of the essayist and critic by the same name) came to America just after the war, in 1785, and spent two years spreading a Socinian version of the gospel, without finding a permanent welcome for a British Unitarian evangelist. He returned to England. Priestley came to America himself in 1794, settling in Pennsylvania, having been driven from England for supporting the French Revolution.[19]

After a second war against England in 1812–14, New England Unitarians found reason to forget the influence of English Unitarians, especially Priestley. For one thing, by then most American Unitarians wanted to make it clear that they were merely liberals, whereas Priestley was thought of as a radical, both in his theology and in his "Jacobin" politics. He had fully supported the French Revolution, while Chauncey's spiritual followers had been appalled by mob rule and attacks on religion and traditional order. Ironically, it was a "Church-and-King" mob in Birmingham, England, that in July 1791 burned Priestley's home, laboratory, and Unitarian chapel and eventually led him to come to America.

Thomas Jefferson thought Priestley the most important English scientist since Newton. He had isolated the gas we now call oxygen. He can also be credited with inventing carbonated soda.[20] Jefferson asked Priestley to settle near Charlottesville. They corresponded on the subject of religion. If anything, Jefferson was more radical than Priestley—more a Deist than a unitarian Christian. Yet he also admired the staunchly Christian Priestley's *History of the Corruptions of Christianity* (1783) and his radical position on the nature of Jesus—as a mortal, pure and simple. Jefferson also shared the suspicion that the soul is a material entity, like a gas, that rises from the body at death.[21] Inspired by Priestley's favorable comparison of the ethics of Jesus with those of Socrates, Jefferson created what he later called *The Life and Morals of Jesus of Nazareth* by going through the gospel accounts, cutting and pasting, leaving out the miracles and ending with the story of the empty tomb, without any resurrection or later appearances of the risen Christ.[22]

The idea that Jesus was simply a man was then called Socinianism. It took its name from the Italian-born biblical scholar, Faustus Socinus (1539–1604). He was leader of a group of radical Protestants in Poland. Socinus anticipated what we now call process theology. He saw God as relational, not static. He rejected the idea of God as impassive and unaffected by what we do or leave undone as Greek philosophy, and not true biblical theology. Jesus was human, but sent by God to change and redeem the world, changing God in the process. Although Socinianism was suppressed in Poland by the Counter-Reformation after 1660, Socinus's stance on the nature of Jesus was espoused both by Priestley and Lindsey. The latter unitarianized the Anglican *Book of Common Prayer* and then organized the first explicitly Unitarian chapel in London even before the American Revolution.[23] Americans such as Benjamin Franklin, John Adams, and Thomas Jefferson attended services there, either at that time or later.

Priestley argued in his historical writing that the traditional doctrine of the Trinity was not universally held in the early Christian church. He also considered it irrational. In New England many liberal, Arminian clergy could agree with that statement but were not radical humanists regarding the nature of Jesus. Instead, they were Arians. Arianism is the position named for Arius, the leader of the losing side when Constantine forced the whole Christian church to adopt a common creed at the Council of Nicaea, in 325 CE. Arius held that Christ was the Word of God and not human, though not part of a co-equal Trinity.

Despite the fact that many of the liberals of the Boston area shared an Arian theology, they were not interested in forcing everyone to be believe just as they did. In fact, they tried to avoid speculative, divisive issues. They were far more interested in promoting a practical piety leading to moral and civic virtue. Like Priestley, they also wanted to distinguish themselves from those "infidels" who found no use at all for the scriptures. They were liberal Christians, but not yet quite Unitarians. They had no desire to form any separate sect. They merely wanted tolerant, inclusive churches. The stronger the liberal influence became, however, the more the orthodox Calvinists denounced them as no different from the English Unitarians. Eventually they embraced that name—but then redefined it for themselves and distinguished it from the Socinian influence that actually had been percolating in America for a half-century before they finally formed the American Unitarian Association in 1825.

Hannah Adams (1755–1831) read the English Socinians before she became an American Unitarian. Like Zelig in the Woody Allen movie, or Forrest Gump, Hannah managed to know every major figure in the development of early Unitarianism. And to make a mark—even while being forgotten. She has two distinctions. She may have been the first person in America, of either gender, to earn a living as a writer. Her most important book, first published in 1784, was also the first attempt in English to provide a comprehensive and objective survey of all known denominations, religions, and beliefs—including theological distinctions like those outlined above. Although a distant cousin of John Adams, Hannah surely illustrates that not all early Unitarians were merchant-class or well-off—just readers. She grew up in rural Medfield, Massachusetts, about half-way between her cousin's home near the coast in Braintree and the Universalist hill town of Oxford, out in central Massachusetts. Her father, Thomas Adams, had graduated from Harvard and owned a house, but was too bookish and shy to succeed as a minister, a lawyer, or even a farmer. So he took in boarders—boys preparing for college admission or read-mission after being sent away for misbehavior or deficiency. He taught them Latin and Greek and mathematics and attempted to sell books to them and to his rural neighbors. Hannah got the same education that the college boys did and wanted even more.

During the Revolution one such student showed Hannah a copy of Thomas Broughton's *An Historical Dictionary of All Religions from the Creation of the World to This Perfect Time* (1742). She was "awakened [in] my curiosity," but also troubled.[24] The book was entirely unsympathetic to most of the views it surveyed. Who was right? How can one ever tell? Religious diversity was increasing, even in her rural neighborhood, with Baptists, Universalists,

Hannah Adams

Quakers, Methodists, and Shakers. She resolved that each religious group should speak for itself. She even wrote to the first Catholic bishop in America, John Carroll of Maryland. Her goal was "to avoid giving the least preference of one denomination above another."[25] The result was *An Alphabetical Compendium of the Various Sects* (1784). It sold out, but her printer soon pocketed all of her profits. One of her readers was James Freeman (1759–1835), the Unitarian (indeed, Socinian) minister of Boston's King's Chapel.[26] Like Lindsey, he had made a unitarian version of the *Book of Common Prayer*. Like Priestley, he favored what we now call "comparative religion." Freeman helped Adams by securing subscribers in advance for a second edition and connecting her to his friend (and fellow Socinian) William Bentley, the minister of East Church in Salem, Massachusetts.

Bentley, ministering to a congregation close by the docks, where trade with India and China was growing, had an insatiable curiosity about the world. He was the only man in America to have learned Persian and Arabic, using dictionaries brought from Europe by sea captains.[27] Thanks to Bentley, Adams's *Dictionary of Religions*, as it was finally called in a fourth edition (1817), managed to include fair descriptions even of Sufi Islam and Persian Zoroastrianism. She also wrote other texts on New England history and world geography, aware that such topics were not even covered in the standard college curriculum, but were of great interest to New England men and women alike as America became more self-aware and as its trade with the world expanded. She gained access to the private library of the exclusive Boston Athenaeum through Joseph Stevens Buckminster (1784–1812), the eloquent young scholar who, as minister of Boston's wealthy Brattle Street Church, was emerging as the first leader of the Boston liberal, proto-Unitarian clergy.

One of Hannah's textbook competitors was Jedidiah Morse, minister of the congregational church in Charlestown. John Harvard had been the first minister there.[28] Morse supplemented his parson's salary by publishing texts not unlike those of Hannah

Adams. Indeed, he felt that she, a mere woman, had no right to compete with him, a learned minister. His works even "borrowed" from her scholarship. Hannah, as quiet as her father, disliked the dispute, but it soon went far beyond the two of them.

In 1805 a controversy arose at Harvard College over the election of a new Hollis Professor of Divinity. Morse had gone to Yale, where staunch Calvinism still prevailed. He led the orthodox Calvinist clergy against the liberals. When one of the latter party, Henry Ware, minister in Hingham, was chosen for the post, Morse was incensed. The college named for his famous predecessor would now breed heretics! Soon he helped to launch an evangelical monthly, *the Panoplist*, to rival the *Monthly Anthology*, started by the Athenaeum liberals. He also helped to gather subscriptions to build an orthodox congregational church in the very heart of Boston, where nearly all the ministers were liberals.

The Park Street Church opened on what was soon called "Brimstone Corner" in 1808. Morse and other Yale-educated Calvinists also organized an orthodox seminary to rival Harvard at Andover, Massachusetts, with a faculty pledged to teach the orthodox creeds and doctrines. The liberal friends of Hannah Adams could not help but point out the contrast between a woman, broadminded, struggling to earn a living, and Morse's ungallant and dogmatic treatment, both of her and of them. They financed a lawsuit on Hannah's behalf against Morse. He was obliged to apologize to her and pay damages, but delayed doing so for years. Meanwhile, Morse's own congregation began to tire of his mean-spirited narrowness. Eventually, they dismissed him.[29]

The liberals tried to keep an inclusive "Standing Order" of congregational churches in Massachusetts, while preserving the individual rights of conscience. In 1780, when John Adams drafted a constitution for Massachusetts, the Standing Order of congregational churches was written into it as the continuing religious establishment. Mind you: If you explicitly joined another organized religious society (Universalist, for example) you could be exempted from paying taxes to support the Standing Order church and its minister. Those ministers, however, were expected to serve not only as pastors to the church itself—made up of communicants who had made a confession of faith and been accepted into membership—but also as the "public teacher of religion and morality" for the entire town or parish. Eighty percent of Massachusetts citizens were at least nominal Congregationalists, so very few raised objections. The clergy, as the spiritual leaders of the Revolution, still had relatively broad public support.

In Boston, however, things were a bit different. There were eight congregational churches—seven were liberal by 1780, with only one (Old South) still orthodox. They relied not on general taxes, but on their wealthy pew owners, for the funds to build larger and more beautiful meetinghouses. They raised generous ministerial salaries by assessing annual pew rents. Successful merchants of Boston generally did not want to be told from the pulpit that they were "utterly depraved" and in need of redemption by divine grace. Instead, they preferred hearing the Arminian assumption of free will, and exhortations to use their success for good moral and civic ends, following Jesus by performing works of "disinterested benevolence."

The Unitarian Controversy split the Massachusetts congregational churches in three ways. It divided the state religiously along geographic lines. Along the coast and in the eastern counties, the parish churches largely ended up in the hands of liberal clergy and lay leaders. Farther west, Calvinist orthodoxy and Yale-educated clergy tended to prevail, challenged here and there by Baptists and Universalists. Nearest and within Boston, the liberal takeover was top-down, affecting the prominent churches, Harvard College, and cultural institutions like the Boston Athenaeum. The orthodox were driven to setting up alternatives. Finally, in some key parishes and towns near Boston the controversy resulted in a "schism from below," when parishioners refused to support ministers who were too narrowly orthodox rather than broadly inclusive.[30]

The first and most dramatic incident of a "schism from below" came in Dorchester, the town just south of Boston (now a part of the city). John Codman had been chosen as the minister of the newly formed Second Church in Dorchester in 1808. Although raised in Boston liberal circles, he had studied the previous two years among the staunch Calvinists of Edinburgh, Scotland. The converted members of the *church* chose him. But the *parish* committee, representing the broader group of pew owners and parishioners, was told by Codman:

> As Arian and Socinian errors have of late years crept into some of our Churches, I think it my duty to declare . . . that I believe the Father, Son, and Holy Ghost to be the one living and true God; and that my faith . . . is conformable to . . . the confession drawn up by the elders . . . of the Congregational Churches in the year 1680.[31]

They simply thanked him for his candor and proceeded to ordain and settle him as their minister. Then they noticed that Codman never exchanged pulpits with most of the other members of the Boston Association of Ministers. He considered them all too liberal. Many parishioners felt denied the opportunity to hear other, more inclusive approaches to preaching. Exchanges were a deeply engrained custom. The lay leaders summoned an "ecclesiastical council," with ministers and lay leaders from other congregations, to settle the dispute, as was the practice in the Standing Order. Even after a second council, Codman refused to budge. He denounced the Boston ministers as "coming from the lowest grade of Socinianism, if not some grades lower."[32] Finally, in 1812, the parish voted, fifty-five to forty-five, to dismiss him. He ignored the vote. Two Sundays later, eight sturdy parishioners stood guard at the foot of the pulpit stairs, to stop Codman from ascending. He simply proceeded to lead worship from below. Meanwhile a substitute preacher, a liberal arranged for by the parish committee, stood by. When Codman finished and left with his followers, the liberal minister began. By the following summer, a compromise was reached. Codman's supporters bought up the pews of the disaffected, who then left and formed the more liberal Third Religious Society in Dorchester.

This moved Jedidiah Morse to new action. In 1815 he published, under the title *American Unitarianism*, an excerpt from English Unitarian Thomas Belsham's *Life of Theophilus Lindsey*. The book included testimony that Lindsey had rejoiced in how widespread Unitarianism was becoming in America, and that he had been in correspondence in James Freeman, William Bentley, and other Socinians or Unitarians for years.

"See," Morse was saying, "John Codman is right! These so-called 'liberals' in Boston may *seem* to avoid being doctrinal, but they are really Unitarians and radicals in disguise." Former President John Adams (1735–1826) received a copy from Morse. He wrote back in his typical way, both humorous and acerbic. Morse claimed that Unitarianism had been in America since 1785. Nonsense, said Adams; the debate between "rational religion" and "revealed religion" was older than that. "I can testify as a witness to its old age," he wrote. He said that as early as 1750 his own boyhood minister in Braintree, Lemuel Briant, and quite a number of other leading ministers "were Unitarians."[33]

Note that Adams was now using the term in a new and broader way, to encompass all liberals who had no particular use for speculative doctrines like the Trinity. Briant was probably only a broad-minded Arminian. Yet during the Great Awakening, the Calvinists in his flock took offense when he preached "On the Absurdity and Blasphemy of Depreciating Moral Virtue." Adams was the son of the senior deacon of the Braintree church, who sent his boy to Harvard to become a minister. Personally, John liked his pastor's affable eloquence—so much so that he later paid tribute to it in a deed he wrote on the house where Briant had lived. When he came home from college, however, his father seemed always to be engaged in trying to mediate between the pastor and his detractors. Finally, Briant was forced to resign. Young John Adams concluded that the life of a minister was too full of controversy; better to become a lawyer!

All the while, his poor cousin Hannah Adams was dwelling among the very Boston liberals that Morse so disliked. Although influenced by Priestley in her comparative studies, she, like them, was peaceable by temperament, not a Socinian humanist, much less a radical. As she later wrote in her autobiography,

> After removing to Boston, and residing in that city while the disputes upon Unitarian sentiments were warmly agitated, I read all that came in my way upon both sides of the question; and carefully examined the New Testament, with, I think, a sincere and ardent desire to know the truth. I deeply felt the difficulties upon both sides of the question; yet prevailingly give the preference to that class of Unitarians, who adopt the highest idea of the greatness and dignity of the Son of God. I have never arrived to that degree of decision that some have attained on that subject.[34]

In other words, she gravitated toward the moderate Unitarians.

Their emerging leader in Boston was William Ellery Channing (1780–1842). Unitarian Socinians like James Freeman and William Bentley had helped Hannah Adams, but she preferred those who "adopted the highest greatness and dignity of the Son of God," that is, the Arians like Channing. Other leaders of Boston religious liberalism had left the scene. John Kirkland, the minister of Boston's New North Church, became president of Harvard in 1810. William Emerson, minister of Boston's First Church (and father of the future "sage of Concord," Ralph Waldo), died in 1811, at only forty-two years of age. Joseph Buckminster of the Brattle Street Church died of epilepsy the following year, at only twenty-eight. So the mantle of Unitarian leadership in Boston fell on Channing, the minister of the Federal Street Church, installed there in 1803.

Channing was in his early thirties. He had grown up in Newport, Rhode Island. His father was a prominent lawyer who served both as Attorney General of the state and as US Attorney. His maternal grandfather, William Ellery, for whom he was named, signed the Declaration of Independence. Raised in a congregation led by Yale-educated neo-Calvinist Ezra Stiles, Channing well understood human sinfulness. After all, on the docks of Newport, within sight of the church, the slave trade was then still in operation. Yet even as a boy he noticed that his father showed little evidence that he truly believed the terrifying depictions of God's wrath commonly heard from the pulpit and from revivalists.

After graduating from Harvard, Channing worked as a tutor on a plantation in Virginia. He acquired chronic tuberculosis, becoming pale and thin, often weighing little over ninety pounds. His uncle Henry Channing, minister in New London, Connecticut, became his mentor in ministry. Listeners soon saw that in the pulpit both his eyes and his soul seemed too enlarged and luminous for his body. He preached the capacity of the soul to grow and expand. His magnetic personality and faith in others, even those prevented from achieving in the world, were especially attractive to women.

Channing married a wealthy cousin, Ruth Gibbs. When he was called to serve at Boston's Federal Street Church as a successor to the scholarly Jeremy Belknap (1744–1798),[35] Ruth's inheritance bought them a Beacon Hill townhouse at 85 Mt. Vernon Street. It proved a good residence for a minister whose congregation was diverse but came to include some of the wealthiest and most civic-minded citizens of Boston.

Like Hannah Adams, Channing held "the highest idea of the greatness and dignity of the Son of God." He was fervent in his reverence and devotion to Jesus. Yet he wanted no creedal tests or required confessions of faith. He felt that the true Christian church is inclusive and catholic in spirit; a church from which no one can be excommunicated except by the death of goodness in one's own breast. So he was hesitant to embrace any sectarian label, especially one that was associated with radicals and Socinians like Priestley. He simply wanted individuals to feel that God desired that their souls grow toward him by expanding in compassion and wisdom.

After Morse's 1815 attack on the Boston liberals as disguised Unitarians, it was only a matter of time before their leader would have to respond publicly. Channing waited for the right time and place. In 1819 he was invited to preach at the ordination of Jared Sparks as minister of a new, liberal congregation in Baltimore, Maryland. Channing called his sermon "Unitarian Christianity." He said that was a term rightly applied to all those who believed that God-given reason should be used in reading the Bible and who found there no warrant for requiring belief in a Trinity.

Channing has been called "the reluctant radical."[36] Not radical after the pattern of Priestley, however, whom he found too much a revolutionary, rationalist, and materialist. Channing by contrast was more spiritual, warm, compassionate, emotional, even mystical —attempting to forge a practical, moderate, inclusive religious liberalism. Anyone who thinks that Emerson's accusation of later Boston Unitarianism as "corpse cold" was meant to apply to Channing probably has neither read much Channing nor realized that he was Emerson's own mentor in ministry.

Yet there was a radical core to Channing's theology. His revision of traditional New England theology shifted emphasis from the fallen character of humanity (Genesis 3) to the idea that all human beings, regardless of their present faults or condition, are made in the image of God (Genesis 1). This reassertion of *imago dei* theology did have truly radical implications.[37] It ultimately would challenge every institution and social arrangement that stood in the way of human beings unfolding the full and God-given potential within their very being. That meant promoting free public education, even for children whose parents could not pay school fees; providing decent care for the mentally ill; dismantling anything like slavery, preferably sooner rather than later; and allowing women to express their own moral and spiritual leadership, among other reforms. Despite all their moderation and social privilege, there was something at the core of the faith of the liberals who now called themselves Unitarians that would tug at Channing and at many of those influenced by him, pulling them in the direction of needed social change and even political conflict.

The Age of
Jacksonian Democracy

1815
1848

Universalism in the Second Great Awakening

The United States grew rapidly in its early years. The non-Native population exploded from 2 million in 1770 to over 8 million in 1815. In that year the Universalist movement had about 125 churches and at least 5,000 adherents, largely in rural New England.[38] Thirty years later the US population reached over 20 million. Remaining Native groups such as the Cherokee had been cruelly displaced by land hunger. America had also become much more urbanized. And Universalism had spread westward, southward, and into the cities at an astonishing rate. When Hosea Ballou (and Andrew Jackson) died in 1845, Universalists claimed over 600,000 people "under influence" of their theology.

Many of these were probably only readers of the many Universalist newspapers and magazines, however, or former members of small, rural Universalist groups that seemed to go out of existence almost as rapidly as they were formed. There were also urban churches. Boston, New York, and Philadelphia each claimed five Universalist congregations. But with only 500 active clergy, and 850 congregations, *organized* Universalism probably never had much more than 100,000 active members.[39] Organization and organizational unity were among the denomination's major challenges.

These were the years of America's "Second Great Awakening." Hellfire and brimstone preaching by Protestant revivalists helped to greatly expand church membership. It also caused many to welcome the Universalist message: There is no hell. Each person came to that idea individually, however. For while debate with orthodox opponents was constant, debate and dissension were also common among Universalists themselves. Turbulent individualism and personal politics in the new denomination mirrored those of the developing nation.

The leading Universalist of this era, Hosea Ballou, in 1817 became minister of the Second Universalist Society on School Street in Boston. The barnlike wooden meetinghouse seated nearly a thousand people in pews and high galleries. Ballou often preached at three Sunday services. He also exchanged pulpits to bolster outlying rural congregations. His down-to-earth preaching style conveyed his deep conviction that there is no punishment to be feared after death.

According to his biographers, Ballou once traveled to a small town to preach. Although his host had embraced Universalism, his hostess remained skeptical of the new ideas. She greeted Ballou in her kitchen while cleaning for the Sabbath:

> She asked, "Do you really believe that *all* men will be saved, *just as they are?*"
>
> When he said that he did, she just shook her head. (One wonders if she perhaps felt that her husband's character might need some further improvement.)
>
> "What is that in your hand, dear woman?" Ballou asked her.
>
> "Why, my mop," she replied.
>
> "Are you going to mop the floor just as it is?"
>
> "Well, of course, I mop it to clean it."
>
> "Ah," Ballou said, "you do not require it to be made clean before you will consent to mop it up. Likewise God saves souls to purify them; that's what salvation is for. *God does not require men to be pure in order that he may save them.*" [40]

While the Unitarians in this era began to preach "salvation by character" (rather than by faith or works), Ballou eventually formulated his position as one of "salvation for all irrespective of character."[41] Ultra Universalism it was called. Sin is punished in this life only. There is no punishment after death, only "death and glory." But other Universalist ministers disagreed with Ballou. Like John Murray and Elhanan Winchester, they believed in the eventual *restoration* of all souls to God, but only after a period of just retribution and spiritual penance. These Universalist Restorationists were horrified by Ballou's Ultra Universalism, and the ensuing conflict became bitter almost as soon as Ballou came to Boston.

Ballou's principal opponents were Paul Dean (1783–1860) and Edward Turner (1776–1853).[42] Dean was the eloquent minister of Boston's First Universalist Society. He had been called to assist and then to succeed John Murray because, like him, Dean was a trinitarian Universalist. In 1823 a regional association of Universalists tried to discipline him for publishing statements that seemed aimed at dividing Universalists. Dean resigned his fellowship briefly, but was soon reconciled. Further attacked by Ballou's followers and accused of being jealous of their "bishop," he and others in 1831 organized a new denomination, the Massachusetts Association of Universalist Restorationists. That year he carried his version of the Universalist message on an evangelical journey to Maryland, Georgia, and South Carolina, where he scandalized other Universalists by allowing himself to be referred to as "bishop." While disturbed by issues like slavery, war, and capital punishment, Dean believed, like Ballou, that each individual should determine the biblical view of such matters, neither involving the church nor "disturbing the state." He also devoted considerable energy to defending Freemasonry, of which he was a major leader, from the charge of being anti-religious or conspiratorial. In 1845, despite his earlier trinitarianism, he accepted a call to a Unitarian pulpit, in North Easton, Massachusetts.[43]

Edward Turner was born in Medfield, Massachusetts, where he attended a school run by Hannah Adams. In 1808 he married Lucy Davis, a daughter of the Davis family of Oxford Universalists. Called to the Universalist church in Charlestown, Massachusetts, in 1814, he became a highly influential and visible Universalist leader by virtue of his work on hymnals and an early history of Universalism, and as the standing clerk and treasurer of the New England General Convention of Universalists from 1815 to 1824. In 1817 he debated Ballou in the pages of a Universalist publication called *the Gospel Visitant*. Ballou had earlier said that he thought a passage in 1 Peter 3:18–20, about Christ visiting "spirits in prison," might refer to a period of limited punishment after death. Now he said it was about reaching unconverted souls and that all punishment was here on earth. Like some other Restorationists, Turner felt discomfort with Ballou's "Ultra Universalism" and soon left the denomination. He served Unitarian congregations in Charlton, Massachusetts, and Fishkill, New York, until his retirement in 1840.[44]

The most notorious Universalist defection, however, and by far the most painful to Ballou, was that of his protégé, Abner Kneeland (1774–1844), the subject of a biography called *The Last Man Jailed for Blasphemy*.[45] Indeed, Kneeland was jailed in Boston— by Unitarians, no less—for proclaiming "blasphemous" ideas that today might be quite common and accepted in Unitarian Universalist congregations: rejecting biblical authority and the existence of the biblical God.

Kneeland, born in Gardner, Massachusetts, the sixth of ten children, had a background quite like Ballou's. By his early twenties he was an itinerant Baptist lay preacher. Through a sister he was introduced to the writings of Baptist-turned-Universalist Elhanan Winchester. Then he met Ballou himself, who became a mentor, preaching at his ordination in Langdon, New Hampshire. He and Ballou collaborated in producing a Universalist hymnal. Ballou wrote the words for an astonishing 193 new hymns; Kneeland, 138. Congregations, however, found their poetry rather more argumentative and didactic than inspiring. It was not reprinted. Accepting the will of God in losses and feeling assured of reunion with one's loved ones in heaven was an important theme of the hymns they both wrote.

Kneeland needed that kind of faith; by his mid-thirties he had been widowed twice. He also began experiencing a crisis of faith in the Bible and its promises. Like Ballou, he had read Thomas Paine and Ethan Allen, who scorned the Bible and the clergy in the name of reason. Ballou had found in their writing good arguments for using reason to explain the Bible, but not to abandon it. Kneeland was not so sure. When the Universalists of Charlestow—supposedly a lucrative post—failed to pay what they had promised him, he resigned his fellowship. For a time, he joined his third wife, Eliza Osborne, in her business selling dry goods. After much correspondence, Ballou persuaded Kneeland to return to the Universalist ministry—to serve a large church in Philadelphia.

Kneeland's message to his new congregation included not only Ballou's "death and glory" universalism, but also a multi-faceted

Abner Kneeland

concern for the suffering and pain on earth caused by injustice and human greed. He became interested in the plight of the urban working poor. He worked at a manic pace for religious and social change. On one occasion he publicly debated Presbyterian clergyman William McCalla for four days about whether Universalist theology is biblically based. He wrote for and edited several Universalist journals. He also read Joseph Priestley on how the Bible has been misused and misinterpreted. He began to doubt again that the scriptures were divinely inspired and not just human fables, and that the reality of suffering in this life was not more important than promises about the life to come.

To challenge the authority of the Bible during this era was to risk being denounced as "an infidel." One could safely debate the interpretation, but not the inspiration of scripture. In 1824 Kneeland met English-born idealist Robert Owen, a socialist and utopian, who reinforced his skepticism on the latter point. Sensing his Philadelphia church unreceptive to any change in his message, Kneeland moved to the Universalist church in New York City. Within two years the congregation there split over his challenges to biblical authority. With his supporters he formed a Second Universalist Society. But when he opened his pulpit to Fanny Wright, co-founder with Owen of the *Free Inquirer* and of an inter-racial commune in Nashoba, Tennessee, "all hell broke loose" as they say, whether people believed in it or not! Ballou himself drafted for Kneeland a letter of voluntary suspension from ministerial fellowship with the Universalists and then had him sign it.

By 1831 Kneeland moved to Boston. He was no longer a Universalist minister. Rather, he assumed a leadership role in the new Society of Free Inquirers. They met on Sunday mornings in a hall just blocks from Ballou's church. Up to two thousand people came to his lectures when he moved them to the Federal Street Theater, close to Channing's church. The Inquirers sponsored scandalous dances on Wednesday evenings. Kneeland's new newspaper, the *Boston Investigator*, openly scoffed at the Bible, as he did in his Sunday morning lectures. His "Philosophical Creed" proclaimed,

I believe . . . that God and Nature, so far as we can attach any rational idea to either, are synonymous terms. Hence, I am not an Atheist, but a Pantheist; that is, instead of believing there is no God, I believe that in the abstract, all is God; . . . it is in God we live, move, and have our being; and that the whole duty of man consists in living as long as he can, and in promoting as much happiness as he can while he lives.[46]

This circulated in 1833. Kneeland also wrote a letter saying either that he did not believe any longer in the Universalists' god, or that he did not believe in any God at all—depending on how one interpreted the placement of a comma.[47] On the basis of the latter interpretation, Kneeland was indicted for the civil crime of blasphemy. His real offense was that he had challenged *social* hierarchy. Like Owen and Wright, Kneeland supported equal rights for women and equality of the races. He suggested that women keep their own names and bank accounts. He spoke out in favor of birth control, divorce, and interracial marriage. The prosecutor at his trial was a Unitarian. So was the judge, as well as the defense attorney. Convicted, Kneeland appealed. A second and third trial each resulted in a hung jury. Finally, in 1838, after a fourth trial in the Supreme Judicial Court (presided over by Chief Justice Lemuel Shaw, another leading Unitarian), Kneeland went to jail for sixty days as a blasphemer.

Channing organized a petition for pardon. It was signed by many luminaries, including Ralph Waldo Emerson, Theodore Parker, George Ripley, Bronson Alcott, and abolitionist William Lloyd Garrison. But more Bostonians signed a counter petition. Kneeland's one-time mentor, Hosea Ballou, stayed silent. Meanwhile, Kneeland's third wife, Eliza, died. When he emerged from jail, he left Boston for Iowa.[48] There he tried to start a Free Inquirer community called "Salubria." It soon failed. Kneeland and a fourth wife had to sell all they possessed in order to satisfy their creditors. He died in Iowa in 1844, at age seventy.

Throughout this period Ballou mentored another protégé who stayed far more loyal to him and who illustrates that not all Universalists remained in the working or middle class. Thomas Whittemore served as an apprentice to a Boston boot-maker when he first encountered Ballou. He ended his long career as a leading Universalist minister and the publisher and editor of Universalism's most important journal. He also held two other roles—president of both a bank and a railway. As a teen Whittemore was something of a "Boston rough," with "a frame of iron, and lungs of brass," his "ready wit, a never-failing flow of spirits, and a genial temperament [that] . . . drew to him hosts of friends."[49]

Thomas Whittemore

In Whittemore, Ballou spotted a successor. He took him into his own home and funded his education. He clothed him for his first (rather unsuccessful) pulpit forays. He arranged for a training pastorate in Milford, Massachusetts. Then he backed Whittemore in starting the first Universalist church in Cambridge and as editor of the *Universalist Trumpet and Magazine*. Whittemore made money as a religious publisher. His *Modern History of Universalism* (1830) was a companion volume to *The Ancient History of Universalism* by Hosea Ballou II, his mentor's nephew. He also revised and published the autobiographical *Life of John Murray*. Although tempted to move west to lead Universalism where it was growing most rapidly, Whittemore stayed in Cambridge, becoming a civic leader. He served in the Massachusetts legislature in 1833, chairing the committee that proposed that the Commonwealth at last cease tax support of the congregational churches.

With the Standing Order divided between Unitarian and Trinitarian Congregationalists, disestablishment succeeded. There was also a proposal to separate "Old Cambridge," around Harvard, from the area where Whittemore's Universalists met, in Cambridgeport. Whittemore led the resistance and advised his fellow citizens to follow Boston's example and incorporate as a city. They did. Whittemore became president of the Cambridge Bank, and later, president of the Vermont and Massachusetts Railroad.

Although his elevated social status put him in contact with Unitarians, he remained critical of them, especially those Unitarian Transcendentalists who tried to base religion on something other than the Bible. He could agree with Unitarian reformers on some practical matters and supported Horace Mann's efforts to establish free public schools. He declared,

> We go for a universal education of the people—the poor and the rich—the farmer and the mechanic and the seaman, as well as the lawyer, the physician and the clergyman. Let all the people be educated. The universal diffusion of knowledge is the only safeguard of our republican institutions.[50]

Whittemore was also an outspoken opponent of capital punishment and one of the founders of the New England General
Reform Association among Universalists. Like many of his contemporaries, he advocated temperance and opposed slavery, though
without being a radical and immediate abolitionist. Like Ballou,
he was also unitarian in his Christology and often excerpted Unitarians in the pages of the *Universalist Magazine*. None of this
narrowed the social or theological gap between the two denominations, however.

Ballou admired the Unitarian leader, Channing. He called
him "the impassioned little saint." Yet Channing never deigned
to communicate with Ballou. In an 1832 sermon, "*The Evil of
Sin*," he even spoke quite disparagingly of "some among us" who
hold "that punishment is confined to the present state."[51] Here
he meant Ultra Universalists like Ballou. Channing felt that their
doctrine, though spreading widely, "tends to diminish the dread of
sin." His was a moral gospel. He and his Brahmin flock disdained
the seeming unwillingness of Ultra Universalists to distinguish
between those who merited reward and those who did not.

Ironically, Ballou's Second Universalist Society a century later
merged with the successor to Channing's church.[52] Many of Ballou's opponents within Universalism, the Restorationists, had
moved toward the Unitarians. From where Ballou and Whittemore sat, it was awful enough to have a defector like Kneeland
become an outright infidel; it was almost worse when some Universalists took a Restorationist line similar to that of the upper-
class, moralizing Unitarians who now dominated religious life in
Boston and Cambridge. Two Universalist intellectuals who took
this path—despite their insightful and deep concerns about social
class inequity—included Orestes Brownson (1803–1876)[53] and
Adin Ballou (1803–1890).[54]

Brownson was born on a farm in Vermont and raised among
Calvinists, discovering Universalism at age twenty-one in upstate
New York. Soon he was not only a Universalist preacher but the
editor of one of its numerous journals. Caught up in a dispute

among New York Universalist ministers over organizing a state convention, Brownson led the opposition. Any organization set up to decide who was an authentic Universalist minister made him nervous, since he himself entertained various doubts about just how a Universalist faith should be formulated or conveyed. So he defended Abner Kneeland during the first flurry of accusing him of infidelity. Like Kneeland, he was drawn to the idealism, socialism, and concern for labor rights expressed by Owen and Wright, though working with their Workingmen's Party left him quite disillusioned. Having read Channing's 1828 sermon, "*Likeness to God*," and experienced "the still small voice" in his own soul, Brownson returned to ministry, but as a Unitarian—and then to journalism, editing and publishing the *Philanthropist*. When that effort failed financially, Brownson took Unitarian pastorates in Walpole, New Hampshire, then in Canton, Massachusetts.

Denouncing the growing economic inequality of the age, Brownson alienated his more conservative Canton Unitarian parishioners. In 1836 he succeeded Joseph Tuckerman as the Unitarians' minister-at-large to the poor of Boston. When the most intellectually restless Unitarians formed the Transcendentalist movement in 1836, Brownson was among them. In his short book, *New Views of Christianity, Society and the Church*, he proposed reforming the church and the ills of society by reinterpreting atonement as Christ's mediation between the material and the spiritual. He did not approve of the spiritual individualism in Emerson's 1838 "Divinity School Address," however. His radical 1840 essay, "The Laboring Classes," predicted class conflict and advocated the abolition of hereditary property and the creation of a public fund to provide educational and occupational opportunities for all young men and women reaching adulthood. Disillusioned with politics after the 1840 elections, Brownson declared the need for a church in communion with the divine mediation of Christ, and in 1844 became a Catholic.[55]

Adin Ballou was a distant cousin of Hosea Ballou. He had come to Universalism through marriage and his reading of Winchester's

Dialogues on the Universal Restoration. Hosea Ballou II (the bishop's nephew) had assured him that despite his uncle's negative attitude toward restorationism, Universalists tolerated a range of views on future punishment. This was true for a time. Adin served in Milford, Massachusetts, in the 1820s, where Whittemore had begun. Then he was called to New York City to clean up the conflict there following Kneeland's departure. After he returned to Milford, his first wife died. He himself barely survived a life-threatening illness. He responded with an eloquent sermon, "The Inestimable Value of Souls." His parishioners sent it to Whittemore to be printed in the *Universalist Magazine.* But Adin Ballou had so strongly endorsed the Restorationist position and argued against Ultra Universalism that Whittemore, rather than print the sermon in his magazine, began a campaign to have his successor removed from the Milford pulpit. Adin Ballou left Universalism along with other Restorationists to form the Massachusetts Association of Universal Restorationists. He edited their new journal, the *Independent Messenger,* and conducted a four-year journalistic battle with Whittemore.

Dismissed from Milford, Adin was called to a Unitarian pulpit in neighboring Mendon. By that time, he had embraced a second meaning of the term restorationism.[56] Adin Ballou yearned for a restoration of the nonviolent community of non-creedal Christianity in the age of the apostles, when all were said to be one in Christ—Jew and Gentile, slave and free, male and female (Galatians 3:28) and when the early Christian community at Jerusalem shared all things in common (Acts 2:44). In 1837 Adin endorsed abolitionism and the following year, a form of pacifism that he later wrote about in his 1846 book *Christian Non-Resistance,* which influenced Tolstoy, and through him, Gandhi and Martin Luther King Jr. By that time he and other reform-oriented Restorationists (as opposed to Paul Dean) had also united around a plan of "Practical Christianity," which imbibed the spirit of the new Transcendentalist movement within Unitarianism.

Adin Ballou had studied the plan for the Transcendentalist community at Brook Farm, founded in 1841. That year he and others purchased a farm in Milford to start a similar type of community and named it "Hopedale." Brook Farm ended after only six years. Hopedale was more successful. Both were instituted as joint-stock communities. Brook Farm had equal compensation regardless of effort, however. Hopedale did not, allowing for reward based not only on investment, but also on personal effort. It lasted until 1856, when its largest investors withdrew and turned its manufacturing into a private firm. The failure of the project broke Adin's heart. His *Practical Christianity: An Epitome of Practical Christian Socialism*, as he called his 1854 justification for the Hopedale experiment, was an attempt to bring Restorationist ideals down to earth. He stayed on as the minister of the Hopedale community, which joined the Unitarians, until he finally retired to do historical writing.

By 1840, the individualistic revivalism of the Second Great Awakening had evolved into a broadly felt need for urgent social reforms. In November of that year a "Convention of Friends of Universal Reform" met at the Chardon Street Chapel in Boston.[57] A thousand hopeful reformers gathered. Some, like Ballou and the founders of Brook Farm, thought human effort and experimentation were needed to realize the Kingdom of God on earth. Others read "the signs of the times" as leading soon to direct divine intervention.[58] William Miller read the Bible as predicting that Christ would come again—on October 22, 1844. He had emerged from the same hill-country Baptists that produced early Universalists. After "the Great Disappointment" of October 23, his follower Ellen White picked up the pieces and creatively formed the Seventh Day Adventists.

Women also played key roles in promoting Universalism during this era, and women's rights and equality were increasingly discussed. The Universalists would be the first denomination to ordain women to the ministry, but that step was still a generation away. Controversies and defections within Universalism took their toll. In 1844 one Matthew Hale Smith (1810–1879) published a book called *Universalism Examined, Renounced, Exposed*, based on twelve years as a Universalist minister. Like his father, Elias Smith, who had also gone in and out of Universalist fellowship, Matthew was probably not entirely mentally stable. He changed his religious affiliation seven times. His brother Daniel, who remained a Universalist, suspected a brain tumor.[59] In any case, one paragraph in his critique merits attention even today:

> Universalist congregations seldom increase. They may retain an existence for years. But after they have reached a certain height, they begin to wane. They start with zeal and perhaps erect a house of worship. Then their downward march begins; and in this is seen the tendency of their doctrine. It removes restraint, loosens the bonds of moral obligation, and takes away the motives for attending public worship. Many, in a little time, learn all that is taught. They become convinced that no one will be lost, and that is all they wished to know. Convinced of this they leave the meeting and spend the Sabbath in doing their own pleasure. The congregation of Universalists is thus continually changing. If new members come in they only take the place of those who, under the influence of the doctrine have learned the folly of all preaching, and have come to the opinion that many better methods have been devised of spending the Sabbath than attending meeting, even though it be to hear the threatenings of the Bible explained away.[60]

Unitarians and the American Renaissance

American Unitarians paid a price for winning over Boston and Harvard so early on. More than their leaders ever intended, Unitarians became localized and caste-bound. For many years their faith spread chiefly where Harvard graduates and the Boston merchant class moved.[61] They also won worldly power that easily led to a cautious conservatism. Yet many Unitarian leaders directed *some* of their power to confronting the great sociopolitical issues of the time. Like people of privilege in every era who see human suffering and injustice, they showed that what matters most is *how* you use your power and influence. Their most restless, creative spirits, the Transcendentalists, not only led an American literary Renaissance, but laid the intellectual groundwork for a "second American revolution" in religion, ethics, and national politics.

If there was one person who knew all of the key figures and bore witness to most of the important events among Unitarians in this era, it was Elizabeth Palmer Peabody (1804–1894). The eldest of the three Peabody sisters of Salem, Massachusetts, Elizabeth is often remembered chiefly for her late-life role in bringing early childhood education to America in the form of the "kindergarten" movement. Long before that, however, she was truly a Renaissance woman. Taught Latin by her father, she went on to master some nine other languages.[62] Her father, Nathaniel Peabody, a respectable but ineffectual physician-dentist, was no reliable provider. Her mother, Elizabeth Palmer, grew up attending King's Chapel; through the experience of other women in her family, she had reason to believe in original sin—or if not that then at least in the wickedness of men. She taught her eldest daughter and namesake to study, think, and fend for herself and to protect her younger sisters.[63] Elizabeth reacted to her mother's Calvinistic pessimism with optimistic determination: If the world is wicked, then let us find the strength within us to set it to rights! Elizabeth herself never married, but she found respectable husbands for her sisters by befriending and even courting, *for* them, two remarkable men—Nathaniel Hawthorne and Horace Mann.

When she was just eight or nine, Elizabeth heard William Ellery Channing deliver a guest sermon at the Second Church in Salem. Here was a Unitarian of no "corpse cold" rationalism, but with a

Elizabeth Palmer Peabody

moving fervor and piety aimed at stirring up listeners to lives of faith and good works. She vowed to move to Boston. At eighteen, she did so, establishing a private school for girls.[64] Despite support for the school from influential Unitarian friends like Eliza Cabot, enrollment remained low. Elizabeth then worked in Maine, as a governess among wealthy Unitarian families. She arranged for her sister Mary, three years younger, to join her in teaching. She guided Sophia, born in 1809, into studying art. In 1825 Elizabeth and Mary opened another girls' school, first in the Boston suburb of Brookline, then later on Beacon Hill. On Sundays they went to Federal Street Church to hear Channing. Elizabeth transcribed his sermons in her own shorthand system and she worked with him to prepare the texts for publication. Eventually he began walking with her on Saturdays to try out his sermon ideas. When her school closed in 1832 because of her partner's financial misman-agement, Elizabeth earned a living by leading "reading parties" and lecturing to Unitarian women on literary and philosophical topics.[65] Peabody probably considered herself a Unitarian before Channing considered himself one. As a young woman she had read Socinians like Joseph Priestley. Embracing the idea that Jesus was fully human left her "with a feeling of strength in my mind, a sense of clearness in my ideas," she wrote in her journal.[66]

Channing's view of Jesus was more elevated. He had embraced the term "Unitarian" only reluctantly—finally doing so in his ser-mon "Unitarian Christianity," preached in Baltimore in 1819. He did this, in part, to bring clarity to the ambiguous relations between congregational ministers, who were by then deeply divided into orthodox and liberal camps—the former calling the latter Unitar-ian. Channing took as his text the biblical admonition to "prove all things; hold fast that which is good" (1 Thessalonians 5:21). He advocated the use of reason in interpreting the Bible and rejected trinitarian creeds as unbiblical.[67] "Unitarian Christianity" was so widely printed and debated that many decided they were on the side of Channing's Unitarian and inclusive spirit rather than in fellowship with those Calvinists who opposed him. In May 1820, the liberal ministers of the Boston area gathered in the Berry Street vestry of Channing's Federal Street Church to form a ministerial conference separate from their orthodox detractors.

Three years earlier, thirteen-year-old Elizabeth Peabody had read through the entire New Testament thirty times in three months, each time in reference to a different disputed point in theology. In most cases, she decided that the more liberal position was the correct interpretation. Needless to say, not everyone agreed. By 1820, the Unitarian Controversy was beginning to divide entire communities and even to provoke litigation. In Dedham, just west of Boston, the parish had voted to settle a liberal minister, despite the objections of a majority of church communicants. The case went to court. The Supreme Judicial Court, made up entirely of liberals, ruled that even the church silver and the meetinghouse belonged to the parish under its new Unitarian minister. The frustrated orthodox had to leave and build their own Trinitarian congregational church.

Five years later, on May 25, 1825, liberal laymen and ministers joined together in Channing's Federal Street vestry with his associate Ezra Stiles Gannett to form the American Unitarian Association (AUA). Coincidentally, the British Unitarians organized their own association on exactly the same day.[68] It was also the twenty-second birthday of Ralph Waldo Emerson (1803–1882). The young Harvard graduate was just beginning his ministerial studies. There had been eight generations of ministers in his family. His grandfather and father, both named William Emerson, had been liberals, but had died prematurely. Channing, by then the dean of liberal ministers, would become a significant influence on Emerson, especially with regard to the goal of religion: the growth and expansion of the soul.[69]

When the AUA was formed, Channing declined to be its president. That honor went to Aaron Bancroft, minister of the liberal Second Parish in Worcester, Massachusetts. The chief organizer, however, was the secretary, Channing's associate, Ezra Stiles Gannett. Some say Channing did not want to lead a sect. Certainly he did call himself "a catholic [*i.e.*, inclusive] Christian" and say that one should "flee the spirit of sectarianism as though it were from hell." But he also may have wanted to show that the new movement had leaders from beyond Boston. On the way back from Baltimore in 1819, he spent a month in New York, visiting his married sister and helping to gather the First Congregational Society of New York (later the Unitarian Church of All Souls). Channing was a theological liberal, but also evangelical in spirit, wanting to spread the good news of a more loving, less Calvinistic God.

That was also the purpose of the new AUA. It was not an association of congregations, but simply of individuals—ministers and wealthy laymen—who supported the publication of Unitarian tracts, sermons, and books, and who gave financial support to new ministers sent as "evangelists" to bring liberal religion to distant places such as Louisville, Kentucky, and St. Louis, Missouri. Resources for such missions, however, were never very great. Evangelists were expected to become self-sufficient rather quickly. Boston-area Unitarians understandably preferred to keep most of their philanthropic resources closer to home. The very first project of the AUA was to support the work of Joseph Tuckerman (1778–1840), Channing's one-time roommate at Harvard, in a ministry-at-large among the poor of Boston.

Often called "the founder of American social work," Tuckerman encountered the poor on the streets and near the docks, since many were new immigrants. His method was first to create trust, then visit people where they lived. He called on widows, invalids, and families alike, sometimes offering modest material assistance. He asked everyone to send their children to his Sunday school and to attend his Sunday evening talks. Realistic about alcoholism and about women and children forced to steal and prostitute themselves, Tuckerman also challenged the Calvinistic fatalism that said neither poverty nor its victims could be changed. "There is no human being, however depraved, who is yet totally depraved," Tuckerman declared, "no one for whom moral efforts are not to be made as long as God shall uphold him in being."[70]

By 1836, he had two associate ministers and three city chapels, with some 730 children enrolled in just one of three Sunday schools. AUA sponsorship was then replaced by support from a local consortium of congregations, the Benevolent Fraternity of Unitarian Churches. They provided funding and coordinated advocacy for reform of prisons, schools, and public charity. The Benevolent Fraternity continues today as the Unitarian Universalist Urban Ministry of Boston, the oldest such organization in the country.[71] Tuckerman, like so many in this era, contracted tuberculosis. As travel to warm, moist climates was the standard medical recommendation, Tuckerman died in Havana, Cuba. He was only one of many pioneering social reformers in Channing's circle, however.

Joseph Tuckerman

Abolitionists like the writer Lydia Maria Child challenged Channing to take a more radical stance in calling for an immediate end to slavery. Horace Mann, who heard Channing preach during a depression that followed the death of his first wife, left a promising career as a politician to implement a state-wide system of free public schools. Dorothea Dix, who began as a teacher, led a national crusade for decent treatment of the mentally ill. All of these activists were connected, not just through Channing, but also through Elizabeth Peabody.

Dorothea Dix (1802–1887) was similar to Peabody in social situation, though not in temperament.[72] Two years Elizabeth's senior, Dix suffered a very unhappy childhood in Maine. Her father was a sometime evangelist, sometime alcoholic; her mother was emotionally ill. At age twelve Dorothea ran away, seeking refuge with her widowed grandmother in Boston, and later with an aunt in Worcester, Massachusetts. She began her own school at fourteen. By 1821 she had heard Channing preach. He inspired her to add to her private school a free evening school for poor children. She also began to write, publishing the books *Conversations on Common Things, Meditations for Private Hours,* and *American Moral Tales for Young Persons.* From time to time she served as governess to the Channing children. Where Peabody was an intellectual and an optimist, Dix distrusted abstract thought and was often sad and lonely. She felt most spiritually alive when directly helping others, but she sometimes worked herself to exhaustion while doing so. After one such collapse, Channing arranged for her to recuperate by traveling to England to visit with Unitarian philanthropists and to ponder their methods for affecting humanitarian issues. When her grandmother died and left her a bequest large enough to make her independent, she was ready for a new project.

One of Channing's ministerial students had attempted unsuccessfully to teach a Sunday class for women prisoners at the East Cambridge jail. When Dix took over the class, she found the conditions at the jail appalling. Minors were housed among adults, convicted criminals with the accused, and many of those jailed had committed no crime—they were simply intellectually slow or mentally ill. She secured an immediate court order to provide the jail with heat and other improvements and set about studying how the mentally ill could best be treated. In a time when respectable women rarely traveled alone, much less visited jails or alms-houses, Dorothea Dix soon challenged every sheriff in Massachusetts.

Hers was one of the earliest social research projects in America. She found the mentally ill "boarded out" to farmers, confined in unheated barns, or chained in cellars, cold and covered in their own excrement. She championed them much as Tuckerman did the poor. She prepared a powerful report to the Massachusetts legislature, polishing it in Channing's own drawing room at 85 Mount Vernon Street. Few legislators approved of women giving legislative testimony, so her fellow reformer (and Channing parishioner) Dr. Samuel Gridley Howe spoke to the legislature.[73] The accuracy of the report, initially received with denial and anger, was readily confirmed. After securing funding to expand the first state hospital for the mentally ill in Worcester, Dix began to travel to other states, seeking similar reforms.[74]

A leading advocate for the hospital in the legislature was Horace Mann (1796–1859), who had been raised in Franklin, Massachusetts, so poor that he could not go to school regularly. When he was fourteen an older brother, Stephen, went skating on a pond one Sunday. The ice broke and Stephen drowned. In his funeral sermon, the local Calvinist minister not only preached that this was punishment for Sabbath-breaking, but also detailed the eternal pains awaiting those who died unconverted and in a state of sin. Horace was traumatized and began examining texts at the local public library (provided by the town's namesake, Benjamin Franklin) to find other ideas about God, life, and religion. He won a scholarship to Brown, the Baptist college in Rhode Island, where he courted his wife-to-be, Charlotte Messer, daughter of the president of Brown. He studied law and, when qualified, set up his practice in Dedham, Massachusetts, joining its newly Unitarian First Parish. One of his first cases found him defending the First Parish in

Milton, where the parish had dismissed their Calvinist minister for refusing to exchange pulpits with more liberal colleagues.

In 1833, Charlotte Mann died of tuberculosis. Horace moved into a Beacon Hill boarding house. His fellow boarders, Elizabeth and Mary Peabody, took him to hear Channing on Easter, 1834. Mann experienced a spiritual resurrection of purpose. Soon he became a member of the state Senate, and then chosen to serve as its president. In 1837 he relinquished a chance to go on to become Governor or a US Senator, to lead instead the first state-wide effort to give a free public education to every child. In 1843, in the front parlor of the Peabody sisters' home at 15 West Street, Boston, where Elizabeth then ran a notable bookstore, Horace married Mary Peabody.[75]

Elizabeth became involved in educational innovation herself. In 1834 she joined Bronson Alcott (1799–1888) in teaching at his new private school on Temple Street in Boston. Calvinist-born and Quaker-influenced, Alcott had married Abigail May, whose brother Samuel was both a Unitarian minister and a leading abolitionist. Alcott was nothing if not an idealist, especially about drawing out the divine potential in children through conversation. Elizabeth described his methods in *A Record of a School* (1835). Alcott also talked with children about scripture. He candidly explained circum-cision, virginity, and sexuality. When he published his own *Conversations with Children on the Gospels* (1836), parents were shocked and withdrew their children from the school. The Unitarian "Pope" at Harvard, Andrews Norton, professor of New Testament, pro-nounced the book "one-third absurd, one-third blasphemous, one-third obscene."[76] Soon he would say similar things of another good friend of Peabody and Alcott: Ralph Waldo Emerson.

The roots of Emerson's 1838 "Divinity School Address" and of the Transcendentalist movement it expressed are complex.[77] Much of what seems a radical break with the previous generation of Uni-tarians actually originated with Channing, especially as expressed in sermons such as "Likeness to God" (1828).[78] Elizabeth Peabody herself embodied such continuities in her friendship with both men. Yet Emerson also knew about discontinuities and the need for new beginnings, especially through his aunt, Mary Moody Emerson, who became a strong influence on him after his father died when he was just a boy.[79] Certainly German idealism was also important.

Emerson's older brother, William, had studied the new biblical criticism in Germany, but returned saying that he could never successfully preach what he had learned. Aunt Mary insisted that Waldo take his brother's place as the eighth generation minister of the family, but Waldo chafed at the artificialities of church ritual and pastoral duty. He served briefly as successor to Henry Ware, Jr., at Boston's Second Church. When his first wife, Ellen Tucker, only 19, died of tuberculosis and left him a substantial inheritance, Emerson felt secure enough to leave the ministry. He told his flock that he could no longer in good conscience administer communion as a memorial to Jesus because he did not believe that Jesus had intended any such ritual. The truth may have been more complex and affected by grief. In any case, he resigned his pastorate and left on a tour of Europe.

The inspiration for his first book came in the Jardin des Plantes in Paris, although he did not complete the book until he was back in the Old Manse in Concord, where his grandfather had watched the American Revolution begin. Revolutionary itself, Nature (1836) says that all revelations of history and scripture are enfolded in the present book of nature and consciousness. It begins:

Our age is retrospective. It builds the sepulchres of the fathers. It writes biographies, histories, and criticism. The foregoing generations beheld God and nature face to face; we, through their eyes. Why should not we also enjoy an original relation to the universe?

Nature appeared the same year that Harvard celebrated its bicentennial. Unitarian ministers gathered for the reunion.[80] George Ripley (1802–1880), then restlessly serving a Boston church, asked those interested in the "new views" coming out of Europe to form a study group. Emerson called it "Hedge's Club" because it met chiefly when Frederic Henry Hedge (1805–1890), minister of the Unitarian Church in Bangor, Maine, could attend. The "new views" stemmed largely from German idealism and romanticism, and Hedge, son of their old philosophy professor at Harvard, had completed a doctorate in Germany. Three women who could translate German were included: Elizabeth Peabody, Margaret Fuller, and Sarah Alden Bradford Ripley.[81]

From his study of European ideas, ironically, came Emerson's 1837 Harvard Phi Beta Kappa address, "The American Scholar," known as "the American intellectual Declaration of Independence."[82] In it he said, "We have listened too long to the courtly muses of Europe. . . . We will walk on our own feet; we will work with our own hands; we will speak our own minds . . . inspired by the Divine Soul which also inspires all men."[83] Few objected—this applied chiefly to American literature; it was cultural patriotism. That year America suffered a major financial panic, and many fortunes were lost. The next year Emerson applied his ideas to faith and religion, in his "Divinity School Address." This time his "new views" caused great controversy.

"Historical Christianity," he said, "has dwelt, it dwells, with noxious exaggeration about the *person* of Jesus. The soul knows no persons." His central message was the same: self-trust. Yet in saying that the meaning of Jesus was only that "one man was true to what is in you and me"; that each minister should be "a newborn bard of the Holy Ghost"; that ministers should supply "to the defects of the church now existing" the only sure remedy—"first, soul, and second, soul, and evermore, soul"—Emerson offended the older ministers of the Divinity School faculty. Andrews Norton denounced Emerson's speech as simply "The Latest Form of Infidelity" in his own subsequent address of that title. For him, the authority of Jesus was demonstrated by the miracles recorded in the Bible. For Emerson, miracles were mere symbols of spiritual power. He wrote, "There is only one miracle," being itself, while "the word miracle, as pronounced by the Christian churches, is Monster. It is not one with the blowing clover and the falling rain."[84]

One young minister who liked what Emerson said was Theodore Parker (1810–1860).[85] Then only twenty-eight, serving a Unitarian parish in rural West Roxbury, Parker had grown up in Lexington. On April 19, 1775, while Emerson's grandfather was a minister in Concord, Parker's served as captain of the Lexington Minutemen. Too poor to pay tuition at Harvard, young Theodore had often walked ten miles from his home, starting at dawn, to hear lectures at the college in Cambridge. He taught himself Latin, Greek, Hebrew, and nine other languages. Like Emerson, Parker had abandoned the idea, held by most Unitarians (and Universalists), that the ultimate authority for religious living is found in the Bible, and that the special authority of Jesus is found in his miracles. In 1841, at an ordination in South Boston, Parker gave a sermon called "The Transient and the Permanent in Christianity." The transient consisted of creeds, forms, and rituals, while the lasting was an ethical imperative: the Absolute Religion, as Jesus taught and embodied it.[86] Others have known the Absolute; so can we all. Spiritual living is above all ethical and radical.

This was all too much for traditional Unitarian Christians, as well as for the orthodox Calvinists who were present or who read Parker's heresies. Most Unitarian ministers in Boston stopped exchanging pulpits with Parker, which Elizabeth Peabody and many others found reprehensible. That fall, supporters invited him to deliver a series of lectures in Boston laying out a systematic Transcendentalist position concerning religion.[87] Concerned that Parker was being heard regularly only by his small flock in West Roxbury, his supporters organized the Twenty-eighth Congregational Society in the City of Boston in 1845, inviting him to be its minister. They rented a large theater, where Parker soon drew such large crowds that services moved to the largest hall in the city, the Boston Music Hall.

Peabody bore witness to the shift from Channing to Parker as Boston's leading preacher. Channing's last years at Federal Street were difficult. In 1834 Samuel May rebuked Channing for not speaking out more forcefully on the issue of slavery. Yet when he began to do so, both from the pulpit and in a pamphlet called *Slavery* (1835), wealthy parishioners involved in the cotton trade, like Nathan Appleton, left his flock.[88] He tried to take a moderate stance out of consideration not only for them but for Unitarian colleagues in the South.[89] He called for gradualism in ending slavery, initially declaring those who demanded immediate abolition too extreme. Yet after a trip to the Caribbean island of St. Croix one winter for his health, he could no longer deny the brutalities of slavery. Lydia Maria Child, sister of Convers Francis, the Unitarian minister in Watertown, Massachusetts, came to see him. She had written about slavery as well, in *An Appeal in Favor of That Class of Americans Called Africans* (1833). She asked Channing just how Christian it was for him to criticize those who sought the immediate abolition of slavery. Channing accepted her censure. He spoke up more; and more wealthy parishioners departed.

The climax of Channing's confrontation with his conservative trustees at Federal Street came after the death of his friend Charles Follen (1796–1840). Born in Germany, Follen had taught at Harvard, married Elizabeth Peabody's friend Eliza Cabot, and become a Unitarian minister—first in East Lexington, then as the interim/candidate minister in New York City. He was an ardent abolitionist, which was why he had not been settled in New York, although the parishioners claimed that the problem was his German accent. When Follen died coming back to Boston, in the burning of the steamer *Lexington*, Channing wanted to hold the memorial service at Federal Street. The trustees refused him permission to use the meetinghouse to honor such a radical. Channing thanked them for their candor, turned over all preaching duties to his more conservative associate, Ezra Stiles Gannett, and refused to accept a salary any longer. All without resigning his post as the chief pastor, responsible for the care of his parishioners' corrupted souls.

An exodus from Federal Street Church ensued. Most abolitionists and reformers were drawn to a newly organized Boston congregation. Just as Emerson saw too many Boston Unitarians as upholding "the best diagonal line that can be cut between Jesus Christ and Abbot Lawrence" (a cotton mill owner), so Elizabeth Peabody and others ended up in the newly formed Church of the Disciples, led by James Freeman Clarke (1810–1888),[90] who seemed to cut a diagonal between Channing and Parker. Like Channing in religion, Clarke was a partisan of continuity over discontinuities and he respected the historic church. His grandfather, James Freeman, had been the minister of King's Chapel. Yet as AUA evangelist to Louisville, Kentucky, in 1833, Clarke edited the *Western Messenger* and helped to spread the "new views" of the Transcendentalists. Returning to Boston, he was one of the few Unitarians who would exchange pulpits with Parker.

James Freeman Clarke

Clarke's new Church of the Disciples, gathered in 1841, came to boast not only Elizabeth Peabody, but also Channing's own physician brother, Dr. Walter Channing; Dr. Samuel Gridley Howe and his wife, Julia; and many other reformers. Despite the individualistic, post-Christian image of Transcendentalism, Clarke managed to fuse the old with the new. The Disciples, under Clarke, organized on the basis of three principles that Unitarian Universalists now take for granted, but which were innovations in the 1840s:

> *The voluntary principle.* No wealthy pew owners would control the new church. Voluntary giving would be the norm. All givers, not just pew owners, would vote.
> *The social principle.* The Disciples would gather not just on Sundays for worship, but also on weeknights for study, spiritual growth, service, music, or committee work.
> *The liturgical principle.* Since liturgy means that worship is "the work of the people," rather than just being listeners, as people were in both Channing and Parker's flocks, the Disciples would encourage lay preaching, responsive readings, unison prayers, congregational hymns, and even (for a time) a prayer book.

If Parker succeeded Channing as Boston's leading preacher, Clarke succeeded him as pastor to the reformers and *literati*. Channing went to Vermont in the summer of 1842, feeling ill. That fall, on the way back home, he died in Bennington. So it was Clarke who presided that July at the wedding of Sophia Peabody to Nathaniel Hawthorne and the next May, at the wedding of Mary Peabody to Horace Mann.[91] As was typical then, both ceremonies were simple family gatherings in the family home at 15 West Street, Boston, where Elizabeth Peabody also ran a bookshop selling the latest European publications. Sometimes the Transcendentalist circle met there; Elizabeth served as publisher for their journal, the *Dial*. Margaret Fuller, the editor, held her "conversations for women" in the same drawing room.[92]

Around the time of Channing's death, Parker published an article in the *Dial* that deeply offended the leading Unitarian ministers of Boston. Parker was asked to explain himself before the Boston ministerial association. This is sometimes portrayed as a Unitarian "heresy trial," but the issue was less about belief than about collegiality. Parker had written about a church council called to mediate between the pastor of the Hollis Street church, John Pierpont, and the trustees. Pierpont was a reformer and temperance advocate, but the Hollis Street trustees had rented out the church cellar for use as a storeroom by some rum dealers. Pierpont repeatedly denounced this publicly. When the council advised the minister to temper his views on temperance, he refused and was forced to leave. Parker's article adamantly condemned the council for not backing Pierpont. He so infuriated the ministers on the council that some wanted him expelled from their ministerial association. Parker refused to resign, even though his congregation had become an independent, "free church," and quite thoroughly "post-Unitarian." By 1845 only Clarke would still exchange pulpits with him, finding that when he did so, fourteen families departed from the Church of the Disciples.

During this time, Elizabeth Peabody remained the link between Channing, Emerson, Parker, and more "broad church" Transcendentalists like Clarke. Meetings of the Transcendentalist circle ended in 1844, when *the Dial* failed financially. Some of Peabody's Transcendentalist friends had gone into utopian experiments in communal living. Brook Farm (1841–1847) in West Roxbury was the best known of these. Having begun trying to accommodate individualism with social reform ideals, it lost members like Hawthorne when there was less time for creative work than expected. Brook Farm ended when a new building for communal living was destroyed by fire.[93] Bronson Alcott also subjected his family and a few friends to a short-lived commune called Fruitlands, in Harvard, Massachusetts. His daughter, Louisa May Alcott, later wrote a hilarious satire of that experiment, *Transcendental Wild Oats*.[94] Adin Ballou did better with his joint-stock commune at Hopedale,

Massachusetts (1841–1856). Even after its economic communalism failed, Hopedale continued as a spiritual community.

Henry David Thoreau (1817–1862), Emerson's younger friend, having also written for the *Dial*, withdrew in 1845 to Waldo's wood lot at Walden Pond to "live deliberately" and to polish his journal of *A Week on the Concord and Merrimac Rivers* (1849). He emerged with notes for *Walden; or, Life in the Woods* (1854). He had earlier withdrawn from the local Unitarian parish. His family attended a short-lived Universalist congregation in Concord instead.

Margaret Fuller (1810–1850) tried her best to keep the *Dial* alive, often filling its pages herself when male Transcendentalists failed to produce contributions they had promised. She was a formidable woman, having been given an excellent education as the eldest child of Cambridge congressman Timothy Fuller. When she was still quite young, her father wrote home to his wife, "Tell Margaret that I love her if she learns her Latin."[95] Brilliant and intense, she could be intimidating. She met Clarke while he was still a Harvard Divinity student. She may have even desired him—but frightened him off. Going west as a Unitarian evangelist, he instead married Anna Huidekoper, the daughter of a wealthy Dutch religious liberal in Meadville, Pennsylvania, who had funded a seminary there.

After her father lost first his political office and then his wealth and health, Margaret became the main support of her mother and her younger siblings. She learned to rock a cradle, peel an apple, and read a book—all at once. Overwhelmed and on the brink of despair, she expressed her commitment to life by adopting as her motto, "*I accept the Universe!*" When Emerson reported this to his British correspondent, Thomas Carlyle, who spoke of the need for an "*eternal yea*" in life, Carlyle reportedly responded derisively, "By gad, she had better!"[96]

Men would unfairly satirize Margaret Fuller as a woman who wanted to be like a man. Nothing could have been less true. She could be self-reliant, but her view of the moral universe was far more relational than the traditional male construct. It was also transcendental—seeing *all* persons, regardless of their relative power, as moral agents, though often unjustly deprived of the opportunity to exercise self-determination. In that sense, her "Conversations for Women" anticipated the women's consciousness-raising groups of the 1970s.

Fuller's relational Transcendentalism also accounts for her pioneering journalism. Like Clarke and unlike Thoreau, she actually went west and visited real Native Americans—people whose annihilation in New England Thoreau wrote about as a mere matter of nostalgia. Her book, *Summer on the [Great] Lakes* (1843) was followed by an essay series in the *Dial* called "The Great Lawsuit: Man *versus* Men, Woman *versus* Women," which was turned into a book, *Woman in the Nineteenth Century* (1845), calling for full women's equality. Then she went to New York to work for Horace Greeley, the Universalist editor of the *New York Tribune*. She investigated and reported on conditions in public jails and hospitals, as had Dorothea Dix. Then she went to Europe, where revolution was in the air, as America's first female foreign correspondent. While covering the Italian revolution of 1848, which briefly substituted a new Roman Republic for the rule of the Pope in the Eternal City, she fell in love with a young radical Italian nobleman, the Marchese Giovanni d'Ossoli, and had a child, Angelo, with him. Returning to America in 1850, all three drowned in a shipwreck off Fire Island, New York.

At the same time, another disciple of Peabody emerged as a successor to Fuller. Caroline Healey Dall (1822–1912) was the young wife of the minister in rural Needham, twelve miles west of Boston. To the astonishment of Needham farmers and their wives, she published her first book, *Essays and Sketches,* in 1848. One essay advocated abolition; another condemned the Mexican War; a third, on women's rights, was called "Sisterhood." Her husband Charles, pastor of the town's only church, was soon asked to resign. Some blamed Caroline's radicalism. Others said Charles could have lost his pulpit by himself, without any help at all from his wife! We will follow their story further in "Unitarians from

Reform to Civil War" (page 81). First Parish in Needham called no more Harvard-educated ministers for some years. Instead, starting in the 1850s they turned to a series of more reassuring, less Transcendentalist clergy—all Universalists.[97]

The Second
American Revolution

1848
1870

Universalism Seeks Unity of the Spirit

Hosea Ballou cited scripture in saying, "If we agree in love, there is no disagreement that can do us any injury; but if we do not, no other agreement can do us any good. Let us endeavor to 'keep the unity of spirit in the bonds of peace.'"[98] But to agree in love was far more easily said than done. Universalists are often portrayed as being community-minded and Unitarians as individualistic. Yet in this period many Unitarians were civic-minded institution-builders, while many mid-century Universalists, like founders such as Caleb Rich, felt less accountable to their fellows than to their own religious experiences. Having used biblical authority to assert that all souls are in the hands of God, many Universalists after 1848 became interested in efforts to communicate with the spirits of departed loved ones. Such experiments were understood not as seeking miraculous suspensions of the laws of nature, but rather as experiential confirmation of a universalist, spiritualist faith that was broadly shared, even beyond the denomination.

Just as Universalism in America had multiple origins, so did American Spiritualism, with its belief in the ability of the spirits of the dead to communicate with the living. Nonetheless, it seems remarkable just how many of Spiritualism's early manifestations in America were among, and spread by, Universalists.[99] Spiritualists are often said to have been primarily women, especially bereaved mothers.[100] Yet among the Universalist spiritualists, male clergy were often prominent. So were would-be scientists.

Consider John Bovee Dods (1795–1872), Universalist minister

and "doctor of electro-psychology."[101] When John was a boy of eleven, his father died. He was adopted by a maternal uncle. Going home from a visit to his impoverished mother, he had a vision of his father. John prepared for the Calvinist ministry and married, but subsequently had visions of a relative who had committed suicide and, therefore, according to orthodox theology, should have been in hell. The spirit told Dods to prepare for "an important work." Soon the Dods's home became the site of so many strange psychic events that he and his wife had to leave. He took up a Universalist ministry in Maine, keeping most of his individual spiritual experiences to himself. His in-laws lived in Richmond, Virginia. Visiting there in 1830, Dods helped to organize an early Universalist-Unitarian group. Then he served churches in Massachusetts, where in 1836 he encountered a French "mesmerist" who induced trances. Dods began to interpret his earlier visions as electro-magnetic phenomena. They were produced by God as the ultimate energy source. A trance could be a kind of sacramental opening to the realm of spiritual truth. He began teaching courses on "mesmerism," or trance induction: ten dollars for men, five dollars for women. In 1850, he published *The Philosophy of Electrical Psychology*, a book so popular that a group of US Senators—including Daniel Webster, Henry Clay, and Sam Houston—called him to Washington DC to lecture. Dods believed that universal human immortality could be demonstrated scientifically, as did many of his contemporaries. Yet the Universalists expelled him from ministerial fellowship. At issue was the Bible.

In 1848 the Universalist General Convention passed a statement of faith requiring all its ministers to affirm the Bible as a "special revelation from God, sufficient for faith and practice."[102] This was partly a reflection of the issue that was dividing Unitarians in the 1840s between those who were more traditional and biblically oriented and the Transcendentalists like Theodore Parker. But it was also meant to deal with individuals promoting their own "special revelations," many of them young, and Universalist ministers who in turn promoted them.

Andrew Jackson Davis (1826–1910) of Poughkeepsie, New York, was a youth of seventeen when he encountered mesmerism and reported a clairvoyant ability to travel through space and time, into the bodies of the suffering.[103] His mother had died while he was still a boy. His father was distant and alcoholic. His local Universalist minister not only sympathized but took the boy on tour. The congregation back home did not approve, nor did organized Universalism. Yet in 1847 several Universalist clergy helped to publish Davis's The *Principles of Nature, Her Divine Revelations, and a Voice to Mankind*. A more traditional and biblical Universalist denounced it as "a second Book of Mormon."[104] Others said that the reason so many Universalists flocked to Davis was that "our organization is so very loose," and called for more "systematic mental discipline," to be brought about by more rigorous clerical training.[105]

Then in 1848 three sisters from a village near Rochester, New York—Leah, Margaret, and Kate Fox—began to display messages from the beyond that sounded like nothing so much as the new electric telegraph. Questions could be posed to the spirits they summoned. Answers came in the form of "rappings" heard by all. A local Universalist minister, Charles Hammond, promoted the Fox sisters while writing for the *Spiritual Telegraph*. When they left Hammond's management, he himself began to receive messages from the spirits of people such as freethinker Thomas Paine. Spiritualist lecturers and clairvoyant mediums quickly proliferated among Universalists. By 1850 John Austin, the former Universalist pastor in Auburn, New York, and by then editor of the spiritualist journal the *Christian Ambassador*, claimed to have some fifty to a hundred (mostly female) mediums training with him.[106]

Perhaps one-third of Universalist clergy would not open their churches to Spiritualist lectures and demonstrations, citing biblical authority. Others were more flexible, calling themselves "Christian spiritualists." Still others left Universalism altogether to join the Spiritualist movement. At its peak, Spiritualism was probably as widespread as Universalism, with many "under influence," but only a fraction of them committed to organized Spiritualism.

Yet Spiritualism also changed organized Universalism. In the 1850s the latter reaffirmed its Christian identity and biblical roots. Many Spiritualists said all differences in religion were reconciled at a higher plane. Organized Universalists insisted that all final religious authority was found in the Bible. In addition, the assertion of messages from restless spirits suggested that perhaps the Restorationists had been right: After death, perhaps still more spiritual work *does* go on, beyond just "death and glory."[107]

Universalists backed away from Hosea Ballou's Ultra Universalism. His own nephew, Hosea Ballou II, also departed from his uncle's stand on two more down-to-earth issues: seminary education and direct church involvement in social reform. "Father Ballou" had opposed both. Properly mentored, grassroots ministers could teach right views of a loving God and then all else would simply follow. His nephew wanted a Universalist college. When a Universalist benefactor named Charles Tufts gave twenty acres of land in Medford, Massachusetts, Tufts College was born. Phineas T. Barnum (1810–1891), the entertainment impresario and entrepreneur, and a strong Universalist, was a life-long donor. The younger Ballou became the institution's first president in 1855.[108]

He also supported the Universalist General Reform Association, founded in the 1840s by New Englanders. By 1857 it had gone national, open to any Universalist who would pay fifty cents a year in dues. They set a daunting forty goals, in four broad categories. Slavery and other "economic and domestic relations" issues, like women's rights, were first. Then came anti-war, nonresistance, Indian affairs, and other "international relations." Third were "social institutions and habits," such as "temperance, education . . . [and] the Sabbath." Finally, Universalists opposed the death penalty and advocated prison reform and rehabilitation.[109] They were led in that last effort by Charles Spear, editor of a pioneering journal called the *Prisoner's Friend*.[110]

The anti-slavery cause was, of course, sectional. Universalist state conventions in South Carolina, Georgia, and Mississippi disassociated themselves from anti-slavery resolutions passed by the national General Convention. But the latter never had any real control over its state conventions. So the Universalists never divided North-South, as many other denominations did. Few Northern Universalists were truly notable leaders in abolitionist circles. Yet in 1851, when William Lloyd Garrison's abolitionist paper, the *Liberator,* reported reactions in Waltham, Massachusetts, to the capture of a fugitive slave, Thomas Sims, it said,

> The bells of the [Calvinist], Methodist, and Universalist churches in Waltham were tolled on Saturday when the news of the man-stealing was received. The bell on the Unitarian Church being clogged with cotton would not sound.[111]

Universalists did not have the direct economic interest in the cotton trade that some Unitarian mill owners did. Still, Universalist ministers were often told by parishioners not to press the antislavery issue too hard. One who was a strong abolitionist, Daniel Livermore, had support from his articulate spouse. Mary Rice Livermore (1820–1905), as a young woman, had lived as a teacher on a Virginia plantation for several years. Having seen slavery first-hand, she was outspoken about abolition. Like many women in the abolition movement, she was also concerned about equal rights for women. Many male Universalists had feminist spouses, as had John Murray. When the first Women's Rights Convention was held in Seneca Falls, New York, in 1848, Universalist Horace Greeley's *New York Tribune* was one of the few papers to take note—although with initial ambivalence. Conceding the right of all people to assert their rights, Greeley wrote, "The best women I know do not *wish* to vote." Yet his wife's name soon appeared at the very top of a petition for woman's suffrage. Urged by her to attend, Greeley was among the few male participants at the first truly national Women's Rights Convention, held in Worcester, Massachusetts, in 1850. He became a thorough convert to the cause and helped it spread.

In 1851 the Universalist Church in Akron, Ohio, hosted a women's rights convention. The ex-slave Sojourner Truth rose to speak. Over the objections of some in the gathering, she was recognized by the chairwoman, Frances Dana Barker Gage (1808–1884). Truth then gave a powerful, impromptu speech in which Gage later claimed that she said, "Ain't I a woman?"[112] Gage, an Ohio Universalist and abolitionist, was herself a gifted orator, activist, and writer.[113] Based in St. Louis in the slave state of Missouri, starting in 1853 she conducted a wide correspondence on behalf of what she and many others called "the triune cause"—abolition, women's rights, and temperance. Back in Ohio in 1860, she helped lead a successful political campaign for the passage

Mary Rice Livermore

of the first women's rights bill in that state. When the Civil War came, four of her sons enlisted in the Union Army. Frances gave speeches in support of the troops. With her daughter, she went to the Sea Islands of South Carolina in 1863 to train freed slaves. There she met and befriended a fellow Universalist, the nurse Clara Barton. They discussed Universalism and how they shared "a burning sense of fairness."[114]

Clara Barton (1821–1912) was born on Christmas Day in the birthplace of Universalism, Oxford, Massachusetts.[115] Her father was a leader in the local Universalist church. Her mother and an older sister were emotionally shaky. When she was eleven her older brother David fell at a building site and was badly injured. Clara nursed him through a long convalescence. Then, a phrenologist, diagnosing character through examination of the skull, recommended that Clara overcome her shyness by teaching school. She was frightened, but she did it, quite successfully. After ten years she felt the need for more formal education. She went to the Clinton Liberal Institute in upstate New York, an institution with strong Universalist ties. Classmates there invited her to try teaching in New Jersey. Encountering gender discrimination, she went to Washington DC as the first female clerk in the US Patent Office. Sexually harassed, overworked, ill with malaria, and finally ousted from her job for political reasons, she returned to Massachusetts. But when war came, she returned to Washington and volunteered as a nurse. Sharing the living conditions and food of common soldiers, she lobbied for better supplies and field hospitals. She was present when the Fifty-fourth Massachusetts Volunteers—the black troops under their young Unitarian colonel, Robert Gould Shaw—were nearly wiped out in the assault of Fort Wagner, South Carolina.[116] Barton and other volunteers were replaced by official army nurses under Dorothea Dix or with the US Sanitary Commission. Her friendship with Frances Gage helped her avoid self-pity. For years afterward Gage corresponded with her, prompting her to write and lecture, advocating for the rights of women, freedmen, and veterans. When the International

Red Cross was formed in 1870, during the Franco-Prussian War, involvement in this new organization became her life work—she became the first president of the American Red Cross.

During the 1850s more Universalist women began to take on public leadership roles. There had been a few women lay preachers, such as Maria Cook, active in upstate New York as early as 1811.[117] Two sisters, Lucy Barns (1780–1809) and Sally Barns Dunn (1789–1858), daughters of early Universalist evangelist Thomas Barns, contributed literature and sermons. Biblical literalism, however, denied women teaching authority or even speech in most churches.

The first woman accepted as a preacher with denominational authority was a Universalist. Although not formally ordained, Lydia Ann Jenkins (1824–1874) was married to a Universalist minister in upstate New York.[118] In 1857 she was reported to be "preaching to good acceptance." Thomas Whittemore wrote a disdainful editorial in the *Trumpet and Universalist Magazine*, saying it would be "better for her to remain at home and tend to her domestic duties," that "St. Paul very pointedly condemned . . . preaching women."[119] Another Universalist journal, the *Christian Freeman*, reviewed a sermon Jenkins gave to the Cayuga Association of Universalists and called her style "smooth" and "flowing" and her sermon "well-arranged," "systematic," and "touching," saying if "the editor of the *Trumpet* had been present, his soul would have been moved and all opposition to female preaching would have departed."[120] Lydia's preaching in New York City was well-received by Horace Greeley, and in 1858 she was a speaker at the New York State Universalist Convention. She was then received as "a preacher of the Gospel" by the Ontario Association of Universalists. Whittemore still objected, but the next year went out of his way to hear her when Jenkins came to Lowell, Massachusetts. Like Greeley, he was won over. Jenkins and her spouse became co-pastors in Clinton, New York, and then itinerant preachers. After the Civil War, while remaining active Universalists, they concentrated on running a homeopathic medical clinic.

Olympia Brown (1835–1926) is better remembered than Lydia Jenkins because she was ordained and her ministry lasted longer, although it began a few years later. She was born in Michigan to Universalists from New England who valued education. They sent her to Mount Holyoke Female Seminary in Massachusetts. Like Emily Dickinson, Olympia found Mount Holyoke rigid and Calvinistic. Antioch College in Ohio was a better fit. The whole Brown family moved there so their younger children could attend as well. Unitarian Horace Mann was the college president. In 1860 he agreed to Olympia's request that Antoinette Brown (later Blackwell; 1825–1921)[121] be invited to lecture and preach. Unrelated to

Olympia Brown

Olympia, Antoinette had been ordained in 1853 by an independent congregation in upstate New York closely aligned with abolitionism. She had expected antagonists among the male clergy, but not those she was to encounter among her female parishioners. By the time she arrived at Antioch, she had left parish ministry and was best known for a pioneering series of articles on women in urban poverty, in Horace Greeley's *Tribune*. Hearing Antoinette preach, Olympia "felt as though the Kingdom of Heaven were at hand."[122]

Olympia applied to the Unitarian theological school at Meadville, Pennsylvania. But the trustees thought it "too great an experiment." Oberlin said that she would be treated as Antoinette had been: she could study there, but not speak publicly. Finally, Ebenezer Fisher, president of St. Lawrence College and its theological school in Canton, New York, said that she could come and that he would leave the question of her becoming a minister "between you and the Great Head of the Church." Olympia finished in 1863, persuading the Universalists to ordain her. No sooner had she begun parish ministry in Weymouth, Massachusetts, then she was involved in women's rights issues. She spent four months in Kansas, giving three hundred speeches, campaigning for women's suffrage. Her congregation generously gave her leave for the effort. Despite getting only one-third of the male voters to support them, she and some other suffragists thought this 1867 effort in Kansas was an early triumph.[123] She continued in the Universalist ministry and lived long enough to vote in an election after the passage of the Nineteenth Amendment in 1920.

Even before the Civil War the growth of Universalism in America had seemed to stall. One almanac in 1849 estimated Universalist membership at some sixty thousand and listed them seventeenth among denominations.[124] The division over Spiritualism was only one factor. Culturally, the assurance of universal salvation was a less urgent concern, or was urgent for fewer people. Hellfire and brimstone preaching had declined, as had the revivals of the Second Great Awakening. Social and political issues had come to the fore.

Universalism aimed to present itself as respectable, middle-class, and biblically grounded. So the differences between Universalists and other religious liberals narrowed. The doctrine that God is a loving parent who would not condemn any soul to eternal punishment had become rather commonplace. Certainly Unitarians and Universalists had that much in common. A few joint congregations, Sunday schools, and other projects had even been tried.

Universalist minister Thomas Starr King (1824–1864) became the most notable transfer to Unitarian ranks in the 1850s.[125] Largely self-taught but eloquent, the twenty-one year old King had been called in 1846 to the Universalist Church in Charlestown,

Thomas Starr King

Massachusetts, where his father had served. "Preaching to aged men and women who have seen me as a boy in my father's pew," he found, "I necessarily cannot command the influence which a stranger would wield." Starting to lecture to supplement his income, he was heard in New York by Henry Whitney Bellows (1814–1882), the leading Unitarian minister there. Bellows was impressed and tried to get King chosen to fill a vacant Unitarian pulpit in the city. But leaders of the second Unitarian church were hesitant to call a pastor who had never been to college. King declined the suggestion that he attend Harvard for a year. But in 1848, aided by letters of introduction from Bellows to the Unitarian notables in Boston, King was persuaded to accept a call from the Unitarian congregation at Hollis Street. That church had been weakened by the battle between its trustees and John Pierpont. King not only healed wounds, his eloquence helped the congregation to thrive once again. Harvard awarded him an honorary MA in 1850, as though to welcome him into the ranks of Unitarians.

By 1859 King's ministry had increased the congregation at Hollis Street five-fold. Theodore Parker called him the best preacher in Boston. He was also sought after as a lecturer. "He is witty," commented his patron, Bellows, "and just profound enough to be intelligible to people who cannot enjoy anything that does not go beyond their own ideas."[126] However, traveling constantly to earn lecture fees to help support a disabled brother and a widowed mother as well as his own family was a drain. Through Bellows, he sought a new, higher-paying pastorate. Offers came from several Unitarian congregations. The one that seemed to King "the more crying call" was to San Francisco. The need was partly political. California was a violent, wealthy frontier state, with many leaders from the slave-holding South. There was no organized Republican party, standing against the expansion of slavery. Within months of arriving, King changed that, helping Lincoln carry the state with a narrow plurality in the 1860 elections. He quickly became a powerful spiritual and civic force, with an influential and growing church. Like Bellows, he had envisioned a unified, liberal Christianity:

"Our mission is to hasten the time when the church in general shall modify her creeds and grant more freedom to thought and organize more charity, and receive again into fellowship the needful forces, which her narrowness has spurned."[127]

After Fort Sumter and succession, King campaigned around California for the preservation of the Union. He was credited with saving California and its gold fields for the Union cause. Acting as Western agent of the US Sanitary Commission, organized by Bellows, he raised millions of dollars for the health and medical care of the Union army and the wounded of both sides. He became exhausted by his exertions, and his own health suffered. King contracted diphtheria and died of pneumonia in March 1864, at the age of only forty.

Had he lived, he almost certainly would have worked with Bellows to fulfill the latter's dream of consolidating the Universalists and Unitarians and other religious liberals in one great Liberal Church of America. Questioned about the difference between the two denominations, King repeated the remark, "The one thinks that God is too good to damn them forever, the other thinks that they are too good to be damned forever."[128] He also said that the only reason that they had not merged already was that they were "too near of kin to be married."

It was still a century too early. Led by Bellows, Unitarians emerged from the Civil War determined to get better organized. Universalist leaders sensed that perhaps they should as well—but on their own. They were aware that they had lost ground. Membership was declining; many churches had closed. Their distinctiveness was less clear and competition was increasing. It was no time to join with a religious group that often seemed to condescend to them. Their position in the religious world at the time seemed somewhere between the Unitarians and the Congregationalists, who were now less strictly Calvinistic and more liberal. So no Universalists rushed to answer Bellows's 1865 call to organize a Liberal Church of America. It was hard enough for him to get the majority of Unitarians together. Instead, Universalists began planning a distinctive gathering of their own. They would celebrate 1870 as a centennial—dating from John Murray's arrival in America. They would meet in force at Gloucester, the site of Murray's church.

In late September 1870, a crowd estimated to be as large as 12,000 Universalists gathered there for three days of speeches, worship, and fellowship. Some 242 ministers—approximately one-third of those then in fellowship—attended. So did many notable lay leaders such as Mary Livermore, Horace Greeley, and Phineas T. Barnum, as well as Israel Washburn, former governor of Maine. There was nominal unity. But state and regional conventions were still much more important than the national General Convention. Southern Universalists stayed away. John Murray's pulpit robe was put on display, along with a rhetorical question: Was there anyone present to fill it? This despite the fact that Murray's deterministic, trinitarian version of Universalism would have been quite poorly received a century later.

Late nineteenth-century liberal religion valued progress far more than it cared about history. Representing the new "National Conference of Unitarian and Other Liberal Christian Churches" was Edward Everett Hale (1822–1909) of Boston, author of *A Man Without A Country* (1863) and the slogan, "Look up and not down, look forward and not back, look out and not in, and lend a hand."[129] Liberal Christianity, Hale said, needed no "mock fusion" of "the two liberal bodies of America," but rather "a broad track," to carry its message on "two wheels."[130] Hale was a "broad church" Unitarian. He also once said, "I am only one, but I am one. I cannot do everything, but still I can do something; and because I can't do everything, I will not refuse to do the something that I can do."[131]

Still, he knew that no one individual could bridge the gap between the post-Civil War Unitarians and their Universalist cousins. Both had become too conserving of their own particular distinctions to cooperate too closely, much less consolidate. What they did share was the difficulty of deciding how most effectively to continue to promote liberal spiritual values in the Gilded Age of post-Civil War materialism.

Unitarians from Reform to Civil War

Many Unitarian congregations in the mid-nineteenth century were neither urban nor prosperous. "I was called to preach supply today in a rural district called Needham, which pretends to be a town," wrote one minister in the 1850s.[132] There Unitarians experienced no major rift with more orthodox members of the parish. "Every man will have a creed of his own," wrote pastor Stephen Palmer (1792–1821). "I have mine, but have no right to impose it upon others, nor have others any right to impose theirs upon me. . . . He who thinks he has no more light to receive, has seen but little; and he who is not open to conviction is in bondage to himself."[133]

Palmer succeeded Samuel West (1730–1807), who served Needham in the American Revolution. On April 20, 1775, West had the pastoral duty of calling on five widows and thirty-five orphans whose husbands and fathers had died at Lexington and Concord. That year he received no salary at all. In 1792 he shocked the parish by accepting a call to the Hollis Street Church in Boston. Needham still owed him over three years of salary.

In 1847 when Needham had trouble attracting a minister, they agreed to build a new parsonage.[134] Charles Henry Appleton Dall (1816–1886), thirty-one, and his wife, Caroline, (1822–1912) twenty-five, needed the job and housing. For a decade Dall had served as Unitarian minister-at-large to the poor in St. Louis and then in his native Baltimore. When Caroline first heard him preach at Christmas, 1842, in Washington, he made her weep. The eldest child of Boston banker Mark Healey, Caroline had learned four languages. Like Margaret Fuller, she relentlessly sought her father's approval. Since her mother suffered from bipolar disorder, and seven younger siblings needed care, Caroline began managing the household at age thirteen. She also taught Sunday school at their Unitarian church and did charitable work among the poor. When her father went bankrupt in 1837, Caroline went to work as a teacher in a private Washington "female academy," where she felt lonely and vulnerable. When Dall asked her to marry him, she confided in her journal that he was awkward and even lacking in "manliness," but she felt called by God to help him in his ministry. Initially, the marriage was tolerable. But Charles could not successfully raise funds to support the work Unitarians sent him to do among the poor. Soon he and Caroline also had a child to consider.

Caroline Dall

In Needham, Caroline delivered a second child, stillborn. Trying to recover by writing, she put her feminist, abolitionist, anti-war, Transcendentalist views into *Essays and Sketches*. When she had a daughter in 1849, Theodore Parker and William Lloyd Garrison sent Caroline congratulations "for a new reformer born into the world." The parish, however, which still included orthodox Calvinists, Trinitarians, Universalists, and conservative Unitarians, told Charles Dall they were unable to pay his salary. Her father had recovered financially but told Caroline that he would help her only if she left Charles and radicalism. She did neither.

Charles found another Unitarian pastorate in Toronto, Ontario. Caroline and the children went with him, though the marriage was strained. She read the memoir of Margaret Fuller that Emerson and others published.[135] On March 20, 1852, she wrote in her journal,

> In Margaret Fuller's biography I see my own life renewed. The same dreams . . . Neither of us appears to have had a natural childhood. Her father and mine were alike impatient, and we were both injured, by the imperative demand for clearness & precision in our statements . . . I read metaphysics at eight. I was awkward, plain, and intractable, and I wondered why God did not give beauty to one who loved it so passionately.
>
> When my husband first knew me, he used to say that I reminded him of two passages of Scripture, "for judgment —am I come"—and "he shall judge the quick and the dead"—so trenchant were my decisions, and so absolute my convictions. This demanding of others, the best that they can do, so often stated of Margaret, was from the beginning true of me. I spared nobody, and myself least of all. . . . No more painful feeling have I ever had than that which often comes over me in conversation—that I really have a great deal to say which I think valuable, that others would not have the patience to hear.

Last night I had been entertaining . . . and talking with several persons not accustomed to meet, and . . . I was obliged to keep the thread of general conversation in my own hands, to prevent their minor threads from tangling. It was on great subjects of religion and politics—the relation of man to God—and of man in God to his fellow men. Charles could do nothing with them—he left all the burden to me, and soon left the room. When I went to bed, serious yet elate[d]. . . he said to me, "I cannot help wishing that when you lead conversation as you did tonight, you had the rare tact not to seem to lead." Tears choked my utterance . . . "Take me as I am," was the longing prayer of my heart—"take me as I am, accept what is fine . . . and be sure that the ages will bury the rest."[136]

For seventy years, until she died in 1912 at age ninety, Caroline kept the longest known diary by an American. She also published twenty-two books. "My Journal—I have kept chiefly to establish my connections with the outward world—as a sort of link between me, & what I was afraid of forgetting." (Needham, July 1, 1848).[137] As with Emerson and others, Caroline's daily examination of conscience and consciousness was a long-standing New England practice.

Margaret Fuller's death in 1850 led some to look to Caroline as her potential successor in promoting women's equality. Then Charles was again forced to resign his pastorate. The Dalls returned to Boston. One day Charles came home from Unitarian headquarters to tell Caroline that he had accepted a post as a Unitarian missioner in Calcutta, India. Caroline and the children were not to follow; he would send home much of his stipend. They remained married, but he visited only five times over thirty-two years and died in India in 1886. Call it a "Boston divorce."

In Boston Caroline Dall edited the new women's rights journal, the *Una*. She organized the huge Boston Women's Rights Convention of 1855 at which Emerson spoke. She even supplied Unitarian pulpits. But other suffragists disliked her. She placed a woman's right to earn a decent living and to be treated well at home ahead of voting rights. Mentors like Elizabeth Peabody chided her for even mentioning issues like prostitution. When Dall was passed over for leadership in a women's rights group, the radical minister Thomas Wentworth Higginson (1823–1911) told her he could not help that she had made herself so very unpopular.

Yet she was not really rigid. While Susan Anthony and Elizabeth Cady Stanton opposed Lincoln's 1864 reelection and new constitutional amendments on civil rights unless they also applied to women, Dall did not. After the war she left the suffrage movement, turning her energies to the American Social Science Association, which she helped to found. In 1867 she published a pioneering book, *The College, the Market, and the Court: or, Woman's Relation to Education, Labor, and Law*. She followed Elizabeth Peabody as head of the Sunday school at the Church of the Disciples. She traveled widely to lecture and report on conditions in hospitals, slums, women's colleges, factories, and prisons. Her efforts deserve greater remembrance.[138]

While Caroline Dall was protesting the Mexican War in Needham, Henry David Thoreau, who went to jail for refusing to pay his poll tax, was in Concord, turning a lecture on the subject into his famous essay, "Civil Disobedience."[139] The most polarizing events, however, were still to come. Daniel Webster, Unitarian senator from Massachusetts, devised the Compromise of 1850, which included the Fugitive Slave Law.[140] President Millard Fillmore, a Unitarian from Buffalo, New York, signed it. Emerson wrote in his journal, "This filthy enactment was made in the 19th Century, by people who could read & write. I will not obey it, by God."[141]

After the first American Revolution the new Constitution both protected slavery and provided for escaped fugitives to be returned.[142] The 1850 law simply added to the enforcement, with slave commissioners appointed through the federal courts. In the conflict between such laws and "the Higher Law" (increasingly

cited by Transcendentalists and those they influenced) abolitionists began to feel that a new American Revolution was now
needed. It has been argued that it broke out on the streets and in
the churches and public halls of Boston in May 1854.[143]

Slave hunters captured a fugitive named Anthony Burns. George
Ticknor Curtis was Boston's slave commissioner and a member of
the Federal Street Church. He cooperated in sending Burns back
to slavery. Curtis's minister was Channing's successor, Ezra Stiles
Gannett. Normally Gannett avoided taking any stand on public
controversies, yet this upset even him. Theodore Parker was minister-
at-large to Boston's fugitive slaves. He had taken them into his congregation and protection before. In 1850 he hid his congregant
Ellen Craft in his own home until she could flee to Halifax and
then to England. In 1851 Parker and the Boston Vigilance Committee tried legal means to intervene in the return of fugitive slave
Thomas Sims, but merely won a delay. So when Anthony Burns
was captured, the Committee voted to block his return and to sum-
mon a public meeting. Five thousand people gathered at Faneuil
Hall. Theodore Parker roared that Massachusetts was being ruled
from Virginia and that citizens of Boston were cooperating. He
invoked the spirit of the American Revolution, ending by saying
that although he was a man of peace, "there is a means, and there
is an end. Liberty is the end, and sometimes peace is not the means
to it. Now, I want to ask you what you are going to do."[144]

News then came of "a mob of negroes . . . in Court Square,
attempting to rescue Burns." The meeting instantly dispersed. An
ax was taken to the jailhouse door. Federal marshals fired, and
fire was returned. Thomas Wentworth Higginson and Bronson
Alcott tried to rally those determined to rescue Burns. Somehow
a federal marshal was killed. Officials invoked martial law and
armed troops marched Burns to a waiting ship. Theodore Parker
was indicted for incitement to riot. Public opinion so supported
him, however, that he could not be brought to trial.

Even some of Boston's most conservative business leaders were
stirred. Amos A. Lawrence, the richest of Boston's cotton mill

owners, denounced the extension of slavery permitted under the Kansas and Nebraska acts. Even Ezra Stiles Gannett now voiced the need for another revolution. He was for obeying the law for now, "but the revolution must come, and such a general revolution is not disobedience." Asked by his daughter what he would do if a fugitive should come to his door, he replied, "I should shelter him and aid him to go further on to Canada, and then I should go and give myself up to prison, and insist on being made a prisoner, [and] accept of no release. For I have decided what to do as an individual against the government, and therefore I should abide the result."[145]

Some called for cancelling the 1854 Fourth of July celebrations. The Massachusetts Anti-Slavery Society, however, summoned "a Grand Mass Meeting of the Friends of Freedom" in Framingham. Speakers included Thoreau, Sojourner Truth, Unitarian suffragist Lucy Stone, and Southern-born Unitarian Moncure Conway, who gave his first antislavery speech. William Lloyd Garrison first read the words of the Declaration of Independence, emphasizing that "all men are created equal," then noted the contrary assertions in the Fugitive Slave Law, the legal decisions about Burns and Parker, and the pro-slavery clauses of the Constitution. Finally, he burned all the latter documents, saving only the Declaration.

In Springfield, Illinois, a Unitarian attorney named William Herndon had corresponded with Theodore Parker. He obtained a copy of Parker's Fourth of July sermon, calling for the fuller realization of American democracy as "government of all, by all, for all." Herndon's law partner, Abraham Lincoln, would later paraphrase those words in his address at Gettysburg.[146] Lincoln, of course, responded to Southern secession after his 1860 election by trying to preserve the Union. Abolition of slavery came only later as a by-product of the war through the Emancipation Proclamation and the post-war Thirteenth, Fourteenth, and Fifteenth amendments.

Strikingly, Unitarians almost uniformly supported the Union cause, despite other deep differences among them. In 1859, there had been reason to worry about their momentum as a religious force. Some were stodgy and conservative. Others had gone well beyond Unitarianism into radicalism and "free religion." For example, Higginson proved too radical a minister for the Unitarians of Newburyport, Massachusetts, resigning there in 1848 and becoming minister of the Free Church of Worcester. Along with Parker and Dr. Samuel Gridley Howe, Higginson was later among "the Secret Six"—admirers of John Brown's abolitionism who raised the funds he used in 1859 to try to capture the federal armory at Harper's Ferry, Virginia, and start an armed slave insurrection.[147] By that time Parker, dying of tuberculosis, had left for the Caribbean, then Italy. He died in Florence in 1860.

The Unitarian alumni of Harvard Divinity School, meeting in 1859 as they had in 1838 to hear Emerson, did not even send a get-well message to Parker, although it was proposed. They were Unitarians; Parker was one of them no longer. Henry Whitney Bellows of New York echoed their concerns about "free religion" in his critical address, "The Suspense of Faith."[148] Bellows said that the Unitarian movement had stalled spiritually, out of anxiety and apathy. Some had taken Protestantism to an extreme form of individualism. But "the Holy Spirit communicates itself more reliably to humanity in general than it does to private individuals."[149] Bellows wanted to be clear: "If I show the wants of our own system, it is not as advocating a return to the systems we have abandoned; if I question the finality of Protestantism, it not in the interest of Romanism; if I speak in the language of a Churchman, it is not as an Episcopalian, much less as one aiming at the re-establishment of a hierarchy."[150] Still, he was accused of being "popish." He simply wanted Unitarians to pull together. An association made up merely of individual ministers and laymen needed to become an effective organization of liberal churches. In the absence of any such structure, Bellows himself had been filling the leadership gap, reaching out to Universalists like Starr King, visiting distant congregations, and helping others find ministers. As the Civil War began, he emerged as the pivotal leader among Unitarians.[151]

Wary of radicalism and disunion, and fearing war with the South, Bellows still bemoaned the growing number of politicians "to whom the higher law . . . is unknown."[152] Like Gannett's church in Boston, Bellows's own congregation in New York included influential merchants and bankers with business ties to the South, plus opinion leaders like philanthropist Peter Cooper and William Cullen Bryant, editor of the *New York Post*. Cooper offered the Great Hall at Cooper Union to Abraham Lincoln in February 1860 for his first speech in the East as a presidential candidate. Bryant introduced the lanky man from Illinois. Lincoln ended his address on slavery and "a house divided" with the words, "Let us have faith that right makes might, and in that faith let us to the end dare to do our duty as we understand it." Bellows pronounced it a better speech than that of New York's own William Seward. Southerners heard it as threat, responding to Lincoln's election with threats of secession. Bellows saw the Union cause as God's own.[153]

So did others. In November 1861, Bellows's friend, James Freeman Clarke, and Clarke's parishioner, Julia Ward Howe (1819–1910), saw Union soldiers in Washington DC, marching and singing the camp song, "John Brown's body lies a-moldering in the grave / His soul is marching on." Clarke suggested to Howe, "Why do you not write some better words to that stirring tune?" The result was the "Battle Hymn of the Republic."

The women of Bellows's church, along with Dr. Elizabeth Blackwell, organized an aid society. Conditions in the Union Army camps were appalling, with more men dying of disease than in battle. Bellows realized that effective aid work had to be carefully coordinated. He assembled four thousand women at Cooper Union, with a steering committee that appointed Bellows to lead a delegation to Washington to lobby for a US Sanitary Commission. Although the War Department dismissed the delegation as "weak enthusiasts, representing well-meaning but silly women," Bellows's ability to organize people of influence overcame all obstacles. The Commission was soon official, with Bellows as president, Samuel Gridley Howe as a commissioner, and Frederick Law Olmsted, who had previously impressed Bellows when creating New York's Central Park,[154] as executive director. While Olmsted worked with the Union army and its superintendent of nurses, Dorothea Dix, Bellows traveled constantly to raise money. Thomas Starr King raised enormous sums in California, which were shared with the Western Sanitary Commission begun by William Greenleaf Eliot, the Unitarian minister in St. Louis. In Chicago Universalist Mary Livermore became the agent of the Sanitary Commission for the Northwest.

A tireless organizer, Bellows had a strong vision for liberal religion and its institutions. He chaired the board of Antioch College, keeping it open after the death of Horace Mann.[155] When King

Henry Whitney Bellows

died suddenly in March, 1864, Bellows traveled to San Francisco for six months to serve as interim minister. Horatio Stebbins, the Unitarian minister in Portland, Maine, substituted for him in New York before taking over in San Francisco. Bellows maintained a correspondence with nearly every Unitarian minister on the continent. After returning from California, at a special meeting of the AUA in Boston, he urged a more effective organization. He then chaired a committee to plan a national Unitarian conference in New York in April 1865, to which each church would send its minister and two lay delegates. His felt that his Unitarian colleagues were divided into four groups:

> *Conservatives* like Gannett, still resentful of Parker and the radicals and suspicious of anything not originating in Boston.
> *Radicals*, "who really think [Christianity] is only one among . . . other religions," reluctant to come, "thinking some test may be applied, some *creed* slipped around them."
> *Evangelicals*, Christians first in identity, Unitarians only secondarily, relatively few in number.
> *Broad Church men*, like Bellows, Clarke, Frederic Henry Hedge, and Edward Everett Hale, "who recognize the elements of truth in all the other sections, & believe in the possibility of welding them together."[156]

When important Unitarian ministers were reluctant to attend, Bellows convinced cooperative colleagues to exchange pulpits and stir up the laity, resulting in 385 delegates attending from 222 churches. Clarke's opening sermon set the tone, and John Andrew, Governor of Massachusetts, presided. Even so, Bellows could not bring all four factions into alignment and had to settle for losing some of the radicals.

The National Conference of Unitarian Churches was not as broad as Bellows had hoped. As three out of the four groups, and

The Second American Revolution

especially most of the lay delegates, clearly preferred, this was a Unitarian *Christian* body. The Parkerite radical Octavius Brooks Frothingham, Bellows's colleague on the West Side of New York City, denounced the Unitarian Conference as cordial but disappointingly "sectarian." At the second National Conference in Syracuse in 1866, the host minister, Samuel May, convinced others to expand the name to "Unitarian and Other Liberal Christian Churches," as a signal of welcome to Universalists. But that wasn't inclusive enough for free religionists, who wanted the name to say "and Independent Churches."[157]

Cyrus Bartol, Caroline Dall's childhood minister at the West Church in Boston, gathered a group to form a "band of disciples of the Spirit." The Free Religious Association (FRA) held its first public meeting in May 1867, with a large and diverse gathering. Emerson signed on as member number one and spoke. Some of the "most splendid gadflies and dissenters" among Unitarians supported the FRA.[158] They had great intellectual gifts and anticipated trends that would become dominant in the next century, including an emphasis on science, humanistic spirituality, and a global perspective on religion. Yet the FRA soon faltered and never rivaled the National Conference as a practical, effective religious body. Even Emerson soon lost interest, saying that perhaps enough creed killing had been done. Many ministers active in the FRA also maintained ties to Unitarianism and the National Conference.

Caroline Dall provided an interesting lay perspective on these Unitarian cross-currents. By 1870 she was trying to study social problems on a scientific basis, through the American Social Science Association. She knew almost every key leader in the FRA. Yet she worshiped at Clarke's Church of the Disciples, which had become Boston's largest Unitarian congregation. She headed the Sunday school and preached from the pulpit. Clarke called it "broad church" Unitarianism. We might call it "high church." Certainly it was still Christian, although liberal. And it was quite dominant among Unitarians after the Civil War. Unitarian church architecture of the era reflected it: often Romanesque revival or

92

neo-Gothic in style. Yet in some Unitarian souls, especially in Eastern cities and in the Midwest, the concern for a more scientific, ethical, and universal basis for religion was still evolving.

The Last
"Gilded Age"of Inequality

1870
1905

Universalism's Liberal Mission

After the Civil War, Universalists still had roughly twice the numbers that Unitarians could claim, but they were not growing. Universalist leaders looked enviously at the funds other denominations raised for mission. The Unitarians could raise over $220,000 in a single year; the Congregationalists, $750,000; and the Methodists, $8 million! Yet the Universalist national mission fund held less than $10,000, despite a request that all the congregations forward 1 percent of their revenues for that purpose.[159] The denomination required a stronger General Convention to oversee the various state conventions.

The leadership *tried* to launch such a national organization at the 1870 Gloucester gathering to celebrate the centennial of John Murray's arrival in America. The Women's Centenary Aid Association led the fundraising effort, the goal of which was a multi-year "Murray Fund" of as much as $1 million. People came from twenty-one states. There were no apparent theological factions, as there were among the Unitarians. The Universalists were uniform in gathering as liberal Christians. They had already said good-bye to their own radical wing, made up not of Transcendentalists, but of post-Christian Spiritualists. *Christian* Spiritualists were still strongly represented. Yet there were differing theological emphases at Gloucester.[160]

As with the Unitarians, the historically minded "broad church" clergy set the tone. President A. A. Miner of Tufts preached the opening sermon claiming that, like the early theologian Origen

of Alexandria (185–254), the earliest Christians were universalists in spirit, as true Christians have been ever since. Miner
built on Hosea Ballou II's *Ancient History of Universalism* and on
Thomas Whittemore's *Modern History of Universalism* while trying to ground Universalism in a form of evolution overseen by a
chastening but ultimately loving God. George K. Skinner, minister in Quincy, Massachusetts, declared that the gathering meant
that Universalism "was now a *church*, and no longer just a loose
denominational organization."[161]

Other speakers put Christian identity ahead of denominational
identity. For them Universalism was simply one expression of the
Church Universal, carrying out a mission *within* the wider Christian Church as well as beyond it. Edwin H. Chapin of New York's
Fourth Universalist Society (the Church of the Divine Paternity)
preached to an overflow crowd of seven thousand at the communion service, reminding listeners that "There is a deeper church
than the Universalist church; it is Christ's church," and "there are
. . . hundreds of thousands who have no fixed, definite views. . . .
They know one thing—that they believe in Christ."[162] His evangelism echoed elements of John Murray's own theology. According
to Elbridge Gerry Brooks of Philadelphia, Universalism's mission
was melding the best of Catholicism and Protestantism to become
"the Church of the Future," harmonizing reason and faith in liturgical forms, but as "the Church *republicanized*," meaning without
bishops or hierarchy.[163]

A third emphasis was on the harmony of Universalism with
American Republican ideals. Listeners were exhorted to work
together to extend those ideals around the globe, now that the
Republic, from its sins of slavery and war, had been restored to
"happiness and wholeness." Noting the Boston Massacre of 1770
coincided with John Murray's arrival, former Governor Israel
Washburn of Maine declared that Universalism alone could maintain the American faith "that all men are created equal, that they
are endowed by their Creator with certain unalienable rights,
. . . [saying] these fundamental principles . . . are identical with

those of Universalism, and . . . inconsistent with those of the old Church."[164] Of the recent defeat of Napoleon III in France, Mary Rice Livermore exuded,

We are pressing on with hot, swift feet to the great, grand time . . . to which the hearts and minds of the whole world reach forward, and we shall have but one worship, that of the Universal Father, who embraces in His nature every form of love known to us, loving creatures of His; when we shall recognize the great tie of brotherhood the world over; when we shall be done with wars and battles.[165]

Despite high attendance and enthusiasm, the Gloucester meeting did not result in a notably stronger national organization. Fundraising largely remained the responsibility of local churches and the state conventions. The Murray Fund raised about $129,000 for missions, yet the largest individual gift, $31,000 from John Buchtel of Akron, Ohio, went to a Universalist college in his own city, to bear his name.[166] Ministers in fellowship with the General Convention and the various state conventions were now required to adhere to the 1803 Winchester Profession of Faith, with its emphasis on scriptural authority. A previous clause that had guaranteed liberty of conscience was dropped. This confessional requirement resulted in a heresy trial of one of the few Universalist Transcendentalists.

Herman Bisbee (1833–1879) had graduated from the Universalist theological seminary in Canton, New York, and was serving the Universalist society in St. Anthony, Minnesota. He began to preach in a Transcendentalist mode after spending time in the East, observing that "religion is the effort which man makes to perfect himself, not the effort that God makes to perfect him."[167] Attacked in the Universalist press for disparaging the Bible and sounding like the "Boston Free Religionists," Bisbee reaffirmed his loyalty to Universalism, but to no avail. The Committee on Fellowship of the Minnesota State Convention of Universalists investigated and recommended his removal; the Convention approved their report, forty-seven to twenty-three. Although his congregation supported him, changing its name to the First *Independent* Universalist Society, Bisbee, who had recently lost his wife and was suffering from poor health, left for a period of study at Harvard and Heidelberg. He returned to ministry as a Unitarian, at the church in South Boston where Parker had preached about "The Transient and the Permanent in Christianity."

Predictably, the next phase of this controversy featured efforts to change the wording of the Winchester Profession. Starting in 1875, proposals to modify a word or phrase or substitute a new statement of Universalist belief were debated at each General Convention. All failed. Many grew resentful over the time being wasted.[168] After all, the purpose of the Convention was to promote the mission, outreach, and influence of Universalism.

The high-water mark of Universalism's numerical and theological influence had been reached thirty years before. Still, the 1870s were probably the high point of the movement's influence in popular culture, politics, and public affairs. The leading force in popular entertainment was Phineas T. Barnum, an active and devoted Universalist. Whatever one may think of his relationship to Tom Thumb or Jumbo the Elephant, he would never have made the comment attributed to him about "suckers."[169] Horace Greeley, the reformer and journalist (who *did* advise, "Go West, young man; go West, and grow up with the country."[170]) ran for president on behalf of both the Liberal Republicans and the Democrats in 1872. He died shortly after losing in a landslide to General Ulysses S. Grant. But from Maine to Minnesota, many Universalists did hold public office. A remarkable number were from one family—the Washburn brothers, raised as Universalists in Livermore, Maine.

Israel Washburn Jr. (1813–1883), the recent governor of Maine, spoke in Gloucester. (His successor served as presiding officer of the Convention.) He had also served in Congress, and was the eldest of the seven Washburn boys. Algernon (1814–1879), the second brother, was a Boston merchant, and later, the family banker. Elihu (1816–1887), the third, represented Illinois in Congress from 1852 to 1869, then served as ambassador to France from 1869 to 1876.[171] He was considered for the Republican nomination for the presidency in 1880 and 1884. The fourth brother, Cadwallader (1818–1882), represented Wisconsin for three terms in Congress, was a Major General at Vicksburg, and returned to Congress before being elected Governor of Wisconsin. His business interests included lumber, railroads, and founding the Gold Medal Flour Company, later called General Mills. Charles (1822–1889), the fifth brother, owned and edited a California newspaper. When he failed to get elected to Congress (to join three brothers there), President Lincoln appointed him US envoy to Paraguay. In 1871 he ran unsuccessfully for Governor of California. He invented an early typewriter and wrote novels. The sixth brother, Samuel (1824–1890), was a sea captain known as "the Commander." William Washburn (1831–1912), the seventh brother, made a fortune in businesses similar to Cadwallader's. The effective founder of Universalism in Minneapolis, he served not only as Congressman, but later as a US Senator. Of these Universalist farm boys from Maine, Andrew Carnegie commented, "Their career is typically American; seven sons, all of them men of mark."[172]

While such Universalist men were making their mark in the Gilded Age, Universalist women were also moving into the public sphere. Mary Rice Livermore (1820–1905) was the most popular female lecturer in America—"the Queen of the Platform." She spoke without notes, yet her lectures were carefully crafted to appeal to a broad audience. "Concerning Husbands and Wives" spoke of equal partnership in marriage and "The Battle of Life" urged people to work for the world that should be. In "Does the Liquor Traffic Pay?" she outlined the social costs of alcohol. Livermore revised annually and delivered over eight hundred times a talk entitled "What Shall We Do with Our Daughters?" urging that the next generation of women be educated for new roles in society.

Livermore founded the Association for the Advancement of Women, served as president of the American Woman Suffrage Association, and for twenty years, until her death in 1895, was president of the Massachusetts Woman's Christian Temperance Union.[173]

Having raised the money for the 1870 Centennial and its mission, Universalist women refused to disband in favor of the ineffectual and male-dominated General Convention. They continued as the Women's Centenary Association (WCA). Their mission was "to assist weak parishes, foster Sunday schools, help educate worthy young students for the ministry, relieve the needs of disabled preachers, minister's wives and orphans, distribute denominational

Augusta Jane Chapin

literature, and to do both home and foreign missionary work."[174] In 1874, when they received a plea for a missionary from six small Universalist groups in Scotland, the very heartland of English-speaking Calvinism, the WCA's president, Caroline Soule, went herself. During her visit, the Scots ordained her to the Universalist ministry. When she left, two men were unable to replace her. She retired in 1893 and returned to Glasgow, where she remained until she died ten years later.[175]

As women advanced Universalism's domestic mission, they also thought globally. Augusta Jane Chapin (1836–1905) grew up in Michigan, in a Universalist family that had moved there from Vermont. She knew as a teenager that it was her mission in life to preach. She learned and later taught Greek, Latin, French, and German. Having heard her eloquence in the pulpit, the Michigan Convention ordained her in Lansing in 1863 at the age of twenty-seven. At the Convention in Gloucester in 1870, she was the sole female ministerial delegate. Elected to the Council, she insisted on non-gender specific rules for ministerial fellowship. Her domestic missions included short-term ministries in Iowa, Wisconsin, Massachusetts, California, Oregon, Pennsylvania, Illinois, Michigan, Nebraska, and New York. During the 1893 Parliament of the World's Religions in Chicago, she chaired the Women's Committee. By 1901, looking back on that experience, Chapin declared, "the Church Universal, which is undying . . . belongs to all nations and to all times. . . . Let the creeds remain as historic landmarks, but let the church the Master founded move on."[176]

Quillen Hamilton Shinn (1845–1907) grew up in what became West Virginia. A well-known Universalist missioner, his effective preaching was consistently grounded in the Bible. After graduating from St. Lawrence, the Universalist school in Canton, New York, in 1870, Shinn served for twenty years in New England, always establishing a wider preaching circuit. He introduced Universalist "Summer Meetings" on the shores of Lake Winnipesaukee in New Hampshire and at Ferry Beach on the coast of Southern Maine.[177] He also organized a Universalist church in Omaha, Nebraska. Appointed by the General Convention as "General Missionary," he visited some thirty-four states and two Canadian provinces,[178] averaging nearly a sermon per day. His *modus operandi* included distributing flyers about his impending arrival with the Universalist gospel, and then, after speaking, gathering the most enthusiastic to start a new congregation. Although some groups endured, many did not. As "the Grasshopper Missionary," Shinn became one of the best known Universalists in the United States. After 1895 the General Convention appointed him "Missionary to the Southern States."

Southern Universalist groups were mostly rural and all-white. Joseph Jordan (1842–1901) was the first African American to be ordained a Universalist minister. As a Baptist minister in Norfolk, Virginia, he read Thomas Whittemore's *The Plain Guide to Universalism* and in 1886 went to Philadelphia to meet with Universalist

Quillen Hamilton Shinn

leaders there. The next year he organized a congregation in Norfolk with about twenty black families, who urged him to establish a day school for their children. He sought aid and recognition from the General Convention. Judged to have a "clear and bright mind" and a character "free alike from pretension and from abjectness," Jordan was soon licensed to preach, ordained, and admitted to full fellowship, as was his congregation.[179] The 1893 Universalist General Convention, meeting in Washington DC raised funds for a church building and school furnishings. Shinn organized a branch of the Young People's Christian Union and declared that "no man can be a Universalist whose love did not take in all races and colors of men."[180]

When Jordan died in 1901, an African-American colleague, Thomas E. Wise, took over.[181] With Shinn's help, Wise established a second mission and school twenty miles away in Suffolk, Virginia, which soon became stronger than the Norfolk school. The schools drew more loyalty than the associated churches; the latter remained dependent upon General Convention aid. When Wise added a third mission and school in Ocean View, north of Norfolk, to serve the African-American community there, the Convention sent a commission to look into finances. They recommended closing the two weaker schools and changing the Suffolk school to emphasize practical trades, as popularized by Booker T. Washington and the Hampton Institute. Wise, who had been to Howard University and had read W.E.B. DuBois, wanted academic training at the schools. Frustrated with the Universalists, he joined the African American Methodist Episcopal Church in 1904, then left the area. The Universalists hired Joseph Fletcher Jordan (no relation to the earlier Joseph Jordan) to take over the Suffolk mission and school.[182]

In the remote Pigeon River Valley of western North Carolina, Quillen Shinn found a small Universalist group that an itinerant preacher had gathered in the 1860s. They held services in local homes and had ordained one of their own, a farmer named James Inman who was in his mid-seventies when Shinn met him and encouraged the erection of a chapel. With initial pledges of only four dollars in cash and eighty hours of labor, plus the work of Inman and Shinn, it took a whole year, but in 1903 Inman's Chapel was dedicated. Like the Suffolk school, it continued for some decades as a national Universalist mission project.[183]

The most distant Universalist mission was to Japan. Throughout the 1880s Universalists discussed sending their message overseas to a non-Christian country. Why should Christian missionaries tell potential converts that their ancestors were all in hell simply because the missionaries had not arrived sooner? Knowing that Meiji-era Japan was eager to learn from the West, George Perin (1854–1921) of Boston's Shawmut Avenue Universalist

Joseph Fletcher Jordan

Church led a mission there in 1890. Accompanying him to help teach English were his congregant Margaret Schouler and George Cate, newly graduated from Tufts and ordained as a missionary by the General Convention. Perin established a related church in Tokyo and a small seminary where he began training seven Japanese Universalist ministers. Although a Unitarian mission begun a year earlier offered to collaborate with Perin, the General Convention found the possibility that Universalist-Unitarian consolidation might begin in Japan "absurd and preposterous."[184] Japanese Universalism grew to a thousand members and eight ministers. But like Shinn's work, it spread itself thin. Today only two small congregations survive.[185]

The first Parliament of the World's Religions convened at the Chicago World's Fair of 1892, marking four hundred years since Columbus first landed in the Americas. Both Unitarians and Universalists participated as leaders. Olympia Brown preached on 1 John 4:20b: "If ye love not your brother whom ye have seen, how can ye love God whom ye have not seen?"[186] But when Chicago-area religious liberals tried to follow the Parliament with an American Congress of Liberal Religious Societies, with Universalist A. N. Alcott of Elgin, Illinois, as secretary, the Illinois Universalist Convention removed Alcott from fellowship for daring to serve "a religious organization not in fellowship with the Universalist denomination."[187] His colleague, J. M. Pullman of Lynn, Massachusetts, addressed the Congress the next year, quoting a frequent barb to Universalism: Having squatted on one of the biggest words in the English language, they should either "improve the property or move off the premises."[188]

Living up to the Universalist name was not easy. It grew harder as the social problems of the industrial age deepened. When George Perin returned from Japan in 1894, his next mission was to expand the ministries of the Shawmut Universalist Church in downtown Boston into "The Everyday Church," featuring programs aimed at the needs of growing immigrant communities.[189]

South of Chicago, in the town of Pullman, Illinois, an industrial strike exploded into violence. Wealthy industrialist George
Pullman (1831–1897), an active Universalist and the brother of
two ministers, had established the town as a paternalistic community for the workers who built Pullman railroad cars. Demand
for rail cars fell after the financial panic of 1893, so Pullman cut
wages and his workers went on strike. Eugene Debs' American
Railway Union boycotted handling Pullman cars. President Grover Cleveland sent in twelve thousand army troops to break the
strike. Eventually, a quarter of a million workers in twenty-seven
states joined the strike resulting in property damage, the deaths
of thirteen strikers, and the wounding of fifty-seven more. By the
time George Pullman died in 1897, he was so unpopular with
workers that even as a Universalist he had to be buried in a lead-
lined coffin in a reinforced steel-concrete vault to prevent more
violence against him on the other side of death.[190]

Apart from missions, principled opposition to the death penalty, and support of prison reform, it is hard to document much
Universalist social activism or growth during this period. Women's
suffrage was repeatedly "laid on the table" at the General Convention. Olympia Brown was forced from her pulpit in Bridgeport,
Connecticut, by the congregation's patron, P. T. Barnum, among
others, for spending too much time on the issue.[191]

The General Convention had never filled the post of General
Superintendent. So in 1898, Isaac Atwood left the presidency of the
theological school at St. Lawrence University to lead the national
Universalist body. The next year he gathered a General Convention
that was even larger than the 1870 gathering. He rivaled Quillen
Shinn in miles traveled. Constantly mediating disputes and discouraged by the tendency of many churches "to cut down expenses, and
'get along with a cheaper minister,'" he stepped down in 1905.[192]
When no one wanted to succeed him, he stayed on as his own
interim replacement. So despite considerable mission work and
the sincere efforts of its leaders, Universalism entered the twentieth
century struggling—organizationally, numerically, and spiritually.

Unitarian Parsonages Move West

While one well-known view of church life is from the pulpit, and another is from the pew, the parsonage provides a fascinating behind-the-scenes view. Historian Cynthia Grant Tucker has explored the lives and views of two groups of post–Civil War Unitarian parsonage women in *Prophetic Sisterhood: Liberal Women Ministers of the Frontier, 1880–1930* and *No Silent Witness: The Eliot Parsonage Women and Their Unitarian World.*[193] In *No Silent Witness,* Tucker takes us behind the parsonage doors of the First Unitarian Church of St. Louis, Missouri, in 1870.

William Greenleaf Eliot (1811–1887) had started his work there as an evangelist, ordained to that calling in 1834 at Channing's Federal Street Church in Boston. Eliot was a direct descendant of John Eliot, the Puritan evangelist to the Native Americans of New England. Three years later he brought out to join him a young wife of equal New England lineage. Abigail Adams Cranch Eliot (1817–1908) shared the name of her grandmother's famous sister, who had exhorted her husband, John Adams, to "remember the ladies." Although William and Abby had fourteen children during their marriage, three died as infants, two as toddlers, two more before the age of ten, and their first-born daughter as well as Abby's own namesake at age seventeen—leaving only five surviving children out of fourteen.

Abigail had to cope with all of these tragic losses by living out the Eliot family motto: "*Tace et Face*"—roughly, "Keep Silent and Work." It has often been said, "If you scratch a Unitarian, you

109

find a Calvinist." The irony is that Abby could not let people in a religious atmosphere still steeped in Calvinism see the Unitarian minister's wife complaining against "the will of God." She worked instead: not only tending her own household, but calling daily on parishioners, organizing Sunday school parties and teas, sewing with the ladies of the church, and only sitting down to rest at home if she had a basket of knitting or mending at hand.[194] Frontier conditions, cholera, congregants' complaints about her husband's leadership of the failed effort to keep Missouri a free, rather than a slave state—nothing of this could be allowed to daunt her or distract her from the mission she had agreed to share.

William's strategy was not to engage in theological debates with the orthodox churches, but rather to outdo them in good works and in spreading a more liberal faith. So he relentlessly promoted local efforts for public health and education. He traveled widely as a Unitarian evangelist, organizing a Western Unitarian Conference (WUC).[195] As he planted and nurtured new Unitarian congregations through Illinois and Wisconsin, he sent home terse notes to Abby, encouraging her to be "cheerful and happy" rather than "Calvinist and blue." Slave-owning Unitarians left the church as the Civil War approached. William supported the Union and organized the Western Sanitary Commission to save the lives of Union soldiers from disease and wounds. By 1870, he was exhausted. He had nurtured many local educational projects—a school for homeless boys, a girls' academy named the Mary Institute (after a daughter who had died), and a college. The last was briefly called "Eliot Seminary," to his great chagrin; later the Polytechnic Institute; then Washington University. In 1870 he became its first Chancellor.[196]

Abby fretted about the church, without her husband as its pastor. She did not much like his successor. She also worried over their eldest son, Thomas Lamb Eliot (1841–1937), who was imitating his father as a Unitarian evangelist to the West. After attending the Polytechnic and Harvard Divinity, he was ordained in St. Louis and went to Portland, Oregon, as the first Unitarian minister on that frontier. He and his wife, Henrietta Robins Mack Eliot (1845–1940, called "Etta"), had named their first child William Greenleaf Eliot Jr. (1866–1956). Grandmother Abby made the daunting trip to Oregon, alone, to visit in 1870. She wanted to see her grandson. Years later she wrote to Tom about her own reaction to losing children: that "Papa said better to have them and see them go than not to have them at all" and that he had promised they would "have them again" in heaven, "and then no more sorrow"—although *she* had found little consolation in that "old story."[197] Blessedly, William Jr. survived to become, along with a younger brother, yet a third generation of Unitarian Eliot evangelists. We will also meet a fourth generation.

Abby Eliot had known her Portland daughter-in-law, Etta, from the time Etta and son Tom met in St. Louis as students at the Polytechnic. Even then she had started helping by reading aloud to him. Something was wrong with Tom's eyes—he could not read long on his own without getting headaches. Having served as secretary to his father while Tom was at Harvard, Etta was familiar with what would be expected of her as a minister's wife. She encouraged women in Portland to join the Unitarian church. She ran the congregation whenever he was away—either spreading the liberal gospel through the Northwest, as his father had in the Midwest, or retiring to a rural cabin along a mountain stream to recover from an episode of melancholy.

Etta was gifted with words. Some Sundays she could be seen mouthing phrases from the front pew while Tom attempted to preach without notes. She was outraged by the poor treatment of Unitarians by other Portland churches. As a former Congregationalist, she even submitted an anonymous essay on "sub-Christian sectarianism" to Henry Ward Beecher's *Christian Union*. When the editors of the Unitarian *Christian Register* asked to reprint it, Tom feared that the disclosure of Etta's identity would mark them both as complainers. *Tace et face*, he said: Let our good deeds do the talking.[198] Etta thus confined her literary efforts to poetry, letters, and juvenile fiction until after her father-in-law died in 1886.

Then she began to plan worship services and to substitute for her husband and son in the pulpit. Etta's loneliness was often painful. She could not complain to Abby, but to her own mother she confessed, "My husband don't talk, and I have no female intimates."[199] Yet she tried not to let her resentment show.

William Greenleaf Eliot Sr. had been reluctant to see women in the pulpit but did not oppose outright their efforts to prepare for the ministry or seek ordination. After 1870 he and Abby fretted over post-war changes in church and society, rude servants, labor strikes, and especially changes in the WUC. In 1870 his colleague John Learned of St. Louis's second Unitarian society, the Church of the Unity, found inspiration less in the Bible and the spiritual example of Jesus than from ethical transcendentalism. If certain ministers sought to be "more than Christian," William worried that they were actually less. In general, William Sr. was inclined to a "broad church" view, as was his friend James Freeman Clarke.

Back East, the leaders of the FRA were promoting "development of self," in contrast to traditional Unitarian Christian doctrine promoting only imitation of Jesus. Octavius Brooks Frothingham and Francis Ellingwood Abbott, leaders of the FRA, even asked to have their names removed from the yearbook of the AUA. The catalyst for the "Yearbook Controversy" had been the editor dropping William J. Potter of New Bedford, Massachusetts, from the ministerial list in 1873, when he said he served a Unitarian congregation but did not call himself a Unitarian Christian nor identify with any denominational label.

The Western Conference protested by passing a resolution declaring its fellowship to be based on "no dogmatic tests," and welcoming "all . . . who desire to work with it in advancing the kingdom of God."[200] Francis Ellingwood Abbott of the FRA could not accept even such a passing reference to the message of Jesus, reminding his Western colleagues that "the spiritual ideal of Christianity is the suppression of self and perfect imitation of Jesus the Christ. The spiritual ideal of free religion is the development of self, and the harmonious education of all its powers to the highest possible degree."[201]

Free religion advocates further divided internally between those basing their convictions on ethical "intuitionism" and those, like Abbott, wanting a more "scientific" basis for faith. By contrast, the Western Conference divided over Unitarian unity, with tension between Unitarian Christians like Eliot and the so-called "Unity men" led by Jenkin Lloyd Jones (1843–1918).

Born in an area of Wales known as "the Black Spot of Unitarianism" for its concentration of Unitarian churches, and with nine uncles serving as Unitarian ministers, Jones (or "Jenk") was brought to rural Wisconsin as a baby when his family emigrated there. Although admitted to the local Protestant church, they refused to subscribe to any creed, causing the minister who admitted them to be disciplined, at which point they collectively resigned. Aversion to any creed was a family tradition. After serving in the Union Army, Jones experienced a "spiritual explosion" that led him to Meadville Theological School in Pennsylvania. His senior paper explored the implication of evolution on theology and religion. After graduating in 1870, he returned to Wisconsin as a traveling missionary and was soon convinced that the WUC needed its own missionary methods and funding, free from control or funding from the Boston-based AUA. When appointed secretary and missionary of the WUC in 1875, he traveled ten to twenty-five thousand miles a year targeting not just displaced Yankees in cities, but German, Norwegian, Danish, and Dutch immigrant groups with liberal religious leaders.

When he began, the WUC served forty-three congregations with a collective debt of $100,000. When he resigned in 1884 to revive Fourth Unitarian Church of Chicago as All Souls Church, the WUC served eighty-seven congregations, owing only $7,000. Mirroring the Universalist itinerant Quillen Shinn, he preached 1,370 sermons in nine years,[202] and lectured widely on topics including women's rights and suffrage, promoting women in ministry. He helped to start the Post Office Mission, mailing sermons and tracts to people living far from any Unitarian church. Beginning in

1878, Jones and William Channing Gannett (1840–1923) of Unity Church (Unitarian) in St. Paul, Minnesota, co-edited the weekly magazine *Unity*, promoting "Freedom, Fellowship, and Character" and published the book *The Faith That Makes Faithful* (1886).

Some Western Unitarians felt that the principles promoted in *Unity* lacked clear focus. Jabez Sunderland (1842–1936) of Ann Arbor, Michigan, Jones's successor as WUC secretary, lamented, "We have tried to make our movement so broad that its constant tendency has been to lose all cohesiveness, or significance, or inspiration, or power, or value."[203] Seeking closer cooperation with liberal Christians in the AUA, Sunderland launched a new magazine entitled *The Unitarian* to "hold to our old freedom from dogmatic creeds and yet stand clearly for belief in God and worship and the spirit of Christ." In his pamphlet *The Issue in the West*, he argued that by "hauling down our Theistic and Christian flags and running up in their place the Ethical only, I am convinced we should seal the fate of Unitarianism in the West." But in 1886 the WUC rejected Sunderland's resolution declaring its purpose to be "promotion of a religion of love to God and love to man" and instead adopted Gannett's non-theistic statement entitled "Things Commonly Believed Today Among Us" the following year:

We believe that to love the Good and to live the Good is the supreme thing in religion;

We hold reason and conscience to be final authorities in matters of religious belief;

We honor the Bible and all inspiring scripture, old and new;

We revere Jesus, and all holy souls that have taught men truth and righteousness and love, as prophets of religion;

We believe in the growing nobility of Man; We trust the unfolding Universe as beautiful, beneficent, unchanging Order; to know this order is truth; to obey it is right and liberty and stronger life;

We believe that good and evil invariably carry their own

recompense, no good thing being failure and no evil thing success; that heaven and hell are states of being; that no evil can befall the good man in either life or death; that all things work together for the victory of the Good;

We believe that we ought to join hands and work to make the good things better and the worst good; counting nothing good for the self that is not good for all;

We believe that this self-forgetting, loyal life awakes in man the sense of union here and now with things eternal— the sense of deathlessness; and this sense is to us an earnest of the life to come;

We worship One-in-All—that life whence suns and stars derive their orbits and the soul of man its Ought,— that Light which lighteth every man that cometh into the world, giving us power to become the sons of God,—that Love with which our souls commune.[204]

Back in the East, Clarke continued to try to mediate disputes between free religionists and his fellow Unitarian Christians. He knew other religions also held spiritual and moral truths. While leading the reform-minded Church of the Disciples, Clarke also held an appointment at Harvard Divinity as professor of natural theology and Christian doctrine, and then later as professor of ethnic religions and the creeds of Christendom. In an era of didactic instruction, he led lively classroom discussions, questioning students about assigned reading and listening respectfully to their answers, summarizing key points, and only then giving his views. Frederic Henry Hedge, Clarke's friend and colleague as professor of ecclesiastical history and minister of First Parish in Brookline, was the first to use the word "ecumenical" in its modern, post-Reformation sense in an English-language text. But Clarke sought unity not only among Christians, but among the religions of all times and places. He published his Lowell Institute lectures in two volumes as *Ten Great Religions* (1871, 1883) and *Events and Epochs in Religious History* (1881).

Despite their differences, Jenkin Lloyd Jones, Jabez Sunderland, and Clarke all viewed religion in both global and evolutionary terms. Neither a Calvinist nor a fatalist, Clarke tended to evaluate other expressions of faith "in reference to universal or absolute religion," using a standard derived from his fellow Transcendentalist Theodore Parker. Clarke judged some faith practices as "ethnic" and partial, others as "progressive" and universal. Among the latter he saw only his own liberal Christianity as able to "reconcile antagonist truths and opposing tendencies," to battle entrenched social evils, to promote democracy, and then to evolve into a universal religion. He seemed to seek a liberal "science of missions." Knowing that Calvinism continued to dominate American theological discourse, Clarke in his later years offered a new five-point summary of the liberal alternative:

> *The Fatherhood of God* (not the sovereignty of God);
> *The Brotherhood of Man* (with all sisters as equals);
> *The Leadership of Jesus* (as exemplar, not as sole divine representative on earth);
> *Salvation by Character* (not by faith, nor works, but by inner change);
> *The Continuity of Human Development* [i.e., Restorationist Universalism] *or The Progress of [Hu]Mankind onward and upward forever.*

I once had a parishioner who grew up, like many Unitarian children from 1890 to 1940, with those "Five Points of Unitarianism" displayed in Sunday school and then memorized. "That last one, you know, I had a hard time believing," she told me. "Good for you," I said. "Doubt is always a part of faith. Hope is good. But inevitable progress? I'll bet two world wars and a great depression made that hard to believe, indeed." She nodded.

Clarke promoted the leadership of women, including his parishioner Julia Ward Howe, who had had a very difficult marriage with her husband, Samuel. Writing in the first 1870 issue of the *Woman's Journal*, founded by Lucy Stone, Julia declared,

> During the first two-thirds of my life, I looked to the mas-
> culine idea of character as the only true one. I sought its
> inspiration, and referred by merits and demerits to its . . .
> verdict. . . . The new domain now made clear to me was
> that of true womanhood—woman no longer in her ancil-
> lary relation to her opposite, man, but in her direct relation
> to the divine plan and purpose . . . sharing with man every
> human right and human responsibility. This discovery was
> like the addition of a new continent to the map of the world
> . . . a new testament to the old ordinances.[205]

Howe was clearly called to preach and tried to form a Woman's Ministerial Conference after the Civil War. She preached
widely, not only in Clarke's pulpit. Opposition came not only
from male clergy, but also from women in the pews. Women
who worked for the church with no recognition at all could easily resent those taking more public roles as leaders. After Clarke
died in 1888 at the age of 78 (he had been born in the same year
as Theodore Parker and Margaret Fuller), Unitarian laywomen
took over mediating the unedifying "I-am-more-inclusive-than-
thou" squabbles among Unitarian clergy. In 1889 they formed
the Alliance of Unitarian and Other Liberal Christian Women.
"We shall *forget theology* in our living faith and burning love,"[206]
declared one of its early advocates. "Help realize what we are all
working for . . . that we *all may be one.*"[207] Abby May,[208] a leading figure in the new Alliance, became related to the Eliots of St.
Louis and Portland when her niece Mary Jackson May (1859–
1926) married Tom Eliot's younger brother Christopher Rhodes
Eliot (1856–1945) during his ministry at First Parish Church in
Dorchester, Massachusetts.[209]

Christopher inherited the old Eliot commitment to Unitarian
evangelism; Mary, the strong social justice mission of the May family. After 1894 their ministry defied the stereotype of well-to-do

Boston Unitarianism. The Bulfinch Place Church in the working class West End began as a chapel in the ministry-at-large to the poor. The parsonage was within walking distance of the slums surrounding the church, where their ministry combined "practical religion" with social work.[210] Their children continued the work. Frederick May Eliot (1889–1958) skillfully led the denomination through the mid-twentieth century, as we shall soon see. His sisters, Martha and Abby—both of whom partnered with other women—provided institutional leadership in public health and early childhood education, respectively.[211]

"Practical religion" was a catch phrase for Unitarians in the late nineteenth century. Unitarians founded or led countless American institutions, including public colleges, universities, schools, hospitals, and other charities and non-profit organizations. Given the Unitarian emphasis on inclusiveness, few were given any sectarian label—such good works were meant to serve everyone. Washington University and Reed College are two enduring examples. Horace Davis, a devout Unitarian whose second wife, Edith, was the daughter of Thomas Starr King, was both president of the University of California at Berkeley and chair of the board of Stanford University, appointed by the founders.

Occasionally some Unitarians were even practical enough to know when *not* to try to improve something! Here is one of my favorite examples: The Grant Administration (1869–1877) placed various Protestant denominations in charge of Indian welfare, assigning Unitarians to the Utes of Colorado. They sent Jabez Nelson Trask, a young graduate of Harvard Divinity School, to the Los Pinos reservation. The Utes didn't know what to make of him in his dark blue, swallow-tail coat and the floppy, broad-brimmed beaver hat and green goggles he wore to protect himself from the sun. Respectful of their traditional way of life, he mainly observed, making little effort to change their culture. White gold-hunters and land-grabbers kept impinging on the Utes. Trask kept reminding the government that the tribe was peaceful. He lasted just over a year, when local settlers demanded that he be removed.

The Utes, who called him "the frog," did not object; but at least he had not tried to convert them.[212]

Other late nineteenth-century Unitarian work in multi-cultural "practical religion" lasted longer. Charles Dall, whose estranged wife, Caroline, we met earlier, partnered with an indigenous Hindu reform movement called the Brahmo Samaj[213] in Calcutta, India. He founded schools for girls and homeless street children, reported on social conditions, published lectures and tracts, and translated Unitarian literature. In 1880, he began corresponding with one Hajom Kissor Singh, from the Khasi Hills of North East India.

The Khasis were never Hindus but a tribal culture, believing in an all-pervading Spirit. The British had brought in Calvinist missionaries from Scotland and Wales. Singh graduated from one of their schools and came to appreciate the teachings of Jesus, though he believed in only one divine Spirit, not a trinity. The missionaries said he was a heretic, a Unitarian. He thanked them for teaching him about how Jesus had come to teach them about how they *should* treat others. Dall then helped Singh to translate Unitarian worship materials and to begin to write many of his own original hymns. The result was a Khasi worship book for "the religion of One God." Schools flourished after the 1896 visit of Jabez Sunderland, an early ally of the Indian independence movement.[214] The Khasi Unitarians now have over thirty congregations and schools, with about nine thousand adherents.[215]

Sunderland's colleague Jenkin Lloyd Jones was general secretary of the planning group for the 1893 World's Parliament of Religions in Chicago. There Americans heard spokespersons for non-Christian religions for the first time. Fannie Barrier Williams, an African-American member of Jones's All Souls Church, addressed the Parliament, denouncing the use of Christianity to try to keep her people docile.[216] After the Parliament, Jones poured some of his endless energy into trying to organize an alliance of liberal Jews, Unitarians, Universalists, and Ethical Culturists. Frustrated at the tepid support among his fellow Unitarians for his latest attempt to transcend all sectarianism, in 1898 he and All Souls declared themselves to be "undenominational." He devoted himself to his congregation's Abraham Lincoln Centre for social services, to the Anti-Imperialist League, and to other reform causes, not to Unitarianism.

Women ministers in the WUC especially regretted this rupture. Jones had helped support and encourage many of them, starting with Mary Augusta Safford and her partner, Eleanor Gordon. Serving in Humbolt, Sioux Falls, and then Des Moines, Iowa, they were central figures in an "Iowa Sisterhood" of women liberal ministers who brought to ministry a distinctive combination of nurture, domesticity, activism, intellect, and practicality. Historian Cynthia Grant Tucker's *Prophetic Sisterhood* traces the remarkable ministerial careers of twenty-one women in this network, whose reach extended well beyond their base in Iowa and the Midwest.

These were important years in the long political struggles for women's suffrage and temperance reform. But during the 1890s concerns arose regarding the supposed "feminization" of American culture. Conscious efforts to restore American "manhood" surrounded the Spanish-American War, epitomized by Teddy Roosevelt and the Rough Riders. Women ministers encountered increased resistance.

In 1886 the AUA built a new headquarters at 25 Beacon Street in Boston.[217] As of 1898, it also had a new man in charge. Samuel Atkins Eliot II (1862–1950) was distantly related to the Eliots of St. Louis and Portland. His namesake and grandfather had helped to incorporate the AUA in 1825; his father Charles Eliot was the president of Harvard. After graduating from Harvard Divinity School, Sam served as a Unitarian missionary in the Pacific Northwest and then successful early pastorates in Denver and Brooklyn. Intensely aware that Unitarians had been slowly declining in numbers, prestige, and cultural influence, Eliot determined that Unitarianism would again grow and prosper. Still in his mid-thirties, he was full of energy and eager to consolidate a hodge-podge of

Unitarian organizations into a cohesive whole, from which new churches might get building loans, and other services.

He first consolidated the AUA and the National Conference of Unitarian Churches. In 1900 his executive role as AUA secretary was given the title President, along with greater authority. He launched a new International Council of Unitarian and Other Liberal Religious Thinkers and Workers.[218] He tried once again to engage Universalists in cooperative ventures, though without much success. Eliot had few illusions about a post-denominational era arriving anytime soon. His own mission was the revitalization of Unitarianism by applying sound business principles to its work. His implicit strategy was to shape a movement that would attract more progressive men of means, ideas, and influence. *Men.*

Eliot's own mother had died when he was nine. He grew up among male academics at Harvard and he focused on starting and strengthening Unitarian churches in other college and university communities. He had no interest in advancing the careers of women ministers.[219] Instead, he raised academic qualifications for ministerial fellowship. Responding to a shortage of effective male ministers, especially in the West, he worked to establish a Unitarian seminary in California. To lead it, he recruited Earl Morse Wilbur from a ministry in Meadville, Pennsylvania. Pacific Unitarian School, later Starr King School for the Ministry, opened with Wilbur alone teaching all subjects. His wife, Dorothea Dix Eliot, known as Dodie, was the daughter of Thomas Lamb Eliot of Portland. She was called "the Deaness" and raised funds and served as house mother and counselor to the earliest students, who were few in number.[220]

In 1900 there were 457 Unitarian churches in the United States and Canada combined. Three hundred one were in New England, and two-thirds of these were in towns of fewer than ten thousand people. Sixty Unitarian churches within ten miles of Beacon Hill provided over half of the AUA's income.[221] In 1900 the AUA gave away over $40,000 to eighty-nine needy churches, while its income just topped $60,000.

Developing an effective mission strategy for large ambitions and limited resources was not easy. The organization wrestled with a series of questions: What constitutes a good growth opportunity for liberal religion? Should the AUA wait to be approached by people wanting to start a church? How soon should one hope for local self-sufficiency? How often? Is it wise to prop up failing congregations? How do you know when to try again? Above all, how do you balance all this with the spiritual mission of turning the hearts of existing members—who *have* some power and influence—toward concern for the situation of the many others, who have little? And is it possible to do that without paternalism, and without making proverbial "pie-crust promises, easily made and easily broken"? Given the gross economic inequalities of the Gilded Age and the imperialist ambitions developing even among American republicans in this era, these were all pressing questions of "practical religion."

In many Unitarian parsonages, these questions were regularly discussed over Sunday dinner. Surely many mission opportunities were lost. At one Unitarian meeting in New Bedford, Massachusetts, a local African-American minister, William Jackson, who had become a Unitarian appeared and asked for fellowship. They took up a collection of forty-nine dollars and sent him away.[222]

One Unitarian systematically asking questions about social mission was Sam Eliot's uncle, Francis Greenwood Peabody (1847–1936).[223] In 1900, while serving at Harvard as professor of "Christian morals" and as college chaplain, he published *Jesus Christ and the Social Question*. Students laughed about his course, "Ethical Theories and Social Problems: A Practical Examination," calling it "Peabo's drainage, drunkenness and divorce," but the questions it raised also stuck with many of them. How *should* liberal Christians (and others) respond to persistent social problems and injustice? A new progressive era in America was dawning, and, stemming from liberal religion, a new "Social Gospel" would prove to be a shaping force.

The Progressive Era

1905
1935

Unitarian Skepticism and Social Reform

In the early nineteenth century, Universalists preceded Unitarians in publishing, organizing, and spreading westward. By the early twentieth century, however, Unitarians were often leading where Universalists followed. This was especially true of two key developments: engagement with modern industrial society's complex needs for social reform, and religious skepticism. Perhaps the two went hand-in-hand.

A Unitarian Universalist minister of the late twentieth century was asked by a parishioner, "What do you consider to be the very *core* of Unitarian Universalism?" The minister reflected: "It might be our tendency to skepticism." The parishioner quickly replied, "I don't believe *that* for a moment!"[224] So it's true!

I believe Unitarian skepticism also accounts for the denomination's twentieth-century engagement in social reform. After all, Unitarians had come into the modern era inheriting Boston Brahmin privilege. But they also taught their children to be critical thinkers; to reject prevailing justifications for the *status quo*; and even to question first principles, which may be why some of its most effective dissenters were minimalists when it came to defining their faith.

Fanny Holmes, wife of Supreme Court Justice Oliver Wendell Holmes, Jr. (1841–1935), was reportedly asked about her husband's religious identity. "Well, here in Washington I suppose everyone must *be* something," she replied, "but we are from Boston, and are Unitarians, which is the very *least* one can be."[225] Her husband had, in fact, lost his inherited Unitarian faith in the carnage of the Civil War. Agnostic and pragmatic, the great jurist said that "the life of the law has not been logic; it has been experience." Human beings "make their own laws; these laws do not flow from some mysterious omnipresence in the sky, and . . . judges are not independent mouthpieces of the infinite."[226] The "Great Dissenter" held sacred both freedom of speech and freedom of conscience. Trained at his father's autocratic breakfast table to think and question, Holmes admitted that "we are all tattooed in our cradles with the marks of our tribe."[227]

The Unitarian tribe also attracted skeptics from other traditions, but "cradle Unitarians," even in an era when their clergy preached "lyrical theism" and an unwarranted optimism, often grew into
NAACP leading twentieth-century dissenters and reformers. At least three such are too often forgotten: Mary White Ovington (1865–1951),
WILPF founder in 1909 of the National Association for the Advancement of Colored People (NAACP); Emily Greene Balch (1867–1961), founder in 1919 (with Jane Addams) of the Women's International League for Peace and Freedom, awarded the 1946 Nobel Prize for
ACLU Peace; and Roger Baldwin (1884–1981), founder in 1920 of the American Civil Liberties Union.

Baldwin grew up in the Unitarian Society of Wellesley Hills, Massachusetts, with parents who were, like Holmes, "agnostic Unitarians."[228] As a youth he attended church "very regularly," and later he told his biographer, "I helped teach Sunday school and I even listened to the preacher. In fact, as I look back I would say that social work began in my mind in the Unitarian church when I was ten or twelve years old, and I started to do things I thought would help other people."[229]

Balch grew up in the First Church (Unitarian) of Jamaica Plain, a suburb even nearer than Wellesley Hills to Boston.[230] Her childhood was somewhat similar:

Grace was not said unless a visiting minister came to dinner. When I was about ten, a prosy old Unitarian divine

126

was followed at the . . . church by Charles Fletcher Dole.
His warm faith in the force that makes for righteousness
became the chief of all the influences that played upon my
life. He asked us to enlist . . . in the service of goodness . . .
whatever its cost. . . . I never abandoned . . . my desire to
live up to . . . the rule of conscience and . . . a warm and
generous sense of the call to service.[231]

Mary White Ovington grew up in the Second Unitarian Church
of Brooklyn, New York.[232] At the death in 1905 of her childhood
minister, John White Chadwick, she noted that he "never lost an
opportunity in speech or in writing to show his full sympathy
with the colored man." But he also denied himself and his listeners "the pleasures of religious sentimentalism," leaving that to his
chief local competitor, Henry Ward Beecher, the liberal Congregationalist at Plymouth Church.[233]

Chadwick preached poetically but only in the interest of
describing "the life of reason." He opened his pulpit to humanistic
Jews like Felix Adler of the Society for Ethical Culture ("Deed, not
creed") and other rationalists. Still, "on economic questions," as
Ovington noted, Unitarians seemed "as sure of the righteousness
of the present competitive system as any dogmatic Calvinist was
sure of heaven and hell." So Balch watched her childhood church
grow "poorer as the conservative element left it," forcing her to
face socioeconomic facts, and feel a "religious call to intellectual
sincerity."[234]

We first follow Ovington's career. When her father's business
faltered in the panic of 1893, Mary left her studies at "the Harvard
Annex" (later Radcliffe College). She returned to Brooklyn and
served as a settlement house leader in the Greenpoint neighborhood and took an active part in the Social Reform Club. The early
essays by W.E.B. DuBois inspired her to read *The Souls of Black
Folk* (1903). Determined to reach out to people of color who were
excluded from most settlement house work, Ovington attended
the Hampton Institute, corresponded with DuBois, and finally

met him at a 1905 conference in Atlanta. She began to research the social conditions of black people in New York City. In *Half a Man: The Status of the Negro in New York* (1911), she concluded that white racism lay at the very root of "the Negro problem."

"If we deny full expression to a race," Ovington wrote, "if we restrict its education, stifle its intellectual and aesthetic impulses, we make it impossible fairly to gauge its ability."[235] For the *New York Post* she covered DuBois and his new Niagara Movement, while helping to organize a "Constitution League," protesting the failure to implement the Fourteenth and Fifteenth amendments or guarantee full civil rights. She traveled throughout the Deep South, regularly meeting with black male leaders despite considerable risks. Finally, provoked by lynching and race riots in places like Lincoln's own Springfield, Illinois, she organized a committee of black and white leaders, women and men, to sponsor a 1909 national conference at the Cooper Union in New York. That became the National Association for the Advancement of Colored People. Ovington served as the NAACP's first acting executive, later as its director of publicity and research, director of branches, and a chief fundraiser.

One of the five incorporators of the NAACP, Ovington's fellow Unitarian and pastor, John Haynes Holmes (1879–1964),[236] later praised Ovington, noting that she "assumed voluntarily in her one person the duties of all the officials we had—director, secretary, treasurer, and publicity agent. With superb devotion and ability, she carried the work to a point where it must have a paid and trained staff if it were really to be the potent force of which we dreamed. Then, with infinite grace, she stepped down that others might follow on."[237] Ovington chaired the NAACP board from 1917 to 1932 and served on the executive committee for fifteen more years, holding together an interracial coalition of strong personalities and diverse ideologies.[238]

Holmes, like Ovington's childhood minister, was a Unitarian radical.[239] In 1907 he took over New York's Unitarian Church of the Messiah, a declining congregation of the privileged. His first published sermon there addressed "Christianity and Socialism." Holmes argued that the religion of Jesus had been socialist and that modern socialism was again touching the hearts of the poor. He led in organizing the Unitarian Fellowship for Social Justice in 1908 and opposed the reelection of Sam Eliot as AUA president in 1912. The next year he penned a hymn on shipboard as he returned from Europe, where he sensed the likelihood of war:

I hear my people crying in cot and mine and slum,
No field or mart is silent, no city street is dumb.
I see my people falling in darkness and despair.
Whom shall I send to shatter the fetters which they bear?

John Haynes Holmes

We heed, O Lord, thy summons, and answer: Here are we!
Send us upon thine errand, Let us thy servants be!
Our strength is dust and ashes, our years a passing hour;
But thou canst use our weakness to magnify thy power.[240]

A firm pacifist, Holmes was not alone among Unitarians in this
stance.

Balch studied at Bryn Mawr and the Sorbonne before founding Boston's first settlement house, bringing social and educational
services into a poor immigrant neighborhood. To shape another
generation of activists by teaching, she studied further at Harvard
Annex (Radcliffe), Chicago, and Berlin. Wellesley College hired
her to teach sociology and economics. In 1905 she took a sabbatical to study Slavic immigrant communities in America and the
socioeconomic conditions in the Austro-Hungarian Empire that
caused record rates of US immigration. Over 1.25 million new
Americans arrived in the United States in 1907 alone, joining a
population then just over 87 million.[241] That year also saw both a
financial panic and a global outbreak of the plague. Her first book,
Our Slavic Fellow Citizens (1910), was "unique not only in presenting the firsthand viewpoints of immigrants but also in countering
the nativist racial assumptions of her society."[242] She had become,
like Holmes, an internationalist, a socialist, and a pacifist. Balch
joined Jane Addams in the US delegation to the 1915 International
Women's Congress at the Hague. She believed that peace took priority even over women's rights, requiring a conference on women's
issues to be reframed. She met with President Wilson about "con-
tinuous mediation" as an alternative to war, but to no avail. When
war finally broke out, Wellesley fired Balch, ostensibly for her pro-
longed absences on behalf of the IWC. Wellesley colleagues, led by
Katherine Lee Bates, author of "America the Beautiful," protested
her firing. Balch and Addams then founded the Women's International League for Peace and Freedom and began to criticize the
terms of the Versailles Treaty that ended the war, fearing that it
would only lead to another. As the chair of the Nobel Prize com-

mittee later said publicly when presenting Balch the Peace Prize, "It would have been wise to listen to what the women had to say. But there were few who would pay any attention."[243]

Democrat Woodrow Wilson had campaigned for reelection in 1916 under the slogan, "He kept us out of war." But very soon he led the United States to join "the crusade to save democracy," alongside Britain and France. Pacifism came under bipartisan attack as unpatriotic. At the 1917 Unitarian General Conference in Montreal, the Republican and former president William Howard Taft served as moderator. "It is the duty of our church," he told delegates, "to preach the righteousness of the war and the necessity for our winning it in the interest of the peace of the world."[244] John Haynes Holmes, chair of the council, countered with a fiery denunciation of the war and advocacy for reconciliation as the only proper religious stance.[245] Taft left the chair in a fury, from the floor demanding a resolution "that this war must be carried to a successful issue." Holmes reiterated his conscientious pacifism: "So long as I live I will have nothing to do with this war or any war, so help me God!" Taft's resolution passed, 236 to 9. The AUA Board soon decided to deny financial aid to any church whose minister was not in support of the war effort.[246]

Holmes withdrew from Unitarian fellowship. When the Unitarian Church of the Messiah burned the following year, Holmes persuaded his congregation to rename themselves the Community Church of New York. Services were held at Town Hall. He soon extended his message to an eager radio audience. He founded a network of post-denominational community churches.[247] Emily Greene Balch also left the Unitarian fold, finding like-minded pacifists in the Society of Friends (Quakers). In time both resumed Unitarian ties.[248]

After years in St. Louis as a social worker and teacher at Washington University, Roger Baldwin came East in 1917 and met both Ovington and Balch.[249] He helped to lead the American Union against Militarism. Divided over how to deal with conscientious objectors, the AUM spun off a separate National Civil Liberties

Bureau, which Baldwin also led, even going to jail for his own pacifist convictions. Holmes served on the board of what became the ACLU for many years. He embraced the work of Margaret Sanger for women's reproductive rights and Planned Parenthood, and was among the first Americans to discover Gandhi and promote his methods of nonviolent activism. By 1930 Community Church of New York had over eighteen hundred members, reflecting a wide diversity of social class, education, ethnicity, race, belief, and politics —a cross section of New York City itself.

In the meantime, the AUA, under Samuel Eliot, had not ignored social or international issues. Starting in 1905 it sponsored a committee on new Americans and soon had eight field workers among Italian, Swedish, Finnish, Norwegian, and Icelandic immigrants.[250] In 1910, through the international organization of religious liberals that later became the International Association for Religious Freedom, the AUA was introduced to the Czech minister Norbert Čapek. He had come to America in 1914 as a liberal Baptist, become a Unitarian, and then returned to Prague in 1921 with AUA help. Aided also by Charlotte Garrigue Masaryk, a US-born Unitarian married to Czechoslovakia's president, Čapek developed the largest Unitarian congregation in the world, claiming 3,395 members by 1932.[251] Immediately after the armistice of 1918, the AUA also reached out to the Hungarian-speaking Unitarians of Transylvania, a territory given to Romania at Versailles. The Romanian government so suppressed the Hungarian minority's civil, religious, and cultural rights that, in the words of Louis Cornish, it was necessary to "stay the hand of ruthlessness and to give these minority institutions a better fighting chance for functioning and for surviving."[252] The Unitarian missionary in Japan, John Day, transferred his work to Japanese adherents and returned home.[253] The AUA also reached out to the Independent Church of the Philippines, a group Taft had taken under wing during his time as US Commissioner there—although that body eventually found a more comfortable home for its liturgy and polity in the Anglican communion.[254]

Post-war prosperity helped American Unitarianism expand. The Unitarian Laymen's League led the way. Started in 1907 to nurture lay groups where no church could be sustained, the League shifted focus after the war to overall Unitarian promotion. By 1924 it had 270 chapters, twelve thousand members, and offices in four regions. The League sponsored Unitarian rallies and mission preachers, including such prominent speakers as Horace Westwood and William Lawrence Sullivan. The latter had been a Roman Catholic priest and teacher until all such were ordered to take an oath in 1910 repudiating modern science, democracy, and biblical criticism. Sullivan refused. As a Unitarian Christian he boldly called on the Pope to live "the Christ-life," not the life of an authoritarian. Sullivan served Unitarian churches in Schenectady, Manhattan (All Souls), St. Louis, and Germantown, Pennsylvania.[255]

Theologically, American Unitarianism in the 1920s ranged from liberal Christianity, often with a strong Social Gospel goal of "realizing the Kingdom of God," to positions more skeptical of any form of nineteenth-century confidence in human progress or in any "lyrical theism." William Wallace Fenn, the Unitarian Dean of Harvard Divinity, argued, in a 1918 lecture called "War and the Thought of God," that God was not the cause of war; human beings were. So a post-war theology would be one in which the assertion of human responsibility and "human freedom will be definitely and emphatically made."[256]   *Whitehead on list.*

Among such new approaches, one was the process thought of (Alfred North Whitehead) History is fluid, he argued, but it promises no inevitable progress. God is the source of freedom. Metaphysics or talk about God must also take into account modern physics. There is a degree of freedom at every level, from the subatomic to the human. No poor logician, Whitehead had co-written, with Bertrand Russell, a new *Principia Mathematica*, taking into account relativity. Russell became an atheist. Whitehead, an English vicar's son, sought a more credible theology, especially after coming to teach philosophy at Harvard. Even before he returned to Britain to deliver the Gifford lectures that would become *Process and Reality* (1929), he gave a series of four influential lectures on religion at the Unitarian King's Chapel in Boston, published in 1926 as *Religion in the Making*. His was a Socinian God—a Creator who had given the created freedom even to change its ongoing Creator. Henry Nelson Wieman, a philosopher of religion at the University of Chicago (and later a Unitarian) helped to popularize such process thought, giving it a more pragmatic emphasis. "Process," however, still seemed both abstract and too close to a promise of "progress." Practical issues took precedence.

Theological realism, articulated in the United States by neo-orthodox theologian Reinhold Niebuhr, represented a second path.[257] Realism emphasized the ways that idealists can unwittingly allow or cause great evils to flourish. Communist idealism could be directly murderous. Other more subtle examples were common. Like Russell and Whitehead, theological realists represented a "revolt against idealism." This was a bracing challenge to Unitarians and other idealists. Yet rather than abandon their ideals, most Unitarians chose the path of ethical humanism. This solved the issue of God and human freedom by putting God aside. Such an approach had long been anticipated among those Unitarians, especially in the Midwest, who emphasized the ethical basis of religion. Their leader, Jenkin Lloyd Jones, died just as the Great War ended, his *Unity* magazine having been closed by censors for advocating war resistance.

The co-founders of American religious humanism were two Western Unitarian ministers: John Dietrich (1878–1957) and Curtis W. Reese (1887–1961).[258] Both first preached humanism during World War I. In 1916, from his pulpit in Des Moines, Iowa, Reese preached about "A Democratic View of Religion," saying this view "holds that this is man's world and that it largely depends on man what the world order shall be like." After 1919 he was Secretary of the WUC, as Jones had been. In that role Reese published *Humanism* (1926) and edited a collection of *Humanist Sermons* (1927).

John Dietrich first called himself a humanist while serving in

Spokane, Washington. Soon he was minister of the First Unitarian Society of Minneapolis. When a traditional Unitarian theist like William G. Eliot Jr. heard Dietrich speak about humanism as "The Content of Religious Liberalism," he rose, trembling, to say, "I would suffer my right arm to be severed from my body before I would take God from my people!"[259] Debates ensued between Dietrich and Unitarian Christian William Lawrence Sullivan. Rights of individual conscience were affirmed and a respectful "unity in diversity" maintained.

During the 1920s the humanist movement spread, especially in and through Meadville Theological School, moved from Pennsylvania to Chicago in 1926. Professor E. Eustace Haydon taught comparative religion at the University of Chicago, discussing it as a human phenomenon. By 1928, with Haydon's help, a new Humanist Fellowship and publication, the *New Humanist*, took humanism beyond its Unitarian roots. In New York City, the flamboyant Charles Francis Potter, after an unhappy pastorate at the Fourth Universalist Society, started a Humanist Society. In California, two Unitarian ministers left the AUA with their followers to form humanist groups.

The advent of the Great Depression challenged all faiths, including humanism, prompting a clear statement of humanist principles. In 1933 the *Humanist Manifesto*[260] appeared· drafted by University of Michigan philosopher Roy Wood Sellars. In its final form it contained fifteen theses in just over eleven hundred words. Sixty-five humanist sympathizers were invited to sign; thirty-four did so before publication, the most prestigious being philosopher John Dewey. Fifteen Unitarian ministers and one Universalist minister signed, all white and all male. The editor of the *New Humanist* declined to sign, explaining, "Any creed excludes, and this is no exception." John Haynes Holmes noted that in the sixth affirmation —"We are convinced that the time has passed for theism, deism, modernism, and the several varieties of 'new thought'"—Sellars *and the others* spoke of matters about which they knew very little. He signed nonetheless.

Humanism did not divide or stall Unitarianism. The Great Depression did. Sam Eliot left the AUA mid-term in 1927 to lead Boston's Arlington Street Church. In 1925 he dedicated a new AUA headquarters building, the present 25 Beacon Street. He had offered joint fellowship to all Universalist ministers who wished it, of whom sixty-five accepted. He started an AUA department of social relations. Eliot assumed Unitarianism's cathedral pulpit— the one Channing had filled—and preached there until 1935, when, at seventy-two, he felt a younger man was needed in the pulpit to bring younger families back into the church. As a result, the church called twenty-seven-year-old Dana McLean Greeley (1908–1970).[261]

At the AUA, Sam Eliot was followed by his executive vice president, Louis Cornish (1870–1950). Cornish was not an Eliot himself, but his mother-in-law was—she had married the minister of King's Chapel.[262] Dana Greeley later joked about the Unitarians and the Universalists being "two families of cousins." Cornish seemed to assume that Eliot's practice of depending upon men (cousins?) of means and influence could continue even into the Great Depression. Not so. Unitarian churches around the country began to close. Wealthy patrons lost fortunes. Ministers' salaries were cut. Programs ended. Mortgages went unpaid. Cornish seemed most interested in traveling to promote international liberal religion. At the annual meeting in May 1934, a lay delegate, Kenneth McDougall of Wellesley Hills, cited desperation among ministers and an inquiry by laymen into foreign missions work to say, "Let there be for the Association a commission of appraisal!"[263] A resolution to that effect passed unanimously.

Only two ministers were appointed to the commission. One was McDougall's pastor, James Luther Adams (1901–1994), later the most influential Unitarian theologian and social ethicist of the century.[264] The other was another Eliot—Frederick May Eliot, then minister of Unity Church (Unitarian) in St. Paul; he served as chair.[265] Only distantly related to Samuel Eliot, he was from the missionary, rather than the Harvard, branch of the family. A great-grandfather went to St. Louis, a grandfather to Portland, and his own father, back into Boston's working class communities. Fred Eliot had been a contributor to Reese's *Humanist Sermons*. He eventually become known as "Mr. Unitarianism" and led what has been called "the Unitarian Renaissance." He also started in earnest the process of consolidating with the Universalists. Before that could happen, however, the Universalists themselves had to meet the Unitarians on more universal, humanistic grounds, gradually reinterpreting their liberal Christian heritage without entirely abandoning it.

Universalism and Modernity

Universalism had not been thriving in the early years of the twentieth century. The number of churches was in steep decline: from 801 in 1894 to 679 in 1916.[266] The coming of roads, highways, and railroads, plus shifts of population to cities and the West, made the closing of numerous small village churches almost inevitable. Madison County, New York, for example, had nineteenth-century Universalist churches in such villages as Morrisville, Cazenovia, Sheds Corners, Hamilton, Madison, Lebanon, Erieville, and Stockbridge. Only two survived until 1905; the last closed just after the Great Depression.[267]

Struggling rural congregations had little surplus to share with denominational missions and institutions. Industrialization and heavy immigration affected the larger urban churches. By the 1890s, for example, Boston had grown to half a million people, immigrants and ethnic populations outnumbering old Yankees three to one.[268] Urban congregations prompted the General Convention to appoint a Universalist Commission on Social Service in 1911. They soon aligned with Social Gospel leaders among mainline Protestants. Walter Rauschenbusch addressed the General Convention in 1913, then Jane Addams of Chicago's Hull House in 1915.

The Commission's secretary, Clarence Skinner (1881–1949), was the most innovative, influential Universalist cleric of this era. He was born in Brooklyn, where his father worked as an editor for the Brooklyn *Eagle*. His grandfather, great-uncle, and great-grandfather all served as noted Universalist ministers.[269] He attended St. Lawrence in Canton, New York, where Universalists had founded both a college and a theological school. On graduating he went into church work without benefit of seminary, as assistant to Frank Oliver Hall at New York's Church of the Divine Paternity (4th Universalist) on Central Park West. Mrs. Andrew Carnegie worshiped there. Skinner then took a pastorate in Mt. Vernon, New York, doubling the membership of a small church and raising sufficient funds for a new building. Mrs. Carnegie donated a matching fund for a new organ, to be played by Skinner's wife, Clara.[270] But in 1910 Skinner moved to Grace Universalist in Lowell, Massachusetts, where he envisioned and created the "Lowell Forum," an evening series on social issues.

Speakers included Stanton Coit, Ethical Culture leader in London; W.E.B. DuBois of the NAACP; and other notable public figures.[271] The Forum drew in hundreds of un-churched people including union members, the press, and more men than were typically seen in churches. Again Skinner's church nearly doubled its membership in a few short years. Lee McCollester, Dean of the Crane Theological School at Tufts, spoke at the forum and then persuaded Skinner to come to Crane as professor of applied Christianity in the fall of 1914. While there he published *The Social Implications of Universalism*.[272]

Its foreword begins, "How to transform this old earth into the Kingdom of Heaven—that's the primal question."[273] Skinner articulated the implications of Universalism for the Social Gospel in eleven chapters serialized in the *Universalist Leader*. "The challenge," he said, is for Universalism to develop "a religion which is throbbing with the dynamics of democracy, a spirituality which expresses itself in terms of humanism, rather than in terms of individualism." He declared that the "traditional Protestant Church is dying" because "the individualism which called it into being is dying."[274] In his chapter on "Hell and Salvation," Skinner not only rejected eternal punishment, but also explained, "Universalism has not abolished the idea of hell. *It has humanized and socialized it.* It has established human misery as the direct consequence of human action. . . . [A] man must not only work out his own salvation; he must work out the salvation of the world."[275] In the chapter called "The New Unity" he wrote, "The sectarian divisiveness of today is not only theologically deplorable, it is a social sin."[276]

In 1917 the Universalist General Convention adopted a Declaration of Social Principles, drafted by Skinner, calling on "all agencies of the church . . . to educate and inspire the community and the nation to a keener social consciousness and a truer vision of the kingdom of God on the earth."[277] It outlined its program for "completing humanity" under four heads:

> First: An Economic Order which shall give to every human being an equal share in the common gifts of God, and in addition all that he shall earn by his own labor.
> Second: A Social Order in which there shall be equal rights for all, special privileges for none, the help of the strong for the weak until the weak become strong.
> Third: A Moral Order in which all human law and action shall be an expression of the moral order of the universe.
> Fourth: A Spiritual Order which shall build out of the growing lives of living men the growing temple of the living God.[278]

These were high ideals indeed! When the United States entered World War I, Skinner declared himself a pacifist. Some colleagues shunned him, but Dean McCollester and President John Cousens of Tufts both defended his rights of conscience. Skinner clearly wanted to challenge Universalism to live up to its large name and "either improve the property premises or move off the premises." Others wanted no part in the process, however.

Serving as part-time pastor of Medford's Hillside Universalist Church, near the Tufts campus, Skinner used the church as a laboratory for his theological students and his new ideals. After the war was over in 1919, both came under attack.[279] Was Skinner simply a pacifist or a real Bolshevik? Skinner had given a speech at Faneuil Hall praising the radical unionists of the International Workers of the World (the IWW, or "Wobblies") and calling the American Legion "anarchists."[280] Hillside swung to the right and sought a new minister. By 1924 they chose Charles E. Clark, formerly of the Universalist Church in Camp Hill, Alabama. He soon welcomed a contingent of robed and hooded members of the Ku Klux Klan at an evening service. Criticized, he defended the Klan against charges of bigotry, calling it "a great Christian Crusade . . . [that has] brought more men to the cross of Christ in the last four years than all the evangelists combined."[281] This was not entirely isolated. Universalist ministers from Muncie, Indiana, to rural Maine were horrified to discover Klansmen among their flocks.

During the 1920s Universalism was conflicted over Christian identity and modernity. The 150th anniversary of John Murray's arrival in America came in 1920. Universalists launched a "Million Dollar Campaign" to double membership, for "a Greater Universalist Church" and "a World Church for World Service." There were large gatherings again both at Gloucester and at Murray Grove, New Jersey. The Women's National Missionary Association bought the Clara Barton Homestead in Oxford, Massachusetts, dedicating it on December 25, 1921, the centennial of Barton's birth, as a camp for diabetic children.[282] But when again neither the membership goals nor the financial ones seemed attainable, the General Convention declared a new "Christ Crusade" promoting universal brotherhood, the Golden Rule, and the Declaration of Social Principles.

"Universalists," said Lewis Fisher, Dean of Ryder Divinity School in Chicago, "are often asked to tell where they stand. The only true answer . . . is that we do not stand at all, we *move*."[283] If only that had been true! Most rural Universalist churches were conservative. Some merged with nearby Methodist and other liberal Christian congregations more confident in their identity and in their finances. There were Universalist missions—to African Americans in Suffolk, Virginia, with Joseph Fletcher Jordan; in

Appalachia at Pigeon River, North Carolina, under Hannah Jewett Powell; and overseas in Japan—but these were not significantly distinct from many other Christian Social Gospel efforts of the same era.[284]

Skinner wanted a radically different model. After leaving Hillside in Medford, he joined forces with his fellow pacifist and humanistic theist, John Haynes Holmes—the Unitarian minister who had left the AUA with his Community Church of New York. Skinner launched a parallel non-denominational Community Church of Boston. The outreach was based on the "Lowell Forum." Invited speakers were deliberately controversial. They included birth-control activist Margaret Sanger, Hindu liberal Sarujini Naidu, Reform Rabbi Stephen Wise, agnostic activist Bertrand Russell, idealist philosopher W. E. Hocking, popular historian Will Durant, and Christian realist Reinhold Neibuhr. They all spoke for the Community Church of Boston, in rented downtown lecture halls. Skinner defended the accused anarchists Sacco and Vanzetti, and the black youths from Alabama known as the Scottsboro boys. By 1926 the average attendance was over twelve hundred per Sunday.[285]

Clinton Lee Scott (1887–1985), another progressive Universalist minister of the 1920s,[286] was then serving the downtown Universalist church in Philadelphia. As many white families moved away, the neighborhood around the church filled with black families, a few of whom began to attend services. Scott filled the building with beneficial outreach programs like those recommended by the Commission on Social Service and its new Declaration of Social Principles. He also wanted an electric sign to advertise the church's programs and its mission. When the lay leaders kept putting him off, Scott insisted that the church's board decide whether to approve the sign while he was at a meeting in Boston. On his return he found a note from the chairman saying, "Dear Pastor: You will find the answer to your request in Matthew, Chapter 12, Verse 39." In his Bible he read, "An evil and adulterous generation seeketh after a sign; and there no sign be given to it."[287] After

O Wen Young

Scott left Philadelphia, the congregation sold their building to an African-American Baptist congregation and built a new church in a white neighborhood.

Most Universalists were neither reactionary nor radical, however. One of the best-known Universalist lay leaders of the 1920s was the lawyer, industrialist, and statesman Owen D. Young (1874–1962).[288] Although his name is no longer widely recognized, in the fateful year of 1929, *Time* magazine named Young "Man of the Year."[289] As chairman of the board of General Electric (GE) and founder of the Radio Corporation of America (RCA), and later of the National Broadcasting Company (NBC), Young called for the business community to respect the rights and dignity of labor and also promoted public-private cooperation in developing utilities and communications. Pressed into public service many times, he provided key leadership in two American delegations to renegotiate the reparations that Germany owed to the Allies after World War I. Some Democrats encouraged Young to run for president of the United States in 1932, but he supported Franklin Delano Roosevelt.

Born on a farm in the Mohawk Valley of upstate New York, Owen Young was raised in the Universalist church in the village of Van Hornesville. He became Sunday school superintendent there at age fifteen.[290] The president of St. Lawrence heard about him from a seminarian doing summer ministry and personally recruited Owen to the college in Canton. As there were no scholarships, the Young family struggled to pay Owen's college costs—$258.80 for his freshman year, including tuition, room, board, and all expenses, including trips back home.[291] He formed close bonds with several future Universalist ministers and sometimes preached for them.[292] He also met his future wife, Josephine (Jo) Edmonds, raised in a Universalist family in Southbridge, Massachusetts.

By the time Owen graduated from St. Lawrence (Class of 1894, age nineteen), he and Jo were enough in love that she transferred to Radcliffe to be near him when he went on to Harvard Law School. But Harvard turned him down when he said that he would have to work while studying. Boston University Law School, on the other hand, enrolled him and gave him a part-time job in its library, paying five dollars a week. Owen rented a room for two dollars and fifty cents a week, thirty-five cents a day for meals.[293] He finished a three-year law course with honors in only two years. Recommended by his dean as an associate to Boston attorney Charles H. Tyler, Young finally married Jo. He represented the investment firm of Stone and Webster in negotiating local power and electric streetcar franchises throughout the United States.

GE, competing in the same field, recruited Young to serve in New York as general counsel and vice president for policy. In 1919, he temporarily resigned from the company when President Wilson asked him to serve on an Industrial Conference about labor unrest in the face of post-war recession and inflation. This conference produced an early bill of rights for labor.[294] Young also helped Wilson by setting up RCA to protect US radio technology from European competition, serving as its founding chairman. In 1922 he became chairman of GE as well.[295]

His management philosophy emphasized generous investment in human resources. Geniuses like GE engineer and active Unitarian Charles Steinmetz might even develop two hundred patents and recombine materials; it was up to managers to invest in those who handled the materials.[296] As he said in a 1923 speech to GE foremen in Schenectady, Young knew "the difference between an income which provides only an uncomfortable house, inadequate food, and insufficient clothes and *no* provision for the future[,] and an income which provides margins for education and health and recreation *and* provision for the future." Young believed not only in a "living wage," but also in a "cultural wage," allowing for enrichment.[297] While chairing the President's Commission on Business Cycles and Unemployment, Young warned that "unemployment is the greatest blot on the capitalistic system."[298] He proved prophetic during the American economic boom years of the 1920s in calling for greater financial restraint. He repeated his mantra, "Think radically and act conservatively,"[299] although few contemporaries understood him.

Young favored heavy taxes on inherited wealth.[300] In a speech
at Harvard Business School in 1927, he called for a day when labor
would hire capital, and not *vice versa*, and when workers would
receive all the profits above the fair cost of the capital that they
hired.[301] People applauded politely, but few comprehended the
full implications of Young's message. During the Great Depression
he supported Social Security, including unemployment insurance,
disability insurance, and old age pensions, having tried to pioneer
such things at GE.

When he found himself well-off during the boom years, Young
gave generously, donating six hundred acres of land adjacent to
St. Lawrence University, leading a million-dollar drive for new
buildings, recruiting Mellons and Bakers and Rockefellers to join
him, and spending half a million himself on a new K–12 school
for his former hometown, plus preserving the Universalist church
there. He also helped build the Universalist National Memorial
Church in Washington DC. In 1929, on "Black Thursday," he
welcomed Nobel Prize winner Madame Curie at his old family
home in Van Hornesville. She had come for an Edison celebration set up by Henry Ford, then spoke in Canton. That very day it
was announced that the "World Peace Tower" of the Washington
church would be named for Young.[302] Soon he owed more in
charitable pledges than he even had. Still, with few exceptions,
he kept all his commitments. After he retired to Florida, he could
sometimes be seen by the side of US Route 1, selling grapefruit to
supplement a relatively modest lifestyle. He was buried from the
Van Hornesville Universalist church. He had helped to preserve
the building there, even though the congregation has long-since
dissolved.

Like many Universalists, those in Van Hornesville had merged
with other Protestants. During the 1920s the national Universalists thought about joining forces with Congregationalists. Sam
Eliot, the outgoing leader of the Unitarians, disdained Universalism's "polite bows to Orthodoxy" and told them so.[303] His tone

offended Universalists. So much for his offer of joint fellowship to Universalist ministers! The president of the 1929 General Convention, Frank D. Adams, warned delegates that they were overly worried about what others thought of them, that they had lost their sense of mission and were hiding behind an "impalpable wall of conservatism"[304]—a message not well-received.

Universalists were clearly in trouble, but did not want to lose their distinctive identity. After 1930 change was inevitable. Funds were so scarce that the general superintendent had little staff and there was no funding for anyone to replace Quillen Shinn as a general missionary or to start new churches. Many existing churches found that they were overly dependent upon wealthy donors now unable to sustain them. Clergy salaries were reduced or eliminated. Despite Universalist pride in having pioneered women's ordination, in 1932 the Universalist general superintendent reported, "There is a tremendous prejudice against women ministers. At the present time I find it practically impossible to get any woman minister a hearing at any salary whatever."[305]

In 1931 a joint commission to explore collaboration with the Unitarians recommended the formation of an umbrella organization, the Free Church Fellowship, for all religious liberals. But there was little funding and less interest. By 1934 it had only twenty-one member congregations, including nine Unitarian, nine Universalist, and three community churches.[306] It disbanded three years later. A joint hymnal commission with Unitarians did produce *Hymns of the Spirit* (1937). The tone was primarily that of the Social Gospel, in both humanist and liberal Christian versions. Very few of the hymns were by Universalists. Far more were by Unitarians and free religionists, or by Protestant Social Gospel hymnodists. When Unitarians initiated the Humanist Manifesto in 1933, only one Universalist, Clinton Lee Scott, joined in signing it. Few Universalists were yet "post-Christian." But a modernized and more inclusive affirmation of faith was finally approved by the General Convention meeting in Washington DC in 1935:

The bond of fellowship in this Convention (church) shall be a common purpose to do the will of God as Jesus revealed it and to co-operate in establishing the kingdom for which he lived and died. To that end we avow our faith in God as Eternal and All-Conquering Love, in the spiritual leadership of Jesus, in the supreme worth of every human personality, in the authority of truth known or to be known, and in the power of men of goodwill and sacrificial spirit to overcome all evil and progressively establish the kingdom of God.[307]

A clause allowing liberty of conscience was included, but so were earlier, more conservative Universalist professions of faith. While Unitarians found all such statements too creedal, Universalists felt them central to their basic historic, spiritual identity. This difference remained a barrier to future merger.

Liberal Religion
and Humanism

1935
1960

The Unitarian Renaissance

It is hard to exaggerate the rather panicky condition of American Unitarianism in 1935. Louis Cornish, president of the AUA, reported: "Churches are being consolidated; churches are being closed."[308] Many ministers were unemployed. Three cities where I later served vibrant churches provide examples. In Knoxville, Tennessee, a Unitarian congregation that met throughout the 1920s simply disbanded. In Dallas, Texas, the First Unitarian Church, founded in 1899, sold its building, suspended services, and had no minister—although its Women's Alliance continued to meet. In New York City, the Unitarian Church of All Souls left a building seating 1,250 on 20th Street to build one at Lexington and 80th Streets seating 600. When the Depression hit, the 20th Street property did not sell and was taxed. Debts, taxes, and mortgages took two-thirds of the church budget, leaving little for programs. The church just barely survived, thanks to one very wealthy and generous family.[309] But few churches had any local rescuers left to call on.

Yet the next twenty-five years have been called "the Unitarian Renaissance" in America.[310] Membership more than doubled; influence spread; hundreds of new congregations were formed.

The 1934 Commission on Appraisal hired as director of studies Dr. H. Paul Douglass, Congregationalist minister, sociologist, and pioneer in an emerging field, "congregational studies." No denominational officials served on the Commission. Lay members included Frederick Melcher, a leading publisher; Aurelia Henry

Reinhardt, president of Mills College in California; and Walter Pritchard Eaton, a professor of drama at Yale. The two ministerial members were the chair, Frederick May Eliot, minister of Unity Church (Unitarian) in St. Paul, Minnesota; and James Luther Adams of the Unitarian Society of Wellesley Hills. Two non-Unitarians included a professor of social work and one of philosophy. The Commission's final report to the AUA, delivered in May 1936, entitled *Unitarians Face a New Age*, began with a stirring defense of the vital mission of Unitarianism and of liberal religion in the face of rising totalitarianism:[311]

> The genius of the Unitarian movement has been its power to adapt the vocabulary and practices of a religion whose roots are sunk deep into the past to new knowledge, new conditions, and new situations. . . .
>
> [T]here can be little doubt of the need in the modern world for some organized expression of the liberal spirit in religion. In a time when revolution and chaos are everywhere threatening, when ideals are again forming an alliance with tyranny and dogmatism, when intellectual confusion and social discontent are blindly trying to fight their way out of situations where only the problem-solving temper of mind can be of real help, when a fresh birth of the nationalistic spirit is everywhere offering its spurious comfort to tired and discouraged people—in a time like ours there is imperative need for a religious fellowship that will bring order and hope and confidence to [those] of the liberal tradition. . . .
>
> Liberal religion must express itself through liberal churches[,] . . . institutions made up of human beings organized to promote the development of spiritual insight and power among their own members and in society . . . emancipated . . . from the tendency to set themselves up as small, select, superior groups. . . .[312]

Effective liberal churches, according to the report, are self-critical, democratic, "characterized by a fresh discovery of the importance of leadership [both lay and ordained], affirmative, worshipful, devoted to life-long spiritual development and religious learning," and convinced "that religion is futile and sterile unless it has direct and effective bearing upon the problems of human society."[313]

Deserved credit for the "Unitarian Renaissance" is often given to Frederick May Eliot, AUA president from 1937 to his death in 1958. He bridged gaps between Unitarian humanists, theists, and Christians. He reorganized the AUA and applied the insights above to efforts aimed at growth. But the words of the report bear the

Frederick May Eliot

unmistakable rhetorical imprint of his colleague, James Luther Adams. Like Eliot, "JLA," as he became known, worked tirelessly to convince Unitarians and others that small differences in "vocabulary and practices" were less important than having an "effective bearing upon the problems of human society." He became the key Unitarian ethicist and theologian of the century.[314] He disseminated his ideas more as an essayist, lecturer, teacher, and mentor than as a book author. His own life story should be better known.[315]

James Luther Adams was no Boston Adams. A grandfather, James Madison Adams, was a Confederate soldier in Virginia whose slave came with him on military recruiting efforts. His son, Jim's father, was a fundamentalist Baptist preacher near Spokane, Washington. When his father left the Baptists for the more narrowly fundamentalist Plymouth Brethren during Jim's teenage years, Jim rebelled by joining a Presbyterian church. After his father became ill and the family impoverished, Jim learned shorthand in order to work for an official of the Northern Pacific Railroad and pay for his education by working at night while studying by day. At the University of Minnesota he was known as a campus atheist and humanist, publishing a mimeo sheet called the *Angels Revolt*.

A Unitarian professor of rhetoric told him, "Jim Adams, you're going to be a preacher. You're talking *against* religion all the time. Don't you see that this is your major passion?"[316] Eventually Adams visited John Dietrich, the Unitarian minister in Minneapolis and a humanist who was both scientific and religious. The younger man began to see some virtue in his own ambivalence and, when offered a chance, attended Harvard Divinity School, although he found the theological curriculum more historical than relevant. But literary humanism as taught by Irving Babbitt showed him how both literature and religion employ varied vocabularies to express both human potential and the reality of human limitations that no individual or society can safely ignore.

In his second year, while Adams served as student minister at Second Unitarian Church in Salem, the minister died of a heart attack. The laity asked Adams to stay. They ordained him in May

1927. He was not quite twenty-six. That summer he used money from a preaching prize to visit Germany, where he witnessed Nazi rallies. When he returned, he married Margaret Young, who would be his wife and life-partner in activism.[317] The Depression soon devastated the country. Although a few of Adams's parishioners were executives, most were middle or lower-middle class. When he plunged into mediating a strike of local textile workers, taking on an issue that other clergy had avoided, the participants respected his fairness.[318]

This helped him to step forward and boldly critique the naïve, genteel passivity and detached idealism that he found pervasive among many of his Unitarian colleagues. What Reinhold Niebuhr as theological realist was then doing for liberal Protestantism, Adams began to do for Unitarianism, seeking greater sociopolitical realism along with greater spiritual depth. The Greenfield Group, a rigorously disciplined clergy study group Adams helped to form, argued the deep issues. Adams began to emerge as a major intellectual leader even before the Commission on Appraisal report was published.

When Meadville Lombard Theological School in Chicago invited him to join their faculty, he responded that he would first need to spend a year in Europe for further study to feel qualified, to which they agreed. He visited T.S. Eliot in England, and while his wife and children stayed in Holland for safety, he spent a year in Nazi Germany meeting with religious scholars like Albert Schweitzer and Rudolph Otto. He saw great philosophers such as Heidegger and many German religious liberals accept National Socialism. He found religious resistance to the Nazi idolatries of blood and soil, chiefly among those who still took the Bible seriously (though not literally), in groups like the Confessing Church movement. He worked with them, sometimes at considerable risk. By the time he returned to America he wanted to be a change-agent himself, giving more spine, substance, and spirit to liberal religion.

Adams taught in Chicago for twenty years, operating at the intersections of humanism, process thought, existentialism, Christian theology, and democratic social reform. He relished music and the arts. His encyclopedic memory and legendary "teaching stories" transformed his work in the classroom. Here is one of the most often repeated stories:

Adams served as a trustee of the First Unitarian Church of Chicago. One fellow trustee, a conservative man with real estate interests, complained often that the minister had no business "mixing politics and religion" by advocating an end to race discrimination in local housing. Adams insisted that the trustees discuss the mission or ultimate purpose of the church. The conservative trustee said that was a question he would leave to theologians like Adams;

James Luther Adams

he just didn't want politics in the church. Adams would not let go. Every member, and especially every trustee, was accountable for the church and its purpose. The discussion continued into the wee hours of the morning until, as Jim told it, "Fatigue and the Holy Spirit combined to have the man blurt out, 'I guess the purpose of a church like this is to get hold of people like me and change 'em.'" Jim led the board in singing "Amazing Grace" before they all went home.[319]

Devoted to democratic dialectic between dissenters and the wisdom of the ages, between small groups and the church universal, Adams hesitated to publish his own thought. He took so long polishing his Chicago PhD thesis (later published as *Paul Tillich's Philosophy of Culture, Science, & Religion*) that his dean finally took the manuscript off his desk, submitting it for him. If, like Tillich and Niebuhr, Adams had published more, he might be better known.[320] But he preferred actively mediating differences and deepening dialogue between humanists, Christians, Unitarians, and potential allies, both religious and secular. As he resisted being pigeon-holed, so he resisted publishing any *magnum opus*. Yet in 1957 he returned to the Harvard Divinity School as professor of Christian social ethics. He taught for a decade there, then at Andover Newton, then back again at Meadville. His students began to collect and publish his essays.[321]

Known as "the happy prophet," JLA continued dialoguing and mentoring until his death in 1994, at age ninety-three. He saw the essential genius of the liberal church in its nature as a voluntary, not inherited, community, devoted to the nurture of other voluntary associations, nurturing not only a priesthood, but also "a prophethood of all believers," in which lay leaders also read the signs of the times in order to join together to shape a little history and not just be pushed around by it. For "by their groups shall ye know them," Adams insisted.[322]

As AUA president, Frederick May Eliot found allies to realize the recommendations of the Commission on Appraisal in three areas:

courageous social action, spiritual development, and church extension. In 1938 he initiated the formation of a Unitarian Service Committee. British Prime Minister Neville Chamberlain, a Unitarian, had tried to keep "peace in our time" by appeasing Hitler at Munich, thus exposing Czechoslovakia to German threats. Since the largest Unitarian church in the world was then in Prague, Eliot acted so quickly "that the Unitarians beat Hitler there," as one minister marveled. Eliot recruited diverse, wise, and influential members for the Service Committee, with Dr. Robert Dexter (1887–1955) of the AUA department of social relations as head.

The first Unitarian Service Committee commissioners were Waitstill Sharp (1902–1983) (JLA's successor as minister in Wellesley Hills) and his wife, Martha (1905–1999). Leaving their children behind with church friends, they traveled first to Prague, then to Vichy, France, and neutral Portugal. Cooperating with everyone from the American Friends Service Committee to resistance leaders to US diplomats, Waitstill rescued a number of leading Jewish intellectuals. Martha brought out groups of Jewish children. The new US Office of Strategic Services (predecessor of the CIA) entrusted Robert Dexter and his wife Elizabeth with both funds and helpful information, encouraging their cooperation with European anti-Nazis, including Communists. What no one fully realized, however, was that Noel Field, a Quaker whom the Unitarian Service Committee eventually promoted to head its work in Europe, was not only a leftist, but most likely also a Soviet agent. After the Cold War broke out, Field fled behind the Iron Curtain. The Service Committee fell into a foggy scandal at a sensitive time.[323] Sadly, this obscured clear recognition of the Sharps' heroism for many years. In 2005 they were finally recognized as rescuers, as "Righteous Among the Gentiles," by the Holocaust Memorial at Yad Vashem, Israel, and by the Holocaust Museum in Washington DC.[324]

When Eliot arrived at 25 Beacon Street in 1937, he found an energetic young man, Ernest Kuebler, in charge of religious education. Together they recruited Sophia Lyon Fahs (1876–1978), then sixty-one, as AUA director of curriculum development.

Raised in a conservative missionary family, Fahs had a long history as an innovator among liberal Protestant religious educators. She had been influenced by educational theorist (and humanist) John Dewey, and conceived of classrooms as small communities in which children could discover and express new insights, rather than as places where teachers were to pour wisdom into children like pitchers pouring water into passive little cups. Fahs developed and edited *The New Beacon Series in Religious Education* to convey an innovative methodology. Like Adams, Fahs worked at important intersections: child development and educational theory, humanistic theology, and progressive biblical studies.

Sophia Lyon Fahs

As one historian has noted, William Ellery Channing may have announced in 1837, when addressing the Sunday School Society, that "the great end in religious instruction is not to stamp our minds upon the young, but to stir up their own"—but it took until 1937 for Fahs to begin to put that revolutionary approach into actual church practice.[325] The New Beacon Series unfolded throughout the war and into the post-war years, when both Unitarian Sunday schools and other liberal churches adopted it. Fahs recruited authors and contributed herself, explaining her over-all philosophy in *Today's Children and Yesterday's Heritage: A Philosophy of Creative Religious Development* (1952), and *Worshipping Together with Questioning Minds* (1965). In 1959, when she was eighty-two, the Cedar Lane Unitarian Church in Bethesda, Maryland, ordained her to recognize the significance of her religious education program in the growth and development of this new and large congregation. She preached her own ordination sermon, noting that she might not have too many more chances. She lived until 1978, dying at 101.[326]

World War II necessarily slowed Unitarian extension work. Travel was rationed. Young ministers served as military chaplains. Older parish ministers were writing to those serving overseas as well as serving their local congregations. Eliot made sure that planning went ahead. In 1944, the AUA established the Church of the Larger Fellowship to serve isolated religious liberals through the mail. Within just two years, over fifteen hundred people were in correspondence, half of them dues-paying members. A new Unitarian church, named for Thomas Jefferson, was planned for Charlottesville, Virginia. And a project called "Unitarian Advance" began work with three committees. The first, headed by A. Powell Davies, the new minister at All Souls in Washington DC, was to be creative; the second, headed by a lay member of the AUA Board, was to investigate and test practical methods for promoting Unitarian growth and ideals; and the third, headed by Raymond Bragg (later head of the Service Committee), was to coordinate efforts with all the Unitarian affiliate groups. All the Unitarian Advance work was nearly derailed by controversy, however.

Stephen Fritchman (1902–1981) headed the AUA's youth work and also assumed the editorship of the AUA publication the *Christian Register*, when its previous head left to start the Church of the Larger Fellowship.[327] Fritchman was clearly a leftist. This was not particularly controversial during the war, when the United States fought with Soviet allies against the Nazis. But as the war ended, he aligned American Unitarian Youth with the Soviet-sponsored World Federation of Democratic Youth. *Register* editorials seemed to echo the Communist Party line. Ministers as progressive as A. Powell Davies of All Souls in DC and Donald Harrington of Community Church in New York raised their eyebrows. Fred Eliot eventually had to intervene.

Other liberal groups also had to deal with insiders who sympathized with totalitarianism. This was not easy for liberals, by definition. In 1940 a self-confessed Communist was forced to resign from the board of the ACLU, with Unitarian John Haynes Holmes casting a key vote.[328] The Fritchman case was even harder.[329] He admitted no external affiliations. The AUA Board at first exonerated him of any misuse of his position. The AUA was not averse to controversy. Fritchman's supervisor, AUA Director of Publications Mel Arnold, wanted Beacon Press to stop publishing mere sermon collections and to put liberal values on controversial issues into print. Then in 1947, Fritchman crossed a line. He wrote an editorial for the *Register* that condemned Western attempts to block further Communist expansion. Communist manipulation in Eastern Europe was already so strong that the next year, in Prague, the Czech Foreign Minister, Unitarian Jan Masaryk, either jumped or was pushed to his death in a modern-day defenestration.[330] Fritchman opposed any effort to block Communist "democracy" in Greece and Turkey. Eliot and Arnold responded by blocking the editorial.

Fritchman resigned, then decided to take his case before the whole AUA annual meeting. The decision of Eliot and the board to remove him was upheld by a democratic vote. Fritchman went on to serve the First Unitarian Church of Los Angeles. During the height of McCarthy-era blacklisting, he staunchly defended those barred from Hollywood for their leftist leanings. He later won denominational awards for his social justice efforts and for distinguished service to the cause of liberal religion.[331] The AUA, rather than dividing over a Communist sympathizer on staff, moved forward. Unitarianism expanded more widely and rapidly than at any time in its history.

Much of that growth can be credited to the Unitarian Fellowship Movement. In 1948 the AUA hired a layman, Munroe Husbands (1909–1984), to develop the program. He was director of fellowships, associate director of extension, and clerk of the Church of the Larger Fellowship. Raised in Salt Lake City, as a teenager Munroe rebelled against both his family's Mormon heritage and the Christian Science church preferred by his mother, a social worker. Wanting her son to be part of a church, she passed on a colleague's suggestion that Munroe "try the Unitarians."[332] The minister was Edwin H. Wilson, a leading Unitarian humanist, who inspired first Munroe and then all his siblings to become Unitarians. Influenced by a mother who loved amateur theater, Munroe left college to train at a radio and theater school in Boston, where he met his wife, Martha. He next headed the speech department of a similar school back in Utah. During the war he served as a Navy recruiting officer and also wrote radio ads. After the war, he and Martha returned to Boston, where they joined First Parish (Unitarian) in Needham because it had a humanist minister. They soon began a local church theater group where they met George Davis, AUA director of extension, who recruited Munroe away from a public relations job with Blue Cross to lead the new AUA lay fellowship program.

Husbands wrote short, provocative ads. The most widely-used began, "ARE YOU A UNITARIAN WITHOUT KNOWING IT?" The Unitarian Laymen's League often paid for and sponsored these in national publications. When people wrote to Boston showing interest, or if the membership of the Church of the Larger

Fellowship showed the possibility of two or three or more gathering together, Husbands would send additional ad copy, suggest holding a public meeting, and arrange for a visit. Each spring and fall he set off in a car loaded with pamphlets for a thirty- to forty-day tour, speaking in a different community every evening. He adeptly handled any hecklers. Before he left town, he appointed the best leaders as interim officers, knowing the democratic process would accompany growth. By 1958 there were 249 new fellowships, and twenty years later, twice as many.[333]

Husbands learned that fellowships should meet in public places, not in members' homes. Those that met privately tended to wither. Starting a religious education program was critical. Some groups used the New Beacon curriculum to raise their children together, but then never went beyond a tacitly closed friendship group. Each newcomer (in a completely unspoken way, of course) had to either be accepted by nearly every existing member or else become an object of quiet controversy or sent away. Ministers knew this tendency of small group behavior but were often regarded by lay fellowships as trying to exercise outside authority. They, in turn, sometimes disparaged lay fellowships as nothing but discussion groups, rather than worshiping congregations, and saw their offers of help repelled in what they interpreted as anti-clericalism. A. Powell Davies (1902–1957), minister of All Souls, Washington DC, would not allow fellowship work in his area. There his powerful sermons were transmitted over phone lines to suburban groups gathered around speakers. Ten new spin-off churches began in the capitol area, each with a church school and soon with a minister. The same process worked in a few other metropolitan areas.

Where the prospects seemed most promising, the AUA extension department would send an organizing minister (Lon Ray Call or Grant Butler) for a period of months, until a permanent minister could be secured. Financial subsidies were modest, although some fellowships grew enough to call ministers on their own.[334] Unitarianism grew after the war, along with colleges and universities and migration to the suburbs. Gender equity was notably absent by later standards, but participation was stronger among men. Currently women often make up 60 percent or more of congregations, but in this era, the gender balance in Unitarian fellowships and churches tended to be closer to fifty-fifty. Although women came to church with their children, male participation was high in Unitarian groups. Like Munroe Husbands, many Unitarian men had delayed their education because of the Depression and World War II. Later, at the high-water mark of the industrial economy, Unitarian men often worked in practical fields like engineering, accounting, or technology. They were drawn to sermons and discussions that integrated the humanities and religion with

Munroe Husbands

pragmatic debates about politics, social issues, and psychology. It did not hurt that many famous Americans were Unitarians—and not just in the past. In the 1950s Unitarians were also disproportionately represented in national politics and the media. And "come-outers" from other denominations were quite welcome. Unitarianism offered the opportunity to join a high-achievement, thinking elite. As one of Husbands' ads read,

> What Is Your Idea of True Religion?
> Unitarianism is a way of life, a life of vigorous thought, constructive activity, of generous service—not a religion of inherited creeds, revered saints, or holy books.
> Unitarianism is not an easy religion. It demands that people think out their beliefs for themselves, and then live those beliefs. The stress is placed upon living this life nobly and effectively rather than on the preparation for an after-existence.
> If you have given up "old time" religion, Unitarianism has the answer for you.

Unitarians had long been in the business of framing deeper moral, religious questions. Beacon Press became a vehicle to do this more publicly. In 1948, the Beacon catalogue had only nineteen books on its backlist—including two hymnals, a number of sermon collections, and four other books by ministers. Although there was no capital to attract new authors, publisher Mel Arnold was determined to publish books that others were afraid to print. His breakthrough opportunity was a book by Yale philosopher Paul Blanshard, *American Freedom and Catholic Power* (1949), in which the author argued that pre-Vatican II Catholic teachings opposed democratic pluralism. Beacon Press thoroughly checked facts and gave Catholic authorities a chance to challenge errors in advance. When Eleanor Roosevelt and New York's Cardinal Spellman publicly clashed over government aid to parochial schools, book sales soared. There were twenty-six printings of the first edition, which sold over a third of a million copies. Beacon gained sufficient resources to acquire other titles and authors of note and by 1956 it had 321 titles on its back-list. Arnold left for Harper to head up the Torchbooks series. The finances of Beacon remained a worry to AUA officials.

In 1958, while on his way to a meeting at All Souls in New York on Beacon Press finances, Frederick May Eliot had a sudden heart attack and died. He was sixty-eight years old and had presided for twenty-one years over a Unitarian Renaissance. The AUA Board nominated Ernest Kuebler, the head of education, as Eliot's successor as president. Kuebler had never served a local congregation, however. Dana McLean Greeley, secretary of the AUA Board and minister of Boston's Arlington Street Church since 1935, was nominated by petition and elected that May by a vote of 823 to 720.

Merger discussions with the Universalists were by that time well underway. A congregational poll showed not only the Universalists, but also some Unitarians, to be hesitant. The Unitarian congregation in Knoxville, Tennessee, for example, racially integrated and involved in the civil rights movement, voted against any merger. A black member was among the group that visited the few remaining Universalist churches in the South, almost all of which were all-white. He reportedly called them "country Methodists with the hell scared out of 'em," and added, "They say there ain't no hell. I'm here to tell you, on the basis of my experience: the hell there ain't!" The Knoxville Unitarian vote on merger was fifteen aye, fifty-seven no, with one abstention.[335]

The overwhelming majority of Unitarian churches voted in favor of merger, however. Differences between Universalists and Unitarians had narrowed in most places. Unitarians were less uniformly Brahmin, and Universalists less rural. Both groups were largely middle-class. Humanism was a strong and growing spiritual common ground. Christians in both groups supported the ecumenical movement. The Universalist traditionalists were the most hesitant and resistant to consolidation. In the nineteenth century they had been more numerous than the Unitarians; now the tables were turned.

103 "missioner"

157 line 5 from bottom "shape with a little"

Gift Card Testimonial and Upda

Hi Church family! Linda Nichols here to tell all of you about the new gift cards available at our gift card table. Just not groceries anymore. I purchased L.L. Bean gift cards to use for Christmas. Well, of course, I had to buy something for myself to be sure the cards were OK. They were very easy to use. I picked up a couple of great swimsuits on sale. I ordered over the internet, and it was simple. I got my

Universalist Humanism and
Unitarian Universalist Consolidation

Although Clinton Lee Scott was the only Universalist to sign the Humanist Manifesto of 1933, he played a key role in the spiritual evolution of Universalism that ultimately made consolidation with Unitarianism possible. "Clint" evolved from orthodox to liberal Christianity and from Christian humanism to a more global religious naturalism, using his gifts of wit and persuasion to mentor a whole new generation of Universalist leaders.[336]

The tenth of twelve children, Scott was born on a farm in the Northeast Kingdom of Vermont near the Quebec border. He lost his father at the age of nine and went to work as an apprentice stonecutter at fourteen. When he attempted to follow an older brother west to acquire an education, the state university in Missouri rejected him due to inadequate high school preparation, so he "rode the rails" as a hobo to return home. His luck changed when he found that he could work while attending Goddard Academy, founded by Universalists, in Vermont. While pumping the organ bellows every Sunday at a local Universalist church, Scott was astounded to continually hear messages of hope from the pulpit. He worked his way through college and divinity school at Tufts while holding a student pastorate in Vermont. He served churches in Buffalo, Philadelphia, and Los Angeles between 1916 and 1926. After his wife, Edith, died in 1925, he and his two daughters moved to Atlanta, where he served the United Liberal Church, serving both Universalists and Unitarians, until 1930.

Reaching out to the wider community there, he sponsored a Sunday evening forum on public affairs to educate his congregation and promote dialogue on contemporary issues. Through his ministry, a former editor of the Ku Klux Klan magazine became a follower and joined the church, renouncing his Klan activities.[337]

In 1930 Scott married Mary Slaughter, a field worker for the Universalist Sunday School Association from Camp Hill, Alabama, where Scott's brother Harold served as the Universalist minister. From 1930 to 1940 the Scotts served the largest Universalist church in the country in Peoria, Illinois. In addition to parish ministry, Clint fought against illegal gambling and local political corruption, resulting in the death of a fellow crusader and death threats against him. Some members of the congregation were apparently unaware of his anti-gambling work, including the dear lady who presented him with a hand-made quilt to be raffled at the church fair. Although she estimated that twenty-five dollars in raffle tickets could be sold, Scott was so scrupulous about avoiding any taint of hosting games of chance in his church that he paid the twenty-five dollars himself![338] After a decade in Peoria, made especially difficult by the meddling of the retired predecessor, Scott sought a new pastorate, only to find few openings because many churches were closing. For two years he served both a Unitarian church in Dayton, Ohio, and a rural Universalist group nearby before being called to Gloucester, Massachusetts, to rescue the "Mother Church" of American Universalism from closing. In 1946, after thirty years in ministry, he published an amusing collection of *Parish Parables*[339] before going on to serve the Massachusetts Universalist Convention as superintendent.

Robert Cummins (1897–1982) became national, or general, superintendent in 1938.[340] After teaching in a Presbyterian school in Bangkok, Thailand, as a young man, he sought a more expansive approach to religion. He had not trained for ministry, but he pastored three rural Universalist churches back in Ohio while also running his own insurance agency. Then he led Cincinnati

Universalists for six years while earning a master's degree. He served Throop Memorial Universalist Church in Pasadena, California, from 1932 to 1938, while earning his master's in theology at the University of Southern California. He brought organizational skill, energy, business experience, and both a national and an international worldview to denominational leadership. Like his counterpart, Frederick May Eliot at the AUA, Cummins sought to reverse an alarming decline. From 1910 to 1939 state conventions declined from forty-three to twenty-four (44 percent), Universalist congregations from 819 to 544 (33 percent), and household units from 52,272 to 39,827 (24 percent).[341]

Cummins reorganized denominational services, centralized responsibility, instituted a system of program evaluation, and recruited Edna Bruner to reinstitute field work for what he had helped rename the Universalist Church of America (UCA). Aware that many Universalists identified themselves as liberal Christians first and Universalists second, he applied for denominational membership in the Federal Council of the Churches of Christ in America, predecessor of the National Council of Churches. Yet he also insisted that Universalism was a still "larger faith" than mere Protestantism. He told his members,

> Universalism cannot be limited either to Protestantism or to Christianity, not without denying its very name. Ours is a world fellowship, not just a Christian sect. For so long as Universalism is universalism and not partialism, the fellowship bearing its name must succeed in making it unmistakably clear that all are welcome: theist and humanist, unitarian and trinitarian, colored, and colorless. A circumscribed Universalism is unthinkable.[342]

Yet how to realize such an idealistic vision in a nation where race prejudice was still deeply ingrained in the social fabric? Jeffrey Campbell, an African American, graduated from St. Lawrence Theological School in 1935, was granted fellowship and ordained,

Liberal Religion and Humanism

even though the state superintendent objected to wasting funds educating a "colored" minister. The *Universalist Leader* vilified Campbell for presiding at the marriage of his sister Marguerite to a white Universalist seminarian.[343] While Campbell achieved dual fellowship with the Unitarians in 1938 (the same year that he ran for Governor of Massachusetts as a Socialist) and served as part-time and interim minister, chaplain, and teacher, no church called him to full-time, settled parish ministry.[344]

If Universalists had a hard time being as inclusive as their name implied, they also had a hard time being included in the ecumenical movement. When the Universalists applied for admission to the Federal Council of Churches of Christ in the USA, their stated relationship to Christianity alarmed other member denominations. They submitted another application, providing more detailed information, but in 1944 the Federal Council of Churches, led by the Presbyterians, voted twelve to six against admission. Universalist leaders felt that they had been treated in a rather unchristian manner when the FCC rejected them for being insufficiently Christocentric and too similar to the Unitarians. St. Lawrence professor Angus MacLean lamented, "After being turned down twice as not being good Christians, we decided to look elsewhere."[345]

While some Christian Universalists such as Seth Brooks of Universalist National Memorial Church in Washington DC and Cornelius Greenway of All Souls Universalist Church in Brooklyn, New York, feared moving in the direction of Unitarian humanism, others like Ellsworth Reamon of Syracuse, New York, sought better relations with the Unitarians. Could Christians in both denominations unite to tame the anti-Christian elements among the humanists?

The new strategies of the Universalist Church of America arrested the decline in membership by the end of World War II. Robert Cummins, Clarence Skinner, Clinton Lee Scott, and their allies created a broader Universalism "greater than Christianity because it is an evolutionary religion," as one minister put it, and "universal rather than partial, because it is one with the spirit of science and is primarily interested in bringing out that which is God-like in man."[346] The *Universalist Leader* devoted an issue to "One World Religion," although an editorial warned against shallow eclecticism, admonishing that "he who believes everything ends up believing nothing," and that "there is no easy route to world religious fellowship."[347] Inspired by the founding of the United Nations, like the Unitarians, the Universalists launched a Universalist Service Committee to initially run work camps and oversee joint relief work in Europe[348] before directing its attention to mission work in minority communities in the United States and overseas.

In 1952 Toribio Quimada (1917–1988)[349] of the Iglesia Universal de Cristo (Universal Church of Christ) in the Philippines looked under "U" in an ecumenical directory for an American church that might help his ministry. The Universalist Service Committee, then led by Carleton Fisher, responded with a package of books that included the series "How to Know Your Bible." The new ideas excited Quimada, and when in 1954 the Iglesia Universal de Cristo excommunicated him for his increasingly liberal ideas, he and nine small groups of followers requested affiliation with the Universalist Church of America. Japanese Universalists sent a minister to visit in 1958, after which he sought further theological education in Dumaguete City on the island of Negros in the Philippines. His congregations continued to thrive even after Quimada was murdered in 1988 by government troops eliminating anyone suspected of inciting rebellion among the poor. Today the Universalist Church of the Philippines has thirty congregations, thirty-four ministers, and two thousand members.[350]

After World War II, Universalists in America struggled to define their denomination's distinctive identity. In 1947 one speaker to the Massachusetts Universalist Convention observed,

In many instances, the only thing that distinguishes the Universalist church from the neighboring Congregational, Baptist or Methodist church in some communities is the

name, not the gospel that is preached, nor the program
of education. . . . If the Universalist Church has no message, no program that is different from other churches in
the community, nothing that is distinctive, then let's unite
with some other church quickly. . . . We have been drifting
and disintegrating. [351]

A younger group of Universalist ministers believed that the
future direction of Universalism lay in honoring its Christian
origins within a wider circumference. Starting as a study group
among recent graduates of Crane Theological School of Tufts University, they called themselves the *Humiliati*, after an Italian religious movement of the twelfth century later suppressed by the
Papacy.[352] These "young Turks" of Universalism were anything but
humble, however, and actively challenged older colleagues who
wanted a circumscribed Universalism within Protestant Christianity. They wore clerical collars and stoles with a new symbol,
a circle with an off-center cross, as though saying, "*Our* Universalism is bigger than *your* Christianity!" Influenced by Clarence
Skinner, who retired as dean of Crane in 1945, and abetted by
Clinton Lee Scott, the Humiliati met annually from 1946 to 1954
seeking new, more inclusive liturgies and actively participating in
denominational politics.

In 1947 the Humiliati sponsored Mary Slaughter Scott for
the UCA Board of Trustees, and in 1951 they endorsed Brainerd
Gibbons of Wausau, Wisconsin, as the new president of the
UCA. Gibbons reflected their concerns when he asked, "Is Universalism a Christian denomination, or is it something more, a truly
universal religion?"

When Robert Cummins left in 1953 to head the US State
Department's International Cooperation Administration, Gibbons
succeeded him as General Superintendent. The UCA began to participate in the Council of Liberal Churches, an organization created by Unitarians and Universalists to combine efforts in religious
education, publishing, and work with teens. The youth of the two

denominations took pride in leading the way, consolidating their respective groups in 1952 to form Liberal Religious Youth.[353]

Although the UCA had its headquarters at 14 Beacon Street (next to Congregational House, then the headquarters of that denomination, and near AUA headquarters), there was no Universalist church remaining in Boston. Second Universalist Church of Boston, founded by Hosea Ballou in 1817, had combined with the Unitarian Arlington Street Church in 1935.[354] Under state Superintendent Clinton Lee Scott's leadership, the Massachusetts Universalist Convention purchased the historic Charles Street Meeting House with funds derived from the sale of closed churches.[355] In 1949 Scott helped start a center for Universalist worship that made the humanistic Humiliati seem conservative by comparison and recruited a minister who would radicalize Boston-area Universalism and influence Unitarians as well.

Kenneth L. Patton (1911–1994) had led First Unitarian Society of Madison, Wisconsin, since 1942[356] and had recruited Madison congregant Frank Lloyd Wright to design a dramatic new meetinghouse for the congregation. When he casually mentioned in a radio sermon that he would "like to resign from the white race and become a colored man," a national magazine featured his efforts to document the extent of race prejudice, bringing him to national attention. He spent two days in Chicago trying to integrate restaurants, country clubs, hotels, and real estate and reported on interracial housing where harmony seemed to prevail. Scott regarded Patton as the most eloquent, poetic exponent of naturalistic humanism—of religion seen in a truly universal perspective.

Patton lent his artistic talent to creating a mural of the great nebula in Andromeda for the chancel of the Charles Street Meeting House and installing sixty-five brass religious symbols drawn from religious and spiritual traditions all around the world.[357] Pews were arranged in the round. Patton wrote non-theistic hymns and responsive readings expressing mystical love for the natural world and humanity's place and potential in it. He published prodigiously through his Meeting House Press. His Sunday addresses

173

on the radio often scandalized more conservative and Christian Universalists. Ironically, the Massachusetts Universalist Convention at first refused membership to the new church that it had created, deeming its public program insufficiently Universalist! Scott had to defend Patton's freedom of the pulpit and Universalism's liberty of conscience to win a narrow vote on continued financial support. The Massachusetts Convention eventually granted admission; however, the Charles Street Meeting House never became a self-sustaining congregation. Patton, who had longed to be an artist, was too much of a "one-man show." He was both too mystical and too irascible to develop lay leadership, make pastoral calls, or even reach out to newcomers. Mary and Clint Scott grew increasingly disappointed in Patton.[358]

Meanwhile, Frederick May Eliot of the AUA had revived the vision of Henry Whitney Bellows for a "United Liberal Church of America." While Cummins and the Humiliati shared that vision, Universalists generally were more hesitant. The first set of process rules required that 75 percent of congregations in both denominations vote to move forward with negotiations, but only 72 percent of the 304 certified congregations voted in the affirmative, so the requirement was lowered to 60 percent.[359]

The compromise Council of Liberal Churches soon proved a poor way for Universalists and Unitarians to cooperate with each other. Both groups tended to give the joint body funds merely representing "what was left, not what was right." Many members and congregations in both groups also tended to do the same. The additional administrative overhead sapped resources from badly needed growth programs. In 1955 in Detroit the Joint Interim Commission on Federal Union reported to meetings of both denominations, recommending that a twelve-member UCA-AUA joint commission on full merger hold yet another plebiscite and determine the will of local members and congregations.[360]

William B. Rice (1905–1970), a Universalist minister serving the Unitarian Society of Wellesley Hills, Massachusetts, presided as chair of the Joint Merger Commission. The term consolidation soon emerged as preferable to merger both for legal reasons and to avoid the implication that one group was absorbing the other. Universalists were particularly sensitive on this latter point, as they had been twice the size of the Unitarians during much of the nineteenth century, yet now the reverse was true. In 1958 the commission sent out a 103-page study guide, *Merger and Alternatives*, to provide historical data to the congregations. The AUA had 606 congregations (361 churches and 245 lay-led fellowships), with a reported membership of 106,751. The UCA had 298 groups (289 churches and 9 fellowships), with a membership of 42,858. While AUA membership had risen 75 percent over the previous twenty years, Universalist membership had declined.

UCA General Superintendent Brainerd Gibbons resigned when the commission was appointed, as he did not see how differences in polity between the two bodies could be overcome. Philip Giles, head of the UCA departments of ministry and church extension, had a more positive view of consolidation and succeeded Gibbons, calling for Universalist Advance to increase local church strength. Ironically, A. Powell Davies, founder of the Unitarian Advance effort, was a leading Unitarian skeptic about merger, viewing the Universalists as too conservative. When Davies looked down 16th Street to his colleague Seth Brooks's Universalist National Memorial Church, his concerns seemed valid. The DC manifestation of Universalism and its leader were highly conservative.

The commission proposed a structure for a new denomination based on a largely Unitarian model: non-creedal, congregational, with annual (not biennial) General Assemblies, a strong president, and regions or districts. Universalist state conventions would continue only as auxiliary organizations. Both denominations were to vote on the plan at simultaneous gatherings in Syracuse in 1959. Seth Brooks did not attend, but other Universalist Christians led the opposition. The first sticking point proved to be whether the new statement of purpose would speak of "love to God and mankind" as "truths taught by Jesus" or from "*our* Judeo-Christian heritage." Humanists and other more universalizing types wanted no mention of Jesus. The compromise still used the formula of the two great commandments, love to God and love of neighbor as one's self, but attributed them to "*the* Judeo-Christian heritage." Not everyone had to own that heritage. Both assemblies had to pass the same language. Unitarians passed the proposal, 518 to 43 (92 percent in favor); then Universalists likewise, 238 to 33 (89 percent in favor).[361]

Paul Carnes (1921–1979), minister of a congregation in Buffalo that was one of the more than forty affiliated with both denominations (and who later served as UUA president from 1977 to 1979), observed, "Something happened to the Universalists. They met the Unitarians and found that the Unitarians are, more or less, just like Universalists except that there are more of them and they make more noise."[362] David Parke, a Unitarian minister then teaching church history at St. Lawrence, arrived in Syracuse and inquired of a policeman as to where the Unitarians and Universalists were meeting. The cop shrugged, "There's some Ukrainians meeting in that hotel."[363] Universalists and Unitarians at last were enough alike to blend their families, but too many Americans still had not heard of them; in many parts of the country they might as well have been Ukrainians.

Boston, the spiritual center and headquarters of both denominations, was the place to celebrate the marriage, of course, which took place a year later in May 1960. Final votes were taken for the new UUA to be fully and legally constituted in May 1961, at which time the Universalists would move into 25 Beacon Street, and new officers, representing both groups, would be chosen. The two denominations celebrated their consolidation at Boston's Symphony Hall. Donald Harrington, minister of the Community Church of New York, who had played a key role in finding the compromise language at Syracuse, gave a pastoral and prophetic perspective on what he called this "milestone moment":

. . . partly a birth, partly a commencement, partly a kind of marriage, which involves also a degree of death, an end of things which have been precious to us and of institutions with which we have been lovingly familiar.

We have achieved a union which is the result of more than a hundred years of striving, and which now, at last, when the time is fully ripe, has come to completion. It is our tremendous potential, born of the world's response to our new relevance, caused by this world's need for a religion which [is] dynamic instead of static, unitive instead of divisive, universalistic instead of particularistic, history-making rather than history-bound, that has made this Unitarian-Universalist merger necessary and inevitable.

He cast an expansive vision of the vital role of liberal religion in shaping the world of the future, and then concluded,

May we, Unitarians and Universalists and men and women of good will everywhere, strive with all our might to make our lives, our churches and fellowships, and our new Unitarian Universalist Association the vehicle of this vision![364]

The Unitarian
Universalist Association

1961
2011

The Marriage During the First Twenty Years

So how did the marriage turn out? Children can be hypercritical of what their parents accomplish for them. So it is hard to be objective about such matters. One can, however, try to capture some of the tone, personalities, and issues the UUA faced in the succeeding five decades. In the early 1960s, for example, the tone was optimistic: *"Liberalism is on the mahch!"*

One has to imagine the Boston accent and stentorian voice of Dana McLean Greeley proclaiming those words. The last president of the AUA became the first president of the new UUA in May 1961.[365] He wanted to make sure that the new denomination had a high profile, and he planned to provide it. Unfortunately, the new UUA body to lift up that profile was young, still awkward, and untested—even more than Dana had been when he first started out in the Unitarian ministry at age twenty-four. Just three years later, in 1935, he had succeeded Samuel Atkins Eliot in Channing's pulpit at the Arlington Street Church. Now he wanted to carry forward the renaissance of liberal religion started by that other Eliot, Frederick May. The atmosphere of the 1960s encouraged optimistic ambitions. Just months before the first UUA election, at his inauguration, John F. Kennedy said (in a speech drafted by Unitarian Ted Sorenson) that "the torch has been passed to a new generation." He ended, "here on earth God's work must truly be our own." If more UUs had been willing to "ask not what your [faith] can do for you, but rather what you can do for your [faith]," things might have gone better for Greeley and the UUA. But in the 1960s and '70s they were not there yet—if they are even now.

Those who planned the consolidation recommended that neither head of the two existing denominations become the first UUA president. Greeley had charisma, leadership gifts, vision, connections, and encouragement. He had only headed the AUA for three years. So he ran. Universalist General Superintendent Phillip Giles did not want to make it an "us *versus* them." So he did not. The UCA Board nominated William B. Rice, who had so ably chaired the Joint Merger Commission. Rice's passions were pastoral. He loved being the chaplain to a local fire department, for example. His chief gifts were facilitative. Greeley, by contrast, was a leader whose gifts were oratorical and prophetic. Martin Luther King Jr. and Coretta Scott King had often gone to hear him preach when they lived in Boston. Greeley narrowly won the election, 1,135 to 980.

Many loved Greeley personally, but also worried over his capacity for managerial prudence. Soon a chief detractor was the new moderator, Marshall E. Dimock (1903–1991), who had served the consolidation process as an expert on management. The moderator was an unpaid volunteer, meant to chair the General Assembly and Board of Trustees. Dimock, however, saw himself as a virtual co-president, demanding an office at 25 Beacon, interfering with staff appointments. Greeley believed the new UUA had to engage in "investment spending." He had a mission on behalf of liberal religion: to convince both Unitarian Universalists and the wider world that UUs were a serious religious, catalytic force for change. He may even have succeeded in that goal—but only at the cost of deficit budgets every year that depleted all endowments and reserves.

There is no documentation for what I am about to say, but I have it on good authority (from the late Malcolm Sutherland, who served as executive vice president of the AUA under Greeley, and later as president of Meadville Lombard Theological School) that in the run-up to the plebiscite on consolidation, opposition began to rumble among the field staff of both denominations. There were then eleven Universalist state conventions that still had state superintendents. There were eight Unitarian regional directors. They understandably feared losing their jobs in the process. The merger plan called for fifty districts, not state conventions, but with only seven regional service centers.[366] Instead, the UUA ended up with nineteen (later twenty-one) districts, each with a district executive. Organizers decided that local "bishops"—and regional boards, and state conventions—were needed to support the denominational consolidation. Could the UUA afford such a structure? Not really.

There were other expenses associated with forging unity. Replacing the subscriber-supported *Universalist Leader* and *Unitarian Register* with a new monthly magazine led to an expensive experiment called *UUA Now*. In order to mollify Universalists, Greeley had recruited as executive vice president a Universalist minister, Raymond Hopkins, who had supported Rice and been a key figure in the Massachusetts Universalist Convention. When budgets annually predicted fund-raising results wildly higher than the previous year's results, Hopkins spoke out for greater caution.[367] The UUA Board went along with the budgets, however; Greeley had chosen many of them (as Eliot had in the AUA) by sitting with the nominating committee. Deficits were covered from unrestricted bequests and endowments—the largest from the Universalist Convention of Massachusetts.[368]

In the context of the 1960s, much of Greeley's "investment spending" seemed justified. He had a global vision and broad ecumenical and interfaith contacts. He was present at the opening of the Second Vatican Council. Albert Schweitzer, when Greeley visited him in Africa, encouraged him to rouse the conscience of the world about the nuclear arms race.[369] Greeley appointed Homer Jack, an activist Unitarian minister who had become head of the disarmament group SANE, to head UUA social responsibility efforts. He appointed Henry Hampton, an African American who later made the award-winning PBS series, *Eyes on the Prize*, UUA associate director of information. Nothing demonstrates better the role that Greeley envisaged for Unitarian Universalism in leading interfaith cooperation for social justice than the UUA response to Dr. King's request for help in assembling religious leaders in Selma, Alabama, in March 1965.

A memorial in the chapel (Eliot Hall) at UUA headquarters recollects that story. Three people who died in the Selma campaign are depicted. The first is Jimmy Lee Jackson, twenty-six, brutally beaten and then shot by a state trooper after peacefully protesting the month before. His death precipitated the first effort at a civil rights march from Selma to Montgomery, on what became known as "Bloody Sunday." Dr. King then called for the nation's clergy to join him. Unitarian Universalist ministers were among the first to do so. Among them, also depicted in the memorial, was James Reeb, thirty-eight, who was beaten and killed by a group of white men armed with clubs.[370] The third person depicted in the memorial is Viola Liuzzo, thirty-nine, a Unitarian Universalist from Detroit, killed by a sniper after the third and final march, while driving a civil rights worker back home.[371] At the head of that march was Dr. King, alongside Dana Greeley and all the national religious leaders—Jewish, Protestant, Catholic, Orthodox—that Dana had called to join them there.[372]

Greeley, strongly committed to nonviolence, early on opposed the Vietnam War and traveled twice to Saigon. Unfortunately, he also persuaded the Unitarian Universalist Service Committee (UUSC) to accept US government funding for a social work training program in Vietnam that turned out to be sponsored by the CIA. (The UUSC subsequently adopted a strict policy of accepting no government funds, to remain independent.) By October 1967, polarizing controversies about *how* to deal with peace and race began to emerge. That month, at the Arlington Street Church, Greeley's successor there, Jack Mendelsohn (b. 1918), hosted an anti-war service initiated by students and addressed by Unitarian youth leader Michael Ferber, Yale chaplain William Sloane Coffin, pediatrician Dr. Benjamin Spock, and Harvard UU historian

George Huntston Williams. The latter preached about the church's history of giving sanctuary to conscientious objectors to war. Students burned draft cards. Conservatives, both in and beyond the denomination, were appalled.

That same month, at the Biltmore Hotel in New York, Homer Jack and the Unitarian Universalist Commission on Religion and Race held an Emergency Conference on Unitarian Universalist Response to the Black Rebellion. There were 135 participants, but only thirty-seven UU African Americans. Almost immediately, thirty of the latter withdrew to form a caucus closed to whites. They emerged with a list of "non-negotiable demands," including the funding by the UUA Board of a Black Affairs Council (BAC),

Arlington Street Church anti-war rally

appointed by the Black Unitarian Universalist Caucus (BUUC), to receive $1 million over four years. The subsequent controversy became complex. Integrationists opposed to black separatism opposed the BAC and formed an alternative group, Black and White Action (BAWA). Polarization over the Vietnam War and over black empowerment hurt UUA fundraising and growth. Annual giving goals were not met. Unrestricted reserves were exhausted, although few knew or cared. The fellowship program was suspended; Munroe Husbands had been let go. It would have been—it *was*—futile to call for reason and prudence. Passions were ignited. As Homer Jack said later, "revolutions are never reasonable or rational."[373] And 1968 surely was a revolutionary year.

At the UUA General Assembly in May 1968, in Cleveland— held just weeks after the assassination of Dr. King—delegates voted 836 to 326 to fund the BAC with $250,000 a year. They also voted to increase funding to theological schools and other programs. They *thought* they had the money and the authority. In fact, they had neither. The bylaws of the UUA made it *seem* as though the General Assembly had final authority for all decisions, rather like a local congregational meeting. Under Massachusetts nonprofit law, the *trustees* had final responsibility for finances. However, that was not yet clear in the young denomination.[374] Efforts to cut the allocation to the BAC or raise part of it outside the budget led to a response from youth and white adults, who formed a group called For Full Recognition and Funding of the Black Affairs Council, or FULLBAC. Black BAWA leader Betty Bobo Seiden challenged their support for separatism and funding: "You say that we blacks are supposed to be off getting ourselves equal to you. I feel equal right now. . . . Can you see how insulted I am that your Lady Bountiful basket is going to give me self-empowerment?"[375]

Others saw things differently. In Cleveland, Ohio, the downtown Unitarian Society had purchased the old building of First Unitarian when the majority of that congregation voted in 1951 to move to suburban Shaker Heights. In 1969 the biracial congregation voted to give their aging building to the BUUC for black community use. Hayward Henry of the BUUC said that other Unitarian Universalist congregations might give "ghetto facilities to blacks, with white constituents moving elsewhere," since the swing to black solidarity had called "the integrated church into question."[376]

To try to keep the peace, the UUA trustees adopted a budget for 1969–1970 with $250,000 for the BAC and $50,000 for BAWA. The BAC declared that it would not accept its allocation if BAWA received any. The 1969 General Assembly became even more contentious than the previous year. There was also a critical election. Dana Greeley had been reelected without opposition in 1965. Now he was ineligible for a third term. Seven candidates— all ministers—barnstormed the country, contending for the office. Robert Nelson West, who had served Unitarian congregations in Knoxville, Tennessee, and Rochester, New York, and been effective on racial justice issues in both places, was the candidate of the most influential clergy—at least after Harry Scholefield of San Francisco developed heart problems. West won a majority of the votes. Second place went to Deane Starr, who had been Universalist minister and district executive, then Greeley's vice president for field services. The election meeting itself was an ugly debacle. Participants seized microphones from one another. The BAC supporters walked out at one point. Only the skill of UUA Moderator (later Congressman) Joseph Lyman Fisher (1914–1992) of Arlington, Virginia, Dimock's successor, persuaded them to return. By the end it was at last known that 25 Beacon Street was heavily mortgaged. A cartoon circulated showing West trying to lead the UUA from a phone booth on the Boston Common.

In 1969 the UUA Board reluctantly reduced its allocation to the BAC from $250,000 for the next year to $200,000, spreading its grant out from four years to five. BAC chairman Hayward Henry saw in this action "a shocking revelation of the institutional racism still rampant at the UUA."[377] The BAC then moved to disaffiliate. The 1970 Seattle General Assembly then rejected a motion to restore full funding, realizing that UUA assistance was coming only because of one wealthy church on Long Island. The BAC then encouraged supporters to boycott UUA fundraising and get local congregations to invest endowments in "BAC bonds." Soon they were mired in internal dissent over how the funds raised were to be or had been used. By the end of the decade, an unedifying series of black *vs.* black lawsuits put both the BAC and the BUUC out of business. Congregational endowments that had bought BAC bonds eventually lost much of their investment. Inflation was high. So was fear of urban violence. Urban churches struggled.

In 1970 the Arlington Street Church called Renford Gaines, one of the denomination's few African-American ministers, by a 54 percent vote. During a turbulent four-year ministry, Gaines changed his name to Mwalimu Imara. After he resigned, Arlington Street for a time had only lay leadership. Feminist songwriter Carolyn McDade numbered among the key leaders. Eventually the UUA offered funding to help its flagship Boston congregation recover. Victor Carpenter, a Boston-born minister who had served in Capetown, South Africa, and had been expelled by the apartheid regime, began at Arlington Street in 1978.

As the 1960s ended, it was clear that Unitarian Universalists were on the march, all right—but far too many, radical and conservative alike, were marching *away* from liberal religion and its institutions. Interestingly, the question of divorce between Unitarians and Universalists simply never arose. Perhaps there wasn't enough property left to divide. Or perhaps the era had just proven that differences in family origin mean relatively little in relation to more pressing issues of justice and even survival.

As Mark Morrison-Reed points out in his book, *Black Pioneers in a White Denomination*, "We do not stand above the social attitudes of our times, as we are prone to believe, but instead flounder about in their midst with everyone else."[378] This was surely true in the 1970s—a difficult decade for liberal religion in all denominations. Many mainline Protestant denominations lost as much as a third of their membership. Unitarian Universalism also lost people. Partisans of one cause or another often blamed a failure to wholeheartedly support their point of view. Cultural commentator Tom Wolfe may have had a deeper insight when he called it "the 'Me' Decade," describing a new American preoccupation with self-awareness and a "collective retreat from history, community, and human reciprocity."[379]

Leading the UUA from 1969 to 1977, Robert Nelson West faced many difficulties: financial crisis, institutional immaturity, rapid cultural change, unproductive polarization, anti-institutionalism among many members, and even governmental harassment in a time of war.[380] On taking office he discovered that the financial situation was even worse than he had known. He had to begin by cutting the budget and staff by 40 percent. All nineteen district executives were let go and replaced with a regional, "inter-district program." The UUA bylaws had been changed. Districts now chose most UUA trustees. An elected financial advisor reported directly to the General Assembly. Informing the constituency became a priority. *UUA Now*, a magazine with only seven thousand subscribers, was replaced by *UU World*, a newspaper sent to all member households.

West did not shrink from courageous action. Beacon Press published the full text of *The Pentagon Papers* (1971) so that readers could see the contradictions between US government statements about the war in Vietnam and its own internal analysis of the conflict. US Senator Mike Gravel from Alaska, a Unitarian, provided the text. The Nixon administration responded by having the FBI seize the donor records of the UUA. As the UUA defended itself, its legal expenses became enormous. Moreover, sales of *The Pentagon Papers* (five large, expensive, rather dull volumes) were poor. Fortunately, there was one Unitarian Universalist congregation in a position to come to the rescue, giving the UUA funds to pay off some debts and to help it stand up to government harassment.

The North Shore Unitarian Society of Plandome, New York (now called the Unitarian Universalist Congregation at Shelter Rock), had unexpected financial resources. The North Shore group had begun as a Sunday school in the 1940s.[381] During the 1950s their minister, Gerald Weary, called regularly on an older, house-bound widow, Caroline E. Veatch.[382] Her late husband had been a geologist. He left her stock in a pre-war German company that had rights to royalties on oil and gas in northern Germany and the North Sea. Weary put her in touch with a Unitarian lawyer who helped her finally receive some income from the stock. Grateful, she left the stock to the congregation. As the oil and gas fields were developed and other legal issues were settled, the congregation began to receive more money than anyone had imagined possible. In 1959 they established the Veatch Program to develop and guide their philanthropy.[383] They made grants to social justice organizations, and they made loans to help new UU congregations build. The UUA under Greeley had been seen as financially irresponsible. West had to beg the Veatch Program for help to deal with bank loans, racial justice, *The Pentagon Papers*, stalled growth, and short-falls in giving. They responded—generously. In 1974 they doubled their annual UUA giving to $600,000. The next year they agreed to West's proposal that, starting in 1977–1978, they match dollar for dollar the giving of all the other UUA member congregations. Without this help, the UUA might well have fallen apart.

One of the cultural phenomena of the decade was a rapid doubling of the divorce rate.[384] This was hardly confined to UUs. Women were fleeing the subordination Betty Friedan had decried in her book *The Feminine Mystique* (1963). Even in the civil rights and anti-war movements, women had felt it. The term sexist emerged, parallel to racist and chauvinist (*i.e.*, nationalist).[385] Along with "the generation gap," polarizing dimensions that went well beyond race or politics entered church life. The existence of male-only groups was deeply challenged. By the end of the decade, the Laymen's League, which had done so much to raise funds for liberal religious expansion, dissolved.[386] The Unitarian Universalist Women's Federation (UUWF), meanwhile, became active at the national level. In Dallas, Texas, its affiliate at the First Unitarian Church raised the funds to bring a case about a woman's control over her own reproductive life. *Roe vs. Wade* went all the way to the US Supreme Court, which issued its decision on January 23, 1973. The UUWF also sponsored the publications *Voices of the New Feminism* (ed. Mary Lou MacDonald, Beacon Press, 1970) and the UUA curriculum *Self-Discovery: Group Explorations in Life Crises* (1970). In 1972, the UUWF proposed eliminating all male-gender language and pronouns from the UUA bylaws.[387] This led to a complex process of re-examining the UUA's founding statement of Principles and Purposes. That took fully another decade.

Meanwhile, Liberal Religious Youth, which had anticipated the consolidation of the Unitarian and Universalist denominations, was not doing well, either continentally or locally.[388] "Youth autonomy" in the era of "the generation gap" had led only to generational distancing. Adults complained, "Why aren't our teens the way *we* were?" One articulate teen from my own congregation served on a national committee to understand the issues. He defined the typical LRY group as having become "a group of abandoned teenagers, told to go off in a corner somewhere by themselves to try to boil music out of a tennis shoe."[389] The best thing that the UUA did for adolescents in the 1970s was to develop and publish a pioneering new curriculum, *About Your Sexuality*, by Deryck Calderwood of New York University. In the spirit of the times, *About Your Sexuality* "let it all hang out," with explicit slides intended to be used judiciously by trained teachers. One minister, under fire in his congregation for other reasons, gave the slides to the press. The congregation, threatened with charges of promoting obscenity by a right-wing district attorney, rallied around him—temporarily.[390]

The sexual revolution of the 1970s affected adults and congregational life in other ways. In many communities Unitarian Universalist congregations led the way in offering programs organized by and for single adults. Often these groups were made up largely of divorced adults hoping to meet new partners. In congregations from Westport, Connecticut, to Atlanta, Georgia, to several communities on the West Coast, singles groups became so large and so heavily made up of people unaffiliated with the host congregation as to become problematic. Boundaries within marriages were challenged, with some couples trying "open marriage." In the name of human liberation, extramarital sexual relationships between adults were justified, and even entered into, by some clergy.[391] As a new young clergy couple, my wife and I often felt conservative, wondering if Unitarian Universalism could survive an imbalance of freedom over responsibility. Fortunately, there were many other leaders, lay and ordained, who kept their eyes on the great potential for just relationships and social transformation inherent in liberal religion.

On many fronts, UU work for human rights stayed prophetic, creative, and courageous. In 1972, as a follow-up to *About Your Sexuality,* the UUA published an adult curriculum called *The Invisible Minority: Homosexuals in Our Society*, which included filmstrips and audiotapes. It received awards from the National Council on Family Relations. Delegates to the 1973 General Assembly voted to establish an Office of Gay Concerns. The Board of Trustees found funding the next year: By a vote of twelve to eleven it started a "gay" office by cutting funds for other programs. It was the first such office ever set up by a religious denomination.[392]

Meanwhile, West had become puzzled by some increasing payments from a series of "India trusts" set up by the late Jonathan Holdeen. They were odd entities—variously described as for "the benefit of people of India," and other causes, with the AUA named as administrator. As "Franklin trusts," they paid only one one-thousandth or one five-hundredth of their income in the first year, reinvesting the rest into ever-growing capital. The Commonwealth of Pennsylvania was residual beneficiary—with the goal of abolishing all taxes there. The trusts were also administered by family and friends of Holdeen, beneficiaries of other trusts he had established. Assets were at times intermingled. West had to go to court to unsnarl this mess, which became the longest-running court case in the history of Pennsylvania—a modern version of *Jarndyce vs. Jarndyce* in Dickens' *Bleak House*. West could

UNITARIAN UNIVERSALIST ASSN.

c/o PSSC
46 Development Road
Fitchburg MA USA

Invoice # 481313
Inv. Date 09/20/2011
Customer PO #

3760460

Ship To: Hamlin, H. Phillips
432 Highland Hills
Knoxville TN 37919

Ship Via: M03 - USPS MEDIA MAIL/DEL.CONFIRM

only start the process—dissolving the accumulation provisions as contrary to basic trust law. The UUA began to receive more trust income. By the 1980s it established the creative UU Holdeen India Program (UUHP). Partners developed by UUHP program director Kathy Sreedhar later won the World Anti-Slavery Award, the Robert F. Kennedy Human Rights Award, the Magsaysay Award for Promoting Democracy in Asia, and many other honors. Litigation over assets misapplied to family investments by former trustees continued. While it went on, little attention could go to the good work being done in India.[393]

During his eight years as UUA president, Bob West received very little thanks for his efforts to reverse the decline of liberal religion. These included "Sharing in Growth" partnerships between larger, healthy congregations and their leaders and smaller groups attempting to grow, a pattern used later in several other forms. There were also notable efforts to improve ministerial recruitment and training, provide pensions and insurance, and expand efforts to make the ministry more inclusive. Soon experienced directors of religious education, most of them women, were recognized as *ministers* of religious education. When his two terms were over, in 1977, West did not return to ministry. Instead he became a law firm administrator.

The contest to succeed West pitted his one-time campaign manager, Paul Carnes, minister of the church in Buffalo, New York, against Jack Mendelsohn, who by then had left Arlington Street Church for First Unitarian Church of Chicago. Gordon McKeeman entered late. Coming from the Universalist side of the family, he was minister in Akron, Ohio. He had served on the UUA Board and had chaired that of the UUSC. Although McKeeman came on strong toward the end, Carnes won the three-way race. He promptly tried to consolidate support, in part by appointing a Mendelsohn supporter, William F. Schulz (b. 1949), minister in Bedford, Massachusetts, as UUA director of social responsibility. He also recruited O. Eugene Pickett (b. 1925), minister in Atlanta, to be UUA director of ministerial education.

Carnes, as a one-time prisoner of war and a cancer survivor, tried hard to be a realist. He raised painful possibilities: selling Beacon Press, rather than incur further annual deficits, and closing the under-endowed Starr King School for the Ministry. First diagnosed with lymphoma in 1963, Carnes thought his illness was safely in remission. But the stressful job of UUA president may well have contributed to the cancer's recurrence in 1978. He tried to keep traveling on UUA business as long as he could. He died in March 1979, at age fifty-eight. Now the UUA Board had to choose a new president. McKeeman and Pickett were the two candidates. Pickett prevailed, fourteen to twelve. McKeeman instead became the president of the Starr King School. It could have been seen as a Universalist *versus* Unitarian race, but few spoke that way. After nearly twenty years of marriage, the two parts of the denominational family were clear that the crises through which they had passed together—and the opportunities still ahead— were far more important.

The UUA Grows Stronger

In the 1980s Unitarian Universalism began to grow again. Several factors seemed to help. Some liberals began to realize that the roots of their values were religious or at least spiritual, and to look for a distinctively progressive alternative. The rise of the religious right played a role. Until the 1970s American fundamentalist Christians had been largely apolitical. Then *Roe vs. Wade* and cases about prayer in the schools mobilized them. Jerry Falwell's Moral Majority (which, as critics pointed out, was never either) stimulated a complex process. Following the "me decade" of the 1970s, there was a stronger sense among liberals that perhaps no socially transforming solutions could be found in being isolated individualists. The baby boomers, born between 1946 and 1964, were also having children. Some were looking for a more inclusive approach to religious education than could be provided in traditional churches and synagogues. With more women working and volunteer time curtailed, more congregations, including lay-led fellowships, admitted the need for professional religious leadership. New funding from the Veatch Program allowed the UUA to strengthen its extension programs, helping many fellowships to call their first minister. New congregations were also started, and a new tone of spiritual commitment and yearning could be sensed among religious liberals. When O. Eugene Pickett became the fourth president of the UUA in 1979, he put it this way:

The old watchwords of liberalism—freedom, reason, tolerance—worthy though they may be, are simply not catching the imagination of the contemporary world. They describe a process for approaching the religious depths but they testify to no intimate acquaintance with the depths themselves.[394]

Women in the UUA were eager both to move beyond "the old watchwords" and to show the way to a deeper and more experiential spirituality. They objected to words in the hymnal, readings, and the UUA bylaws that made women feel left out: brotherhood, man, mankind, not to mention the use of male pronouns. Supplements to the hymnal using gender-inclusive hymns and readings were published. Changing the statement of Principles and Purposes, however, with words that had been so painstakingly arrived at and agreed to at Syracuse in 1959, required a vote of two successive General Assemblies and a two-thirds vote. An elaborate revision process, with an appointed commission and much vetting and debate of proposed language, was necessary. The process took several years. The effort, however, produced an entirely fresh statement of Unitarian Universalist values and spirituality, with two significant innovations. First, it revived the religious concept of covenant as a relationship of trust and mutual commitment. It said that the congregations of the UUA "covenant to affirm and promote" seven broad principles. Second, it celebrated the theological diversity of Unitarian Universalism by characterizing not one, but five (and later six) Sources for "the living tradition we share." Although some critics feared a merely superficial eclecticism, the new Principles and Purposes proved to be more indicative of a growing desire in the denomination for renewed commitment—to high ideals, greater spiritual depth, and pluralism.

Gene Pickett had been born and raised a Maryland Methodist. He was influenced by the ministry of A. Powell Davies and attended Meadville Lombard Theological School in Chicago. He

met and married Helen Rice. Pickett had served UU congregations in Miami, Richmond, and Atlanta.[395] Much of the growth
of Unitarian Universalism that began again in the 1980s was in
the Sunbelt, but this was less by design than because of changing demographics. Congregations in northern New England, in
upstate New York, and in some "rust belt" cities were shrinking,
even closing, but with Northerners and retirees moving South and
West, the center of gravity of the UUA also moved in those direc-
tions. The value of providing a strong alternative to fundamental-
ism became clear when the UU Congregation of Atlanta, which
Pickett had served, and then All Souls Unitarian Church in Tulsa,
Oklahoma, became two of the largest churches in the UUA. Veatch
funds began to support a program of starting new urban congregations led by ministers of color, not only in Tulsa and Atlanta, but
also in Washington DC, Los Angeles, and elsewhere. Results were
not always satisfying or lasting, but the effort to re-engage with
racial diversity and justice was sincere. The Unitarian Universalist
ministry was becoming markedly more diverse.

The percentage of women entering theological school
increased dramatically, and by the end of the decade women
made up a majority of the new ministers granted fellowship
each year. There had been women ministers in the 1890s who
were quietly partnered with other women, but the first openly
gay male ministers were granted fellowship beginning in 1978.
Traditional Women's Alliance programs were in decline in many
congregations, but the more feminist-oriented Women and Religion program kept many younger and working women engaged
with Unitarian Universalism.

After a conference called "Common Ground," involving the
remnants of Liberal Religious Youth and the many unaffiliated
youth groups that had developed in congregations, Young Religious Unitarian Universalists (YRUU) began in 1983. In short,
while 1980s conservatives were using "wedge issues" to try to
divide American progressives on the basis of race, gender, sexual
orientation, and age, Unitarian Universalists in the same period

found ways to reassert a principled commitment to justice and inclusion, and to begin to heal some divisions.

Bob West had not dared to try to start a UUA capital fundraising campaign in the 1970s. Pickett launched a campaign called "Visions for Growth," which raised some $4 million. He worked closely with William F. Schulz, who served as his executive vice president. Together they fended off distractions and rebuilt a UUA service structure that could again be trusted by its donors and constituents. Unfortunately, Pickett was not as lucky in having a good relationship with UUA Moderator Sandra Mitchell Caron (1935–1999), a lawyer who served as deputy superintendent of banking for New York State. When Pickett's term of office ended in 1985, the election to succeed him was rather awkward. Sandy Caron, while still serving as moderator, ran for UUA president against Schulz. Caron was not only the first woman, but also the first layperson, to seek the UUA presidency. With strong support from the ministers, Schulz was easily elected. Pickett succeeded George Marshall as minister of the Church of the Larger Fellowship, also serving a term as president of the International Association for Religious Freedom.

Schulz was raised a Unitarian in Pittsburgh, Pennsylvania, where his father was a law professor. He studied sociology at Oberlin College and was doing a pre-seminary student ministry in Kent, Ohio, in 1970 when four students were killed there by the National Guard during an anti-war protest. After earning a doctor of ministry degree at Meadville Lombard, Schulz served briefly at First Parish in Bedford, Massachusetts, before Paul Carnes appointed him UUA director of social responsibility. He became executive vice president at only twenty-nine, and president at thirty-six. A gifted speaker and writer, Schulz engaged in public debates with the religious right, and worked assiduously to continue the growth and raise the public visibility of Unitarian Universalism. He also worked persuasively with the North Shore Unitarian Universalist Society, who in 1985 transferred to the UUA a $20 million unrestricted endowment, and in 1987, a further $9 million endowment for theological education.

Schulz challenged humanists of the UUA, among whom he counted himself, when he declared a need for a religious "humanism in a new key." "Reason is still a cherished standard in our religious response," Schulz wrote, "but is coming to be supplemented by our immediate apprehension of the Holy and by our conviction that the Holy is embodied in the abundance of a scarred creation."[396]

When running for president against Sandra Caron, Schulz had announced that, if elected, he would appoint Kay Montgomery, a former administrator of the Unitarian Universalist Congregation of Atlanta, as his successor in the role of executive vice president. He did so, and she went on to serve through three succeeding administrations. Schulz also had a close partner in leadership in Moderator Natalie Webber Gulbrandsen (1925–2002), a former president of the UUWF and a member of the Wellesley Hills congregation. Both shared an interest in other cultures and in the

John Buehrens, Denny Davidoff, Natalie Gulbrandsen, William Schulz

global community of liberal religionists. Schulz tried to find ways to deepen cooperation with groups overseas. The UUA Board was persuaded to admit congregations in Australia, New Zealand, and the Philippines, and to drop from the full name of the "Unitarian Universalist Association of Congregations" the final phrase—"in North America." In 1989, when a revolution in Romania toppled the regime of the dictator, Nicolae Ceausescu, Schulz and Gulbrandsen led a delegation, including UU member of Congress Chet Atkins, to visit and bring support to the long-oppressed Hungarian-speaking Unitarian community there. North American congregations were invited to form partner relations with congregations in Hungary and Transylvania. This program, some have observed, may have done more than any amount of multicultural training could have to teach American UUs that liberal faith could be expressed authentically in multiple forms of worship and belief.

In the 1980s Unitarian Universalists began to adopt new forms of worship themselves. The custom of lighting a chalice at the beginning of worship and meetings spread rapidly. Feminists contributed the water ceremony many congregations began to use at the beginning of each new year in September. The flower communion developed by Czech Unitarian minister Norbert apek in the 1920s had made its way to America already in the 1940s, but it too spread. Candle-lighting and the sharing of joys and concerns in worship were also innovations of the era. There had been a great deal of experimentation, starting in the 1970s. Now some consensus around simple ritual and meaningful liturgy began to emerge in many congregations. There were some differences of opinion, of course, but nothing on the scale of the "worship wars" that broke out in many other denominations between traditionalists and innovators. By the time a new hymnal commission was appointed in 1987, there was also broad consensus that the 1964 hymnal and its "man-centered" religious humanism needed to be made more inclusive. Not everyone was pleased with the result, called *Singing the Living Tradition*—especially regarding the revisions to familiar hymns and carols—but its 1993 publication was generally well-received. Sales surpassed all expectations. Toward the end of his tenure, Schulz launched a new UUA capital campaign called "Handing on the Future," aimed at raising at least $10 million. The Veatch Program had made it clear that they wanted to see other Unitarian Universalists start to contribute to the long-term growth and health of Unitarian Universalism.

The election of Schulz's successor took place at the 1993 UUA General Assembly in Charlotte, North Carolina. Schulz went on to become the executive director of Amnesty International, USA, for twelve years, becoming a leading figure in human rights and in 2001 publishing *In Our Own Best Interest: How Defending Human Rights Benefits Us All.* In 2010, he became president and CEO of the UUSC.

Carolyn Owen-Towle and I were the two candidates to succeed Schulz. Owen-Towle was co-minister with her husband, Tom, of a large congregation in San Diego, California. Carolyn had been president of the UU Ministers Association and chair of the board of the UUSC. My own ministries had been to congregations in Knoxville, Tennessee, and Dallas, Texas, before becoming, in 1987, co-minister with Forrest Church at the Unitarian Church of All Souls in New York City. He and I had together written *Our Chosen Faith: An Introduction to Unitarian Universalism* (1989). Based on the Sources of Unitarian Universalism in the statement of Principles and Purposes, it quickly became a standard introduction for newcomers, showing those afraid of superficial eclecticism a deeper confluence among the varied streams of liberal religion.

The contest was close. I was elected by a mere ninety-nine votes out of over twenty-five hundred cast. Elected without opposition as UUA moderator was Denise Taft Davidoff (b. 1932), a trustee-at-large who had followed Natalie Gulbrandsen as president of the UUWF. We began our joint leadership at the 1993 General Assembly in Charlotte, North Carolina. The host district, named for Thomas Jefferson, had invited people to a "Thomas

Jefferson Birthday Ball" on the night of the elections—historic cos-
tumes optional. African-American UUs justifiably asked if perhaps
rags and chains would be appropriate attire for them. Within an
hour of the election results, Denny and I were locked arm-in-arm
with people protesting the planned party.

Getting predominantly white Unitarian Universalists to engage
with issues of anti-racism and anti-oppression became a major
theme of the following years. Davidoff, like a number of other
UUA Board leaders of the 1990s, had been part of FULLBAC in
1969. I had been part of the Urban Church Coalition and was
determined to balance social activism with good stewardship
both of money and morale. I reorganized the UUA executive staff
and appointed the first people of color to serve at that level. Mel
Hoover co-directed a new department of faith in action, combin-
ing social justice and anti-oppression work. William G. Sinkford
(b. 1946) became director of district services—soon expanded to
include extension efforts as well. Anti-racism training was controversial, but was required of UUA staff, trustees, and other "gate-
keepers," from the Ministerial Fellowship Committee to the UUA
President's Council, a body of major donors.

The policy of admitting indigenous UU groups overseas, such
as the UU Church of the Philippines, struck me as fraught with
potential for paternalism, cultural insensitivity, and countless
other issues of equity. I recruited Kenneth Torquil MacLean, who
as a UUA trustee had cast the sole vote against that policy, to serve
as my special assistant for international relations. In 1995 Ken
helped establish the International Council of Unitarians and Universalists as a more appropriate organization for groups in India,
Romania, the UK, the Philippines, and elsewhere to partner with
the UUA and with one another. Toward the end of the decade, as
the age of the Internet introduced more spiritual seekers around
the world to Unitarian Universalism, new groups emerged in Latin
America, Africa, Asia, and Europe. The relationship between the
UUA and the Canadian Unitarian Council was also changed to
allow Canadians to devote more attention to the growth of reli-

gious liberalism in their own context than to cross-border relations and financial arrangements.

Unitarian Universalism in the United States was growing in many places. One of the first challenges I faced was to expand the capacity of the UUA to lend money to congregations that were building new facilities. Members of the Presidents' Council provided the expertise for the UUA to multiply its lending capacity by using the income stream from existing building loans to secure a much larger amount of capital. The 1990s economy was good, and many UU congregations were renovating, building, and expanding. I preached at the dedication services for well over a hundred new, newly acquired, renovated, or expanded UU facilities, large and small. The congregation in Bethlehem, Pennsylvania, sold its A-frame in the woods and moved to a downtown building that had been a Methodist church. The congregation in Fargo, North Dakota, re-purchased a small church they had built early in the 1900s and then sold during the Depression. In Savannah, Georgia, the congregation also recovered its historic church building. But in Las Vegas, Nevada, I found myself blessing a converted Moose Hall, while in Ann Arbor, Michigan, and Williamsburg, Virginia, the new buildings were designed by award-winning architects. These visits offered me the opportunity to encourage generous donors to go beyond brick-and-mortar, and to hear a vision of a stronger, more influential UU movement, made possible with more scholarship funds for ministers, greater support for growth efforts in promising areas without a UU presence, and stronger infrastructure for communications and social witness. In 1997, as I was elected to a second term, I was able to announce that the "Handing on the Future" campaign had exceeded its goal, raising $13.6 million.

Working very cooperatively with the moderator and the General Assembly Planning Committee, I persuaded them to use each annual meeting in my first term to put the focus on some area of UU life where improvements at the congregational level were clearly necessary, where examples of good congregational practice could also be shared. Attendance at annual General Assemblies went up from the low 2,000s to nearly 5,000, and each issue focused on seemed to improve. Fundraising and generosity was the first theme. Average giving by UUs to their religious communities in the 1990s went up by over 65 percent.[397] Young adult and college ministry was the second. The number of UU campuses with a UU group presence went from only 19 to 135. High school youth work was next. The number of congregations with active youth groups more than quadrupled.

In my second term, I asked the UUA Board to appoint a strategic planning team charged with evaluating other challenges blocking Unitarian Universalism from "Fulfilling the Promise," as we titled the effort. A survey of grass-roots opinion was coupled with serious evaluation by the board, staff, and President's Council of our work in communications, marketing, extension, and public witness. The UUA's anti-oppression work was reframed so as to include not only anti-racism, but also multiculturalism and anti-oppression efforts on behalf of bisexual, gay, lesbian, and transgender people. "Add one more category to the name of that office," I told its new director, Keith Kron, "and it'll be an 'Office of Queer Concerns.'" "That would be fine," Kron replied. Meg Riley, Kron's predecessor, became UUA director of social witness.

I was outraged at a letter the UUA received from Boy Scouts of America (BSA) headquarters. Having been a Scout myself, attending a World Jamboree when I was 12, I had valued that organization for its role in making me sensitive to the natural world and to inclusive good citizenship. The letter, however, told the UUA that our "Religion and Life" award—the UU equivalent of other BSA awards given by other religious communities to Scouts who deepen their understanding of their own faith tradition and practice—would no longer be recognized. Why? Because our curriculum encouraged UU Boy Scouts to challenge homophobia, even in the BSA itself. Unlike other national youth organizations, the BSA had discriminatory policies with regard to sexual orientation. I asked UUs not to walk away from Scouting, but to stay engaged in challenging them to give up discrimination and again become worthy of public support.

In 1996, at the General Assembly in Indianapolis, I arranged with the moderator to interrupt debate in a highly irregular fashion as the Assembly debated whether or not to admit to the floor a new resolution in favor of equal civil marriage rights for same-sex couples. (The UUA much earlier supported ministers doing religious blessings of such unions.) I invited to join me on the platform all those present who, as partners in a same-sex union, were being deprived of such a basic human right. The resolution was admitted and passed overwhelmingly. That General Assembly then put the UUA on record as the first religious body to endorse equal marriage rights. At the Millenium March for Equality, on the National Mall in Washington DC, I was the only non-gay religious leader invited to speak. I asked the half million people present to stand and wave if they had ever been in a UU meetinghouse—for any reason. Nearly the entire crowd did so. When my term of office concluded in 2001, I chose to return to parish ministry at the First Parish in Needham, Unitarian Universalist—near where my parents had retired and where my wife was serving as an Episcopal priest. I became national co-chair of Freedom to Marry.

The election to succeed me was between two members of my own senior staff: Director of Ministry Diane Miller, and William G. Sinkford, director of congregational, district, and extension services. Sinkford was elected by a nearly two-to-one margin, becoming the first African-American president of a historically white denomination. Diane Olsen (b. 1943) became UUA moderator, but after a year and a half, resigned the position. Gini Courter (b. 1957), the chair of the UUA finance committee, was chosen by the board to succeed her. Although the president and the new moderator once again had tensions, Sinkford made adroit use of the UUA's enhanced capacities for effective public witness. He had grown up in First Unitarian Church of Cincinnati during a period when that congregation had an African-American director of religious education. As a student at Harvard, he had been national president of Liberal Religious Youth. In the 1970s, however, when he perceived UUism withdrawing from engagement with racial justice, Sinkford withdrew from UUism; he later spoke openly about that history. He also recognized the need once again to revamp the UUA's relationship with its high-school-age youth, to strengthen its effectiveness in passing the spiritual commitment to justice and human rights from generation to generation.

In 2000 Sinkford and I watched the UUSC select an African-American woman, Valora Washington, as its CEO. He and I had often discussed how white liberal organizations can choose people of color whom they then set up for failure. Washington resigned after only three years, having failed to win the confidence of UUSC staff and donors. She was succeeded by Dr. Charlie Clements, who had earlier led UUSC programs challenging US policies in Central America. He served until 2010. Sinkford worked closely with Clements, a genuine human rights hero who, at great personal risk, had helped blow the whistle on US secret wars in both Cambodia and Central America. The two traveled to Africa to bear witness to failures of the United States and the international community to stop the genocide in Darfur.

Following the terrorist attacks of September 11, 2001, Sinkford led Unitarian Universalists around the country in reaching out to Muslim and Sikh Americans, visiting and protecting mosques and gudwaras. When Hurricane Katrina devastated New Orleans in 2005, a UUA-UUSC joint appeal raised some $3 million dollars. One-third of these funds went to help three local UU congregations re-gather, if not rebuild. The other two-thirds helped efforts to organize the poor in New Orleans as they advocated for their human rights. The UUSC increased its overall budget by 50 percent.

Unfortunately, both organizations had to deal with financial instability that began to affect all nonprofit endowments after stock market turmoil early in the new twenty-first century. Sinkford finally completed a $32 million "Campaign for Unitarian Universalism" that I had launched and greatly expanded the practice of "umbrella giving," so that funds raised by the UUA, especially in the form of deferred gifts, could be shared with the UUSC, local congregations, seminaries, and other UU organizations. Growth in Unitarian Universalism slowed as the economy stalled. Church school enrollments decreased as the children of the baby boom were replaced by those of a smaller demographic, called Generation X.

Sinkford also led the UUA in the ongoing struggle for equal marriage rights. When Massachusetts became the first state in the union to allow same-sex marriage, he personally presided at the wedding of the lead plaintiffs, Hillary and Julie Goodridge, in the UUA chapel. As the legislature next door voted against amending the state constitution to ban such marriages, the headquarters building at 25 Beacon Street bore a large banner favoring equal marriage.

Peter Morales (b. 1946) left a successful ministry at Jefferson Unitarian Church in Golden, Colorado, and a place on the UUA Board to join Sinkford's staff as UUA director of district services and extension. His own assessment led him to question whether the strategies in place would work. The twenty-year effort to help lay-led fellowships with the desire and potential to grow into small pastoral churches had proven expensive on a cost-per-new-member basis. The UUA had also largely run out of fellowships with the motivation to grow in that way. Efforts to imitate evangelical methods by "planting" large, new minister-led congregations were both expensive and not always successful. Marketing efforts in metropolitan areas and in national publications, when evaluated, showed that the problem in most UU churches wasn't getting visitors; it was effectively welcoming and assimilating them. With an average adult membership of only 150, the typical UU congregation was good at maintaining its single-cell character, but not at growing, especially in diversity. That growth seemed to be confined to large and urban congregations that had succeeded in attracting young adults from Generation Y.

Morales resigned from the UUA staff after two years, returning to his Colorado church, where he achieved notable success in overcoming all these obstacles. Starting in 2008, all religious and charitable institutions began to face the challenge of what soon became known as "the Great Recession." Endowments dropped with the collapse of a speculative bubble in debt-financed housing and other assets. Unemployment rose even among the well-educated. Growth for UU congregations became even more difficult.

The race to succeed Sinkford in 2009 was between Laurel Hallman and Morales. Hallman had led First Unitarian Church of Dallas since 1987 and had doubled its membership and increased its racial/ethnic diversity. Morales had started in Golden as recently as 1999, but had done the same there, even with his two-year hiatus in Boston. Hallman was best known for her video curriculum, *Living by Heart*, designed to introduce Unitarian Universalists to deeper daily devotional and meditative practice. Morales, who grew up in a non-Catholic Hispanic family in San Antonio, Texas, had edited and published small-town newspapers before going to Starr King School for the Ministry. Morales was elected by a substantial margin.

O. Eugene Pickett, William Sinkford, Robert West,
John Buehrens, William Schulz, Peter Morales

He soon faced the unenviable task of asking all UUA departments to trim their budgets and staffing by up to 25 percent in order to deal with a drop in endowment income and donations.

As the UUA approached its fiftieth anniversary, which would be in 2011, it was time for the children of the marriage between the Universalist Church of America and the American Unitarian Association to assess the health of their blended family. One thing was clear: Very few people any longer claimed to be children of one side or the other. Even if some heritage Universalists were still annoyed by the tendency of some people to shorten the long, ten-syllable label, Unitarian Universalist, to just the first word, UU identity was actually quite strong—much stronger than in other progressive religious denominations. A member of the United Church of Christ, for example, if asked about religious identity, would be much more likely to say "Protestant" or to name their local congregation than to name their denomination. Members of Reform Jewish congregations similarly might respond, "Jewish," or name their synagogue. Unitarian Universalists, by contrast, tend to name themselves as such—even if they are not current members of a local congregation.

Surveys of religious identity in the United States conducted in 1990 and 2001, in fact, showed that an estimated six hundred fifty thousand or more Americans identify as Unitarian Universalists. Unfortunately, when the American Religious Identification Survey was repeated in 2008, UU statistics were not separated out. The UUA was no longer treated as a Judeo-Christian denomination at all, but rather lumped among "new religions."[398] Still, there were just over one thousand UU congregations in the United States. Once you subtract congregations in other countries jointly affiliated with the UUA, the Canadian Unitarian Council, or the International Council of Unitarians and Universalists, the certified members of US congregations numbered about one hundred sixty thousand adults, plus some fifty-five thousand children and youth.

So, many contemporary UUs are like the six hundred thousand people that the Universalists of the early nineteenth century counted as "under influence," although not active in member congregations. Or like Thomas Jefferson in rural Virginia, "contented to be a Unitarian by myself." Many who have been raised as Unitarian Universalists are not currently church-goers. Fretting over retaining the commitment of UU young adults has become a denominational obsession, but the same issue is often seen in other denominations. Episcopalians, for example, estimate that less than one out of ten young people confirmed in their churches become active communicants as adults.

Religious mobility has been increasing rapidly in the United States. After World War II only 5 percent of all religiously active Americans were active in a religious movement other than the one they had been raised in; by 1995, this number had increased to some 45 percent. Unitarian Universalists in that period simply led the way, noting as early as 1967 that only 10 percent of active members had been raised as Unitarians or Universalists. That has not changed much. Concern about UU congregations being "the church of the revolving door" has abated somewhat as all religious groups experience the same difficulties of operating within a consumerist culture. Another factor that undoubtedly affects Unitarian Universalist commitment and loyalty is a relatively high level of geographic mobility. Many UUs never successfully make the transition from a congregation where they were active to a congregation in a new location that may not be very different in basic values, but where the worship style, programs, ministry, or even architecture are "just not the same." The high level of mobility goes along with having high educational levels. Almost half of all UUs have graduate degrees.[399] Average household income is also higher than in any other American denomination. There may be considerable social-class and educational diversity within local congregations, but the dominant tone in the denomination is that of the educated professional class.

Some would conclude that, in that sense, the Unitarian heritage prevails in the family. What is different, however, is that classic American Unitarianism was very much an inherited form of faith. There is an amusing story told about a Unitarian woman from Beacon Hill, a wealthy neighborhood in Boston, attending a suffrage rally on Boston Common, wearing a particularly striking and elegant hat. One of the younger suffragists admired it, asking "Wherever did you get that wonderful hat!" The matron replied, "My dear, Unitarian ladies of Boston's Beacon Hill do not 'get' their hats. They simply *have* them." The same could be said of their faith. It went where they went, not further.

Today's Unitarian Universalists are much more like the Universalist side of the family in wanting their faith to be shared widely. When asked about their aspirations for Unitarian Universalism, 63 percent of eight thousand individuals surveyed in 1998 chose as their answer, "Become a visible and influential force for good in the world." Certainly the Universalist emphasis on the saving power of love, and not simply cold reason, is evident in efforts like the UUA's public witness campaign, "Standing on the Side of Love," which unites the demand for equal marriage rights with advocacy for immigration reform that does not divide families and that provides a path to citizenship for the undocumented. That emphasis on the power of love is also evident in contemporary UU worship—the Unitarian James Freeman Clarke might join the Universalist *Humiliati* in celebrating that UU worship has become both more liturgical and more participatory, with an emphasis on being spiritually inspiring and emotionally moving. The days of "fiddle and lecture" Sunday mornings seem to be over. Reason is still deeply honored, but "corpse-cold" rationalism is little mourned by most newer and younger Unitarian Universalists.

After fifty years, the blending of the family seems complete and rather solid, with a good deal to celebrate. There is still unfulfilled potential, of course. And what the children and the newcomers will do with this heritage in the next fifty years remains to be seen. The liberal religious tradition is nothing if not democratic and adaptive. Every generation has had to change and adapt the living tradition they have inherited. May understanding our past better help us to avoid repeating the errors of those who have gone before us, and make us wise and persistent as we sing in one of our treasured hymns, "What they dreamed be ours to do, / hope their hopes and seal them true."

For Further Reading

Here is a short list of some important works about Universalist and Unitarian history in general. For more specific studies of particular people and events, please see the endnotes.

Bowers, J.D. *Joseph Priestley and English Unitarianism in America.* University Park, PA: Pennsylvania State University Press, 2007.

Buescher, John. *The Other Side of Salvation: Spiritualism and the Nineteenth-Century Religious Experience.* Boston: Skinner House Books, 2003.

Emerson, Dorothy May. *Standing Before Us: Unitarian Universalist Women and Social Reform, 1776–1936.* Boston: Skinner House Books, 1999.

Howe, Charles. *The Larger Faith: A Short History of American Universalism.* Boston: Skinner House Books, 1993.

Morrison-Reed, Mark. *Black Pioneers in a White Denomination, Third Edition.* Boston: Skinner House Books, 1992.

————. *Darkening the Doorways: Black Trailblazers and Missed Opportunities in Unitarian Universalism.* Boston: Skinner House Books, 2011.

Robinson, David. *The Unitarians and the Universalists.* Santa Barbara, CA: Greenwood Press, 1985.

Ross, Warren R. *The Premise and the Promise: The Story of the Unitarian Universalist Association.* Boston: Skinner House Books, 2001.

Tucker, Cynthia Grant. *No Silent Witness: The Eliot Parsonage Women and Their Unitarian World.* New York: Oxford University Press, 2010.

———. *Prophetic Sisterhood: Liberal Women Ministers of the Frontier, 1880–1930.* Boston: Beacon Press, 1990.

Ulbrich, Holley. *The Fellowship Movement: A Growth Strategy and Its Legacy.* Boston: Skinner House Books, 2007.

Williams, George Huntston. *American Universalism*, Fourth Edition. Boston: Skinner House Books, 2002.

Wright, Conrad. *The Beginnings of Unitarianism in America.* Boston: Beacon Press, 1955.

———, ed. *A Stream of Light: A Short History of American Unitarianism.* Boston: Skinner House Books, 2001.

———, ed. *Three Prophets of Religious Liberalism: Channing, Emerson, Parker.* Boston: Skinner House Books, 1994.

Dictionary of Unitarian Universalist Biography website: http://www25.uua.org/uuhs/duub.

Acknowledgments

The First Parish in Needham, Unitarian Universalist, the congregation that I have served as Minister since 2002, made this book possible. You will encounter some of their rich history here in the fifth chapter. They graciously granted me three months of sabbatical leave in 2010—time which I devoted to this project. My capable research assistant, Holly Hendricks, facilitated quick completion of the work. Her deep knowledge of our heritage and of archival, online, and library resources was invaluable. She also secured most of the images used in this volume.

My wife, Rev. Gwen Langdoc Buehrens, a priest in the Episcopal Church, has been patiently supportive of my devotion to my own denomination for over thirty-eight years. During this project she was indulgent even when I hollered from my study, "Not just now, dear! I'm in the midst of writing!" I am blessed to have her as a partner in life and ministry.

Bobbie Alicen, daughter of the late Munroe Husbands, provided me with biographical material and a photo of her father. His work has been celebrated in *The Fellowship Movement: A Growth Strategy and Its Legacy* by Holley Ulbrich (Skinner House, 2008), but here his personal spiritual journey is told as well, thanks to Bobbie.

Eminent colleagues in Unitarian Universalist history were good enough to read a full draft of this book and offered their comments and counsel. My deep thanks go to David Robinson, Cynthia Grant Tucker, Dan McKanan, Susan Ritchie, and Peter

Hughes. All of them are *migliori fabbri*—far better historians than I. Peter Hughes led me to the discovery of the real source of a quotation long attributed to John Murray. I also want to thank Mary Benard and Marshall Hawkins of Skinner House Books for their editorial encouragement and careful oversight of this project.

In the short scope of a history aimed at the general reader, it was simply not possible to include all of the stories that I would have liked to use. So I remain solely responsible both for the multiple sins of omission and for those errors of fact or interpretation that remain.

Notes

Introduction

1   The first use of the term *Unitarian* (as applied to a group of people) seems to have been in Hungarian-speaking Transylvania, in the early 1600s. The first use of *Universalist* for a group seems to have been in America, in the 1780s.

2   Paul Conkin, *American Originals: Homemade Varieties of Christianity* (Chapel Hill: University of North Carolina Press, 1997).

3   The one exception is David Robinson, *The Unitarians and the Universalists* (Westport, CT: Greenwood Press, 1985). It includes a biographical dictionary of leading figures.

4   George Santayana, *The Life of Reason, Vol. I, Reason in Common Sense* (New York: Scribner's, 1905).

5   There is a website with links at www.famousuus.com. The Harvard Square Library has sections on Notable American Unitarians and Notable American Universalists at www.harvardsquarelibrary.com. The UU Historical Society has the *Dictionary of Unitarian Universalist Biography* at www25.uua.org/uuhs/duub/index.html. The latter two, with well-edited, carefully researched articles, have been of great assistance in this study.

The Multiple Origins of Universalism in America

6   The site of the Thomas Potter farm and chapel is Murray Grove, a Unitarian Universalist retreat center in Lanoka Harbor, NJ. For the full story, see www.murraygrove.org.

7   Judith Sargent Murray, *The Gleaner*, quoted at www.jsmsociety.com.

8   In 1984, in Natchez, MS, UU minister Gordon Gibson found Judith's extensive letter books. Her role as a pioneering religious feminist has been lifted up through the exertions of historian Bonnie Hurd Smith. See the Judith Sargent Murray Society at www.jsmsociety.com.

9   In England the General Baptists (or Universalists) joined forces long ago with the Unitarians. See www.unitarian.org.uk/intro/history.shtml. In America, General Baptists are today theological conservatives. See www.generalbaptist.com/#/identity/statements-of-faith. So are Christian Universalists (www.christianuniversalist.org) and "Biblical Unitarians" (www.biblicalunitarian.com), anxious "not to be confused with Unitarian Universalism."

10   John C. Morgan and Nelson Simonson, "George de Benneville," *Dictionary of Unitarian and Universalist Biography*, www25.uua.org/uuhs/duub/articles/georgedebenneville.html.

11   Ibid.

12   Charles A Howe, "Benjamin Rush," *Dictionary of Unitarian Universalist Biography*, www25.uua.org/uuhs/duub/articles/benjamin-rush.html.

13   Stephen A. Marini, *Radical Sects of Revolutionary New England* (Cambridge, MA: Harvard University Press, 1982).

14   Peter Hughes, "The Davis Family of Oxford, Massachusetts," *Dictionary of Unitarian and Universalist Biography*, www25.uua.org/uuhs/duub/articles/davisfamily.html.

15   Gordon S. Wood, *Empire of Liberty: A History of the Early Republic, 1789–1815* (New York: Oxford University Press, 2009), p. 470.

16   Alfred Storer Cole, *Our Liberal Heritage* (Boston: Beacon Press, 1951). This epitome of Universalism was then picked up by Henry Cheatham in a book written for young people, *Unitarianism and Universalism* (Boston: Beacon Press, 1961) and attributed to Murray rather than the "Time-Spirit" speaking to Murray, as Cole had. Cheatham even made it seem that Murray had spoken these words in Thomas Potter's chapel.

Early Universalism in America

17   See especially the work of historian C. Conrad Wright, from *The Beginnings of Unitarianism in America* (Boston: Beacon Press, 1955)

through *The Liberal Christians* (Boston: Beacon Press, 1970) and *The Unitarian Controversy: Essays in American Unitarian History* (Boston: Skinner House, 1994).

18   Chauncey published his major theological work, *The Mystery Hid from Ages and Generations*, in London anonymously in 1784, long after he completed it. He affirmed an innate moral sense in man, human free will, a plan of universal salvation and the spiritual equality of all God's children.

19   J.D. Bowers, in *Joseph Priestley and English Unitarianism in America* (University Park, PA: Pennsylvania State University Press, 2007), has shown just how extensive this influence was. Priestley helped organize the First Unitarian Church of Philadelphia in 1796. The Priestley Memorial Chapel in Northumberland, PA, raised by his son, is in the community where the family settled, in the upper Susquehanna Valley. Other English Unitarians who came to America included Rev. William Hazlitt, father of the famous essayist and critic by the same name; and George Keats, a founder of Unitarianism in Cincinnati and a brother of poet John Keats.

20   See Steven B. Johnson, *The Invention of Air: A Story of Science, Faith, Revolution, and the Birth of America* (New York: Riverhead Books, 2008).

21   Efforts to weigh the body before and after death, in order to determine the weight of the soul, were discussed in the late eighteenth century, influenced by the Swedish engineer and mystic Emmanuel Swedenborg (1688–1772).

22   Thomas Jefferson, *The Jefferson Bible: The Life and Morals of Jesus of Nazareth*, ed. Forrest Church (Boston: Beacon Press, 1989).

23   See Charles Howe, *For Faith and Freedom: A Short History of Unitarianism in Europe* (Boston: Skinner House, 1997).

24   Elizabeth Curtiss, "Hannah Adams," *Dictionary of Unitarian and Universalist Biography*, www25.uua.org/uuhs/duub/articles/hannah-adams.html.

25   Ibid.

26   King's Chapel, the original outpost of the Church of England in Boston, founded in 1686, became "congregational in polity and unitarian in theology," while remaining "Anglican in worship," when in 1785 it revised its *Book of Common Prayer* to replace Trinitarian

formulae with scriptural passages and then two years later ordained James Freeman without the involvement of a bishop.

27 Bentley translated correspondence with Muslim rulers on the Barbary Coast of North Africa for Thomas Jefferson, who had such a high regard for his fellow Unitarian (both used the term) that he asked Bentley to be the first president of the University of Virginia. Bentley declined to leave his beloved Salem. See J. Rixey Ruffin, *A Paradise of Reason: William Bentley and Enlightenment Christianity in the Early Republic* (New York: Oxford University Press, 2007).

28 When John Harvard died in 1638, he left his books and half his estate to the "new college in Cambridge," founded two years before, "dreading to leave an illiterate ministry to the churches, when our present ministers shall lie in the dust," as the founders of the college put it.

29 This came in 1820. There are further ironies. Morse's son, the famed inventor of the telegraph, Samuel F. B. Morse, became a Unitarian. The seminary he helped to start, now Andover Newton Theological School, today has Unitarian Universalists among its students, faculty, and trustees.

30 Peter S. Field, *The Crisis of the Standing Order: Clerical Intellectuals and Cultural Authority in Massachusetts, 1780–1833* (Amherst: University of Massachusetts Press, 1998).

31 Ibid., p. 187.

32 Ibid., p. 191.

33 John Adams to Morse, May 15, 1815; copy in the Charles Follen Papers, Collection 2, Massachusetts Historical Society; quoted in Field, *Crisis of the Standing Order*, p. 143.

34 From her 1832 memoir, quoted by Curtiss, "Hannah Adams," *Dictionary of Unitarian Universalist Biography*, www25.uua.org/uuhs/duub/articles/hannahadams.html.

35 Jeremy Belknap was both historically minded (he wrote a history of his native New Hampshire) and a patriot and activist.

36 Jack Mendelsohn, *Channing: The Reluctant Radical* (Boston: Little, Brown, 1971; later reprinted by Skinner House).

37 Dan McKanan, *Identifying the Image of God: Radical Christians and Nonviolent Power in the Antebellum United States* (New York: Oxford University Press, 2002).

Universalism in the Second Great Awakening

38   Stephen A. Marini, *Radical Sects of Revolutionary New England* (Cambridge, MA: Harvard University Press, 1982), p. 94.

39   Paul K. Conkin, in *American Originals: Homemade Varieties of Christianity* (Chapel Hill: University of North Carolina Press, 1997), p. 101, says, "no more than 300,000." Others consider that estimate overly generous.

40   Adapted from Ernest Cassara, *Hosea Ballou* 3rd Edition (Cambridge, MA: Cornerstone Press, 2003), p. 148; and in turn from Thomas Whittemore, *The Life of Rev. Hosea Ballou* (1855), Vol. II, pp. 287–88.

41   Article published after his death in the *Universalist Trumpet*, Vol. XXII, August 18, 1849.

42   Peter Hughes, "The Origins and First Stage of the Restorationist Controversy," *Journal of Unitarian Universalist History*, Vol. XXVII, 2000, pp. 1–57.

43   Peter Hughes, "Paul Dean," *Dictionary of Unitarian Universalist Biography*, www25.uua.org/uuhs/duub/articles/pauldean.html.

44   Peter Hughes, "Edward Turner," *Dictionary of Unitarian Universalist Biography*, www25.uua.org/uuhs/duub/articles/edwardturner.html.

45   Stephan Papa, *The Last Man Jailed for Blasphemy* (Franklin, NC: Trillium Books, 1998).

46   Ibid., p. 1.

47   To Whittemore, in December 1833, Kneeland wrote "Universalists believe in a god which I do not; but believe that their god, with all his moral attributes, (aside from nature itself,) is nothing more than a chimera of their own imagination."

48   Interestingly, Kneeland told the remnant of his Free Inquirers to go and join the Unitarians!

49   Characterization by his later contemporary, the Universalist minister John G. Adams, quoted by Ernest Cassara in "Thomas Whittemore," *Dictionary of Unitarian Universalist Biography*, www25.uua.org/uuhs/duub/articles/thomaswhittemore.html.

50   Also quoted in Cassara, "Thomas Whittemore."

51 William Ellery Channing, *Complete Works* (Boston: James Munroe and Co., 1843) Volume IV, pp. 151–67.

52 Second Universalist was weakened by dissension in 1845 over who should succeed Ballou. The congregation endured, however, until 1935, during the Great Depression, when it merged with the Unitarian congregation of the Arlington Street Church, the successor to Channing's Federal Street flock.

53 Patrick Carey, *Orestes A. Brownson: American Religious Weathervane* (Grand Rapids, MI: Eerdmans, 2004); Lynn Gordon Hughes and David Voelker, "Orestes Brownson," *Dictionary of Unitarian Universalist Biography*, www25.uua.org/uuhs/duub/articles/orestesaugustusbrownson.html.

54 Peter Hughes, "Adin Ballou," *Dictionary of Unitarian Universalist Biography*, www25.uua.org/uuhs/duub/articles/adinballou.html.

55 Carey, *Orestes A. Brownson.*

56 See Paul Conkin, "Restoration Christianity," in *American Originals*, referring to the Christian Connexion, the Campbellites, and the Disciples of Christ. Some Unitarians also identified with this religious impulse and founded Meadville Theological School and Antioch College in cooperation with Restorationists. Many of the latter later aligned with the inheritors of Trinitarian congregationalism in a United Church of Christ/Disciples alliance.

57 See Ralph Waldo Emerson, "Chardon Street and Bible Conventions," *Dial Essays*, 1842, in "Uncollected Prose," www.emersoncentral.com/dial1842.htm.

58 Cf. ibid., "Signs of the Times."

59 Russell E. Miller, *The Larger Hope, Vol. I: The First Century of Universalism in America, 1770–1870* (Boston: UUA, 1979), pp. 196–99.

60 Matthew Hale Smith, *Universalism Examined, Renounced, Exposed* (Boston: Tappan and Dennet, 1842), p. 279.

Unitarians and the American Renaissance

61 John Weston, "Beyond Boston," unpublished essay, 2000.

62 Bruce Ronda, ed., *Letters of Elizabeth Palmer Peabody: American Renaissance Woman* (Middletown, CT: Wesleyan University Press, 1984). In language ability, Peabody was like Rev. William Bentley

of her native Salem. In having to earn a living herself, never marrying, she was like Hannah Adams. See chap. 2.

63   Megan Marshall, in *The Peabody Sisters* (Boston: Houghton Mifflin, 2005), shows how Elizabeth not only vetted the men her sisters married, Nathaniel Hawthorne and Horace Mann, but first courted them herself!

64   The family had earlier spent two years in rural Lancaster, MA, where Elizabeth first taught.

65   In this Peabody paved the way for her younger friend, Margaret Fuller.

66   Marshall, *The Peabody Sisters*, p. 91.

67   Reprinted in Conrad Wright, ed., *Three Prophets of Religious Liberalism: Channing, Emerson, Parker* (Boston: Skinner House, 1994) along with Emerson's "Divinity School Address" of 1838 and Parker's "Transient and Permanent in Christianity," 1841.

68   Frank Schulman, *This Day in Unitarian Universalist History* (Boston: Skinner House, 2004).

69   David Robinson, *Apostle of Culture: Emerson as Preacher and Lecturer* (Philadelphia: University of Pennsylvania Press, 1982).

70   Jedidiah Mannis, "Joseph Tuckerman," *Dictionary of Unitarian Universalist Biography*, www25.uua.org/uuhs/duub/articles/josephtuckerman.html.

71   www.uuum.org.

72   Wayne Viney, "Dorothea Dix," *Dictionary of Unitarian and Universalist Biography*, www25.uua.org/uuhs/duub/articles/dorotheadix.html.

73   Often eclipsed by his more famous wife, Julia Ward Howe, Dr. Howe directed the pioneering Perkins School for the Blind. He later said, "We should be cautious about establishing such artificial communities . . . for any children and youth; but more especially should we avoid them for those who have natural infirmity. . . . Such persons spring up sporadically in the community, and they should be kept diffused among sound and normal persons. . . . Surround insane and excitable persons with sane people and ordinary influences; vicious children with virtuous people and virtuous influences; blind children with those who see; mute children with those who speak; and the like." (speech in Batavia, NY, 1866).

74 Dix was eventually heard by legislatures North and South. Many states established hospitals at places named for her. In 1854 she went to Europe, discouraged, and was received by the Pope, who heeded her report and compared her to St. Theresa. In the Civil War she served as Superintendent of US Army Nurses and was allowed to cross enemy lines. She died in 1887.

75 Horace and Mary Peabody Mann went on their honeymoon to Europe with Dr. Samuel Gridley Howe and his wife, Julia Ward Howe.

76 Charles A. Howe and Peter Hughes, "Bronson and Abigail Alcott," *Dictionary of Unitarian and Universalist Biography*, www25.uua.org/uuhs/duub/articles/bronsonalcott.html.

77 Conrad Wright, *Three Prophets of Religious Liberalism: Channing, Emerson, Parker* (Boston: Skinner House, 1994).

78 Robinson, in *Apostle of Culture*, p. 50, says, "Emerson began almost where Channing left off," with the idea of "self-culture" an important link between them.

79 Paula Cole, *Mary Moody Emerson and the Origins of Transcendentalism* (New York: Oxford University Press, 1998), sees continuities from "New Light" spirituality to Transcendentalism.

80 One such minister was Samuel Gilman, Harvard class of 1811, who composed for the occasion the hymn "Fair Harvard, Thy Sons to Thy Jubilee Throng." He served the Unitarian Church in Charleston, South Carolina, from 1819 to his death in 1859. His wife adapted to slave-holding culture. Gilman never defended slavery from the pulpit, but feared disunion was inevitable.

81 Joan Goodwin, *The Remarkable Mrs. Ripley: The Life of Sarah Alden Bradford Ripley* (Boston: Northeastern University Press, 1998).

82 So dubbed by Oliver Wendell Holmes Sr., the Unitarian physician and writer whose father, Abiel Holmes, had been the last Calvinist minister of First Parish in Cambridge, where Emerson gave the address.

83 Emerson, "The American Scholar," www.emersoncentral.com/am-scholar.htm.

84 Emerson, "The Divinity School Address," www.emersoncentral.com/divaddr.htm.

85   Dean Grodzins, *American Heretic: Theodore Parker and Transcendentalism* (Chapel Hill: University of North Carolina Press, 2002).

86   Later Parker decided that this was not true after all, that Jesus had made theological errors.

87   Theodore Parker, *A Discourse of Matters Pertaining to Religion* (Boston: C.C. Little and J. Brown, 1842).

88   Appleton remained a Unitarian, but went to King's Chapel. His daughter, Fanny, married Henry Wadsworth Longfellow (and later died tragically). Leading members of other cotton-mill families, especially after 1850, left Unitarianism altogether and became Episcopalians.

89   John Macaulay, *Unitarianism in the Antebellum South: The Other Invisible Culture* (Tuscaloosa: University of Alabama Press, 2001).

90   Gregory McGonigle, "James Freeman Clarke," *Dictionary of Unitarian Universalist Biography*, www25.uua.org/uuhs/duub/articles/jamesfreemanclarke.html; Arthur S. Bolster Jr., *James Freeman Clarke: Disciple to Advancing Truth* (Boston: Beacon Press, 1954).

91   Clarke also presided in 1847 when Elizabeth Shaw, the daughter of the Chief Justice of Massachusetts, married the novelist Herman Melville.

92   The building at 13–15 West Street, Boston, still stands. Efforts are underway to have it declared a protected historic site. In recent decades it has housed a series of restaurants.

93   Aaron McEmrys, "Brook Farm," *Dictionary of Unitarian Universalist Biography*, www25.uua.org/uuhs/duub/articles/brookfarm.html.

94   Louisa May Alcott, *Transcendental Wild Oats* (1873), http://womenshistory.about.com/od/alcottlouisamay/a/lma_transcend.htm.

95   Paula Blanchard, *Margaret Fuller: From Transcendentalism to Revolution* (Reading, MA: Addison-Wesley Publishing Company, 1987); Joan Goodwin, "Margaret Fuller," *Dictionary of Unitarian Universalist Biography*, www25.uua.org/uuhs/duub/articles/margaretfuller.html.

96   Thomas Carlyle, "The Everlasting Yea," *Sartor Resartus* (1831), and subsequent correspondence with Emerson. *Sartor Resartus* was serialized in *Fraser's* magazine, London, 1833–1834, and published as a book in 1838.

97   Ruth Sutro, "A Succession of Short Term Ministries," in *History of First Parish in Needham*, www.uuneedham.org/AboutFP/documents/FirstParishHistory5.pdf.

Universalism Seeks Unity of the Spirit

98   Ephesians 4:3; Hosea Ballou, *Treatise on Atonement*, 1805, 1832 (reprint, Boston: Skinner House, 1986), pp. 239–40.

99   John B. Buescher, *The Other Side of Salvation: Spiritualism and the Nineteenth-Century Religious Experience* (Boston: Skinner House, 2004).

100   Anne Braude, in *Radical Spirits: Spiritualism and Women's Rights in 19th Century America* (Boston: Beacon Press, 1989; 2nd Edition, Bloomington, IN: Indiana University Press, 2001) shows that spiritualists were often social activists, with a call needing no sanction by male clergy.

101   Buescher, *The Other Side of Salvation*, p. 3ff.

102   Charles A. Howe, *The Larger Faith: A Short History of American Universalism* (Boston: Skinner House, 1993), p. 48.

103   Buescher, *The Other Side of Salvation*, pp. 20–39.

104   Thomas Jefferson Sawyer, in *the Christian Messenger*, cited in Buescher, *The Other Side of Salvation*, pp. 40–41.

105   Buescher, *The Other Side of Salvation*, p. 46.

106   Ibid., pp. vii, 85ff.

107   Ibid., pp. 130–32.

108   Howe, *The Larger Faith*, pp. 49–51.

109   Ibid., p. 52. Barnum almost certainly did *not* say "There's a sucker born every minute." He did say, "A human soul is not to be trifled with. It may inhabit the body of a Chinaman, a Turk, an Arab or a Hotentot—it is still an immortal spirit!" This in support of the 13th Amendment.

110   John Buescher, "Charles Spear," *Dictionary of Unitarian Universalist Biography*, www25.uua.org/uuhs/duub/articles/charlesspear.html.

111   Howe, *The Larger Faith*, p. 54, citing the *Liberator.*

112   There are disputes over just what Sojourner Truth said in Akron, and how.

113 Sandra Parker, "Frances Dana Barker Gage," *Dictionary of Unitarian Universalist Biography*, www25.uua.org/uuhs/duub/articles/frances-gage.html.

114 Ibid.

115 Joan Goodwin, "Clara Barton," *Dictionary of Unitarian Universalist Biography*, www25-temp.uua.org/uuhs/duub/articles/clarabarton.html.

116 This is the story told in the 1989 film *Glory* and memorialized by the bas relief monument to the 54th Massachusetts Volunteers by sculptor Augustus St. Gaudens, on Beacon Street across from the Massachusetts State House.

117 Peter Hughes, "Maria Cook," *Dictionary of Unitarian Universalist Biography*, www25-temp.uua.org/uuhs/duub/articles/mariacook.html.

118 David Robinson, *The Unitarians and the Universalists*, p. 199 n. 33; pp. 282–33.

119 Charles A. Howe, "Lydia Ann Jenkins," *Dictionary of Unitarian Universalist Biography*, www25-temp.uua.org/uuhs/duub/articles/lydia-annjenkins.html.

120 Ibid.

121 JoAnn Macdonald, "Antoinette Brown Blackwell," *Dictionary of Unitarian Universalist Biography*, www25.uua.org/uuhs/duub/articles/antoinettebrownblackwell.html.

122 Laurie Carter Noble, "Olympia Brown," *Dictionary of Unitarian Universalist Biography*, www25-temp.uua.org/uuhs/duub/articles/olympiabrown.html.

123 Other suffragists, including Lucy Stone and Abby Kelley, disagreed and found the Kansas campaign an embarrassing exercise in racist pandering.

124 *American Almanac and Repository of Useful Knowledge* (Boston: Gray and Bowen, 1849), cited in Cynthia Grant Tucker, *No Silent Witness: The Eliot Parsonage Women and Their Unitarian World* (New York: Oxford, 2010), chap. 1, n. 3. Tucker says that Unitarians in 1849 had half the Universalist numbers and that by 1887 both had declined by a further fifty percent. Other sources put Universalist membership at 45,000–65,000 in the 1890s and the Unitarians at 60,000–75,000.

125 Celeste DeRoche and Peter Hughes, "Thomas Starr King," *Dictionary of Unitarian Universalist Biography*, www25-temp.uua.org/uuhs/duub/articles/thomasstarrking.html.

126 Bellows to his wife, Eliza, July 22, 1858; cited in Walter Donald Kring, *Henry Whitney Bellows* (Boston: Skinner House, 1979).

127 Cited in DeRoche and Hughes, "Thomas Starr King."

128 In actuality, the *bon mot* can be traced to Thomas Gold Appleton, a Unitarian and the brother-in-law of Henry Wadsworth Longfellow. See George Huntston Williams, *American Universalism* 4th Edition (Boston: Skinner House and Unitarian Universalist Historical Society, 2002), p. x, n. 4.

129 Lend-a-Hand Societies were created all over the US, inspired by Hale.

130 Williams, *American Universalism*, p. xi.

131 Used as an affirmation in *Singing the Living Tradition* (Boston: UUA, 1993), #457.

Unitarians from Reform to Civil War

132 George B. Emerson, journal entry, Universalist Archives, Andover-Harvard Theological Library, Cambridge, MA.

133 www.uuneedham.org/AboutFP/documents/FirstParishHistory3.pdf.

134 www.uuneedham.org/AboutFP/documents/FirstParishHistory5.pdf.

135 Ralph Waldo Emerson, William Henry Channing, and James Freeman Clarke, eds., *The Memoirs of Margaret Fuller Ossoli* (Boston: Phillips, Sampson and Co., 1852).

136 Helen R. Deese, ed., *Daughter of Boston: The Extraordinary Diary of a Nineteenth-century Woman, Caroline Healey Dall* (Boston: Beacon Press, 2005), pp. 155–61.

137 Ibid., p. 105.

138 Meanwhile, Charles Dall did his own important work in India—on women's rights, education, and with Indian leaders interested in liberal religion. Before he died he met a young man from India's Khasi Hills, Hajom Kissor Singh. Singh had rejected the trinitarian missionaries and declared for "the religion of one God." Dall

gave him Unitarian worship materials. That collaboration led to an indigenous Unitarian movement that today numbers 37 congregations and some 9,000 Unitarian Khasis, who still honor his memory. Cf. Spencer Lavan, *Unitarians and India: A Study in Encounter and Response* (Boston, Beacon Press, 1977).

139   First published by Elizabeth Peabody in 1849. Thoreau had also withdrawn from First Parish in Concord (Unitarian), unwilling to support the ministry of Rev. Barzillai Frost, whom his friend Emerson had caricatured in his Divinity School Address. The Thoreau family—but not it's most famous member—joined the new Universalist congregation in Concord, which later merged back into First Parish. When Thoreau died in 1862, his funeral was held at First Parish.

140   Webster's speech of March 7, 1850, in favor of the Compromise, calling it necessary to preserve the Union, was endorsed by nearly a thousand leading citizens of Boston. Abolitionists differed. Theodore Parker said, "No living man has done so much to debauch the conscience of the nation." Horace Mann called Webster "a fallen star! Lucifer descending from Heaven!" Forced to resign from the Senate, Webster became Secretary of State in Millard Fillmore's cabinet. He died in 1852.

141   Joel Porte, ed., *Emerson in His Journals* (Cambridge, MA: Belknab Press, 1982), pp. 408–9. Dated July–Oct., 1851.

142   US Constitution, article 4, section 2, paragraph 3.

143   Albert J. von Frank, *The Trials of Anthony Burns: Freedom and Slavery in Emerson's Boston* (Cambridge, MA: Harvard University Press, 1998).

144   Ibid., p. 61.

145   Ibid., p. 271.

146   Garry Wills, *Lincoln at Gettysburg: The Words that Remade America* (New York: Simon & Schuster, 1993).

147   During the Civil War Higginson led a regiment of freed slaves, the First South Carolina Volunteers. After the war, he devoted himself to rights for freedmen and women and to literature, becoming a mentor to poet Emily Dickinson. He never again served a church.

148   Henry Whitney Bellows, "The Suspense of Faith" (1859), in *An American Reformation: A Documentary History of Unitarian Christi-*

anity, ed. Ahlstrom and Carey (Middleton, CT: Wesleyan University Press, 1985).

149 Ibid., p. 393.

150 Ibid., p. 373.

151 As Frederic Henry Hedge said of Bellows after his death in 1881, "He was our Bishop, our metropolitan . . . by universal consent of the brethren. . . . He ordered us hither and thither, and we surrendered ourselves to his ordering." See:http://www25.uua.org/uuhs/duub/articleshenrwhitneybellows.html.

152 Bellows, "The Suspense of Faith," p. 379.

153 Walter Donald Kring, *Henry Whitney Bellows* (Boston: Skinner House, 1979), pp. 218–23.

154 Ibid., pp. 240–41.

155 Eventually Antioch shed its Unitarian ties, as did Harvard. So did Washington University in St. Louis, founded by William Greenleaf Eliot, and Reed College in Portland, Oregon, founded by his son, Thomas Lamb Eliot, minister of the Unitarian Church in that city.

156 Kring, *Henry Whitney Bellows*, pp. 309–10, based on Bellows's own analysis in a letter to a colleague.

157 David Robinson, *The Unitarians and the Universalists* (1985), p. 107.

158 Ibid.

Universalism's Liberal Mission

159 Miller, *The Larger Hope*, Vol. I, p. 844. This is an estimate; the Convention also admitted that there were "no statistics worth the name." Cf. p. 852.

160 This typology derives from George Huntston Williams, *American Universalism* (1970; 1976; 2002), which began as a bicentennial essay for which I assisted Dr. Williams in his archival research.

161 While *church may* imply Christian identity, the animosity of some Unitarian Universalists toward the term *denomination* is misplaced. The term does not suggest being part of Protestant Christianity. American Judaism and Buddhism also speak of having denominations (such as the Buddhist Church of America). Nor does *denomi-*

nation say anything about the structure of organization. It simply refers to a religious group sharing the same *name*, from the Latin word *nomen*. To say, "we are an association, not a denomination" is to mix categories. Rather we are a denomination *structured* as an association of congregations.

162 Edwin Chapin, "The Church of the Living God," quoted in Williams, *American Universalism*, pp. 12–13.

163 Elbridge Gerry Brooks, quoted in Williams, *American Universalism*, pp. 16–17.

164 Israel Washburn, quoted in Williams, *American Universalism*, p. 20.

165 Mary Livermore, quoted in Williams, *American Universalism*, p. 22. Response to the Franco-Prussian War of 1870 was strong among American liberal women. Clara Barton began her campaign for a US affiliate of the International Red Cross. Julia Ward Howe issued her Mother's Day Proclamation for peace, a sharp contrast to her "Battle Hymn." Livermore was one of the most sought-after platform speakers in America in this era.

166 Miller, *The Larger Hope*, Vol. I, p. 854. It later was secularized and became the University of Akron.

167 Howe, *The Larger Faith*, pp. 64–65.

168 Miller, *The Larger Hope*, Vol. II, pp. 88–89.

169 The phrase, "There is a sucker born every minute," attributed to Barnum, came instead from a rival. See www.historybuff.com/library/refbarnum.html.

170 In an 1865 editorial, addressing young clerks laid off by the federal government at the end of the Civil War. There is a dispute about whether Greeley borrowed the phrase, however.

171 Elihu Washburne was the only brother who spelled his name with an "e." He married a Presbyterian and adapted to his wife's affiliation.

172 Theodore A Webb, *Men of Mark: The Washburn Brothers of Maine* (Boston: Unitarian Universalist Historical Society, 1985).

173 Charles A. Howe, "Mary and Daniel Livermore," *Dictionary of Unitarian Universalist Biography*, www25.uua.org/uuhs/duub/articles/livermorefamily.html.

174 Howe, *The Larger Faith*, pp. 68–69.

175 Howe, *The Larger Faith*, p. 73; Dorothy May Emerson and Alan Seaburg, "Caroline Soule," *Dictionary of Unitarian Universalist Biography*, www25.uua.org/uuhs/duub/articles/carolinesoule.html.

176 Beverly Bumbaugh, "Augusta Jane Chapin," *Dictionary of Unitarian Universalist Biography*, www25.uua.org/uuhs/duub/articles/augustajanechapin.html.

177 Charles A. Howe, "Quillen Shinn," *Dictionary of Unitarian Universalist Biography*, www25-temp.uua.org/uuhs/duub/articles/quillen-hamiltonshinn.html.

178 Generally speaking, the history of Universalism and Unitarianism in Canada is beyond the scope of the present work. See Phillip Hewett, *Unitarians in Canada* (http://img.uua.org/mfc/Hewitt_Unitarians_Canada.pdf.) Of the fifty congregations in the Canadian Unitarian Council in 2010, only three have Universalist roots.

179 Willard Frank, "Joseph Jordan," *Dictionary of Unitarian and Universalist Biography*, www25-temp.uua.org/uuhs/duub/articles/josephjordan.html.

180 Ibid.

181 Willard Frank, "Thomas E. Wise," *Dictionary of Unitarian and Universalist Biography*, www25-temp.uua.org/uuhs/duub/articles/thomasewise.html.

182 Howe, *The Larger Faith*, pp. 86–87. The Suffolk school continued under Joseph F. Jordan and his daughter, Annie B. Willis, and as a denominational project until, in 1969, the new UUSC withdrew support. It continued for fifteen more years as a nonprofit with public-private funding.

183 After James Inman died in 1913, the Universalist National Women's Missionary Association sent Rev. Hannah Powell to serve Inman Chapel and the school and social services of "Friendly House." Both finally closed in 1947.

184 Howe, *The Larger Faith*, p. 84.

185 Ibid. After the consolidation of the Unitarians and Universalists in 1961, Japanese Universalists insisted on their identity as Christian Universalists and declined overtures from the new (predominantly humanist) UUA and from the International Association for Reli-

gious Freedom. The International Council of Unitarians and Universalists (www.icuu.net) includes them.

186   Howe, *The Larger Faith*, p. 78.

187   The seventeen groups Alcott led were Universalist (6), Unitarian (3), Independent (3, all post-Unitarian), Jewish (3), Ethical Culture (1), and Quaker (1). See Howe, *The Larger Faith*, p. 79.

188   Howe, *The Larger Faith*, p. 80.

189   The building of the Shawmut Universalist Church, organized in 1838 as Fifth Universalist, can still be seen at 76 Warrenton Street, off Stuart Street in Boston's Chinatown. It is now the Charles Playhouse. See http://archive.uua.org/aboutuua/boston/map_center.html.

190   See www.pullman_car.com/history/george_pullman.html.

191   Laurie Carter Noble, "Olympia Brown," *Dictionary of Unitarian Universalist Biography*, www25.uua.org/uuhs/duub/articles/olympia-brown.html.

192   Charles A. Howe, "Isaac Morgan Atwood," *Dictionary of Unitarian Universalist Biography*, www25.uua.org/uuhs/duub/articles/isaac-morganatwood.html.

Unitarian Parsonages Move West

193   Cynthia Grant Tucker, *Prophetic Sisterhood: Liberal Women Ministers of the Frontier, 1880–1930* (Bloomington, IN: Indiana University Press, 1990); *No Silent Witness: The Eliot Parsonage Women and Their Unitarian World* (New York, Oxford University Press, 2010).

194   Cynthia Grant Tucker, *No Silent Witness*, pp. 28 and 38.

195   Charles H. Lyttle, *Freedom Moves West: A History of the Western Unitarian Conference* (Boston: Beacon Press, 1952).

196   Eliot resisted an attempt to give the St. Louis university his own name. Twenty-two years later, in Portland, his son Tom resigned his pulpit there. He devoted himself to developing a cultural institute into Reed College, using a bequest from his parishioner, Amanda Wood Reed.

197   Abby Eliot to Thomas Lamb Eliot, October 13, 1889, cited in Tucker, *No Silent Witness*, p. 28, n. 14.

198 Tucker, *No Silent Witness*, p. 66.

199 Henrietta Robins Mack Eliot to Rebecca Robins Mack, n.d. (1871), in Tucker, *No Silent Witness*, p. 64, n. 26.

200 George Willis Cooke, *Unitarianism in America* (Boston: American Unitarian Association, 1902), p. 209.

201 Francis Ellingwood Abbott, *Fifty Affirmations*, number 47, cited in Cooke, *Unitarianism in America*, p. 211.

202 Cathy Tauscher and Peter Hughes, "Jenkin Lloyd Jones," *Dictionary of Unitarian Universalist Biography*, www25.uua.org/uuhs/duub/articles/jenkinlloydjones.html.

203 1885 report by Sunderland, as secretary to the Western Unitarian Conference.

204 www.famoususs.com/writings/things_commonly_believed.htm.

205 Joan Goodwin, "Julia Ward Howe," *Dictionary of Unitarian Universalist Biography*, www25.uua.org/uuhs/duub/articles/juliaward-howe.html.

206 Tucker, *No Silent Witness*, p. 46, n. 57. Emphasis added.

207 Ibid., p. 46, n. 57.

208 See Abby May's rather stern portrait in the first floor Fifield Room of Pickett-Eliot House, honoring the contributions of the Alliance to the purchase of the building wherein it hangs.

209 Two sons and a daughter remained in St. Louis. Henry Ware Eliot (1843–1919) "choked" on going into ministry but still sang in the choir and ran the Sunday school. His youngest child, Thomas Stearns Eliot, the famous poet, scandalized the family by becoming an Anglo-Catholic. But the difference between his faith and that of his grandfather was nominal, not substantive. Edward Cranch Eliot (1858–1928) became a lawyer and president of the American Bar Association. Rose Greenleaf Eliot Smith (1862–1936) married an art professor at Washington University.

210 They lived on West Cedar Street, now a fashionable address on Beacon Hill, but then much more modest.

211 These were Martha May Eliot, MD (1891–1978), who, along with her life partner, Dr. Ethel Dunham, pioneered in pediatric and public health measures as Chief of the US Children's Bureau and

at the World Health Organization and UNICEF; and Abby Adams Eliot, EdD (1892–1982), who, supported by her life partner, Alice Holman, reformed the training of preschool educators in the US.

212 Ted Fetter, "The Unitarians and the Utes," unpublished sermon, May 9, 2010.

213 The founder of the Brahmo Samaj, Ram Mohan Roy (1774–1833), both opposed traditional Hindu practices like *suttee* (widow suicide) and fought for self-rule. He was close to Unitarians. While petitioning Parliament, he died attended by British Unitarian minister J. Estlin Carpenter, whose daughter Mary became a leading advocate for the education of women in India.

214 Spencer Lavan, "Jabez Sunderland," *Dictionary of Unitarian Universalist Biography*, www25.uua.org/uuhs/duub/articles/jabezsunderland.html.

215 Melinda Seyavedra and Marilyn Walker, "Unitarianism in India," www.icuu.net/resources/downloads/unit9_india.pdf.

216 June Edwards, "Fannie Barrier Williams," *Dictionary of Unitarian and Universalist Biography*, www25.uua.org/uuhs/duub/articles/fanniebarrierwilliams.html.

217 Not to be confused with today's 25. The first 25 Beacon was neo-Romanesque in style. It stood where Bowdoin Street now intersects with Beacon. When the Massachusetts State House was expanded in 1924–1925, the AUA was traded a lot on the opposite side of the State House and allowed to move their street address to their new, larger building.

218 This body developed into the International Association for Religious Freedom (IARF).

219 Tucker, *Prophetic Sisterhood*, p. 150ff.

220 Tucker, *No Silent Witness*, p. 102.

221 David Parke, "A Wave at the Crest," in *Stream of Light: A Short History of Unitarianism* 2nd Edition, ed. Conrad Wright (Boston: Skinner House, 1989), pp. 97–98.

222 Mark Morrison-Reed, *Darkening the Doorways: Black Trailblazers and Missed Opportunities in Unitarian Universalism* (Boston: Skinner House, 2011).

223 Samuel A. Eliot, ed., *Heralds of a Liberal Faith*, Volumes I–III.; Vol. IV, author, "Francis Greenwood Peabody," www.harvardsquarelibrary.org/Heralds/Francis-Greenwood-Peabody.php.

Unitarian Skepticism and Social Reform

224 I owe this story to Rev. Kenneth Torquil MacLean, who cites it as personal experience.

225 The source of this anecdote, perhaps apocryphal, is lost. But as they say in Italian, *"Se non e' vero, e' ben trovato."* ("Even if it's not true, it's a good story!")

226 Francis Biddle, *Justice Holmes, Natural Law and the Supreme Court* (New York: Macmillan, 1961), p. 49.

227 The jurist was the son of Dr. Oliver Wendell Holmes, subject of *The Autocrat of the Breakfast Table* and member of King's Chapel. He was the grandson of Abiel Holmes, Calvinist minister of First Church in Cambridge and fierce opponent of Unitarian liberalism.

228 Robert C. Cottrell, "Roger Baldwin," *Notable American Unitarians*, www.harvardsquarelibrary.org/unitarians/baldwin.html. Cottrell also wrote *Roger Baldwin and the American Civil Liberties Union* (New York: Columbia University Press, 2000).

229 Peggy Lamson, *Roger Baldwin: Founder of the American Civil Liberties Union* (Boston: Houghton Mifflin, 1976), p. 6.

230 Jamaica Plain, along with West Roxbury, became part of the City of Boston in 1874.

231 Freely arranged from a lengthy passage in a memoir by her sister, Alice Balch Stone, quoted by Mercedes M. Randall in *Emily Greene Balch: Improper Bostonian* (New York: Twayne, 1964), p. 48. Emphasis added to the phrase from Charles Dole, since it is a likely quotation. Dole served the Jamaica Plain church for over forty years, starting in 1881. He wrote a number of books on religion and social issues. His son James D. Dole, "the Pineapple King," in Hawaii founded Dole Foods. Charles Dole died in Hawaii in 1927.

232 Carolyn Wedin, *Inheritors of the Spirit: Mary White Ovington and the Founding of the NAACP* (New York: John Wiley, 1998).

233 Debby Applegate, *The Most Famous Man in America: The Biography of Henry Ward Beecher* (New York: Doubleday, 2006).

234 Wedin, *Inheritors of the Spirit,* pp. 12–16.

235 Dorothy Senghas and Catherine Senghas, "Mary White Ovington," *Dictionary of Unitarian Universalist Biography*, www25-temp.uua. org/uuhs/duub/articles/marywhiteovington.html.

236 Paul Sprecher, "John Haynes Holmes," *Dictionary of Unitarian Universalist Biography*, www25.uua.org/uuhs/duub/articles/john-haynesholmes.html.

237 Wedin, *Inheritors of the Spirit*, pp. 86–87.

238 Ovington was particularly instrumental in keeping DuBois engaged with the NAACP until he chose the path of black separatism in the 1930s.

239 No close relation to Oliver Wendell Holmes, John Haynes Holmes was named for his maternal grandfather, John Haynes, who had been treasurer of Theodore Parker's congregation. He saw himself as a spiritual successor to Parker.

240 "The Voice of God," #316 in *Hymns of the Spirit* (1937) and #214 in *Hymns for the Celebration of Life* (1964), is not in *Singing the Living Tradition* (1993). Holmes wrote more than a hundred hymns.

241 "The Story of US Immigration: Ellis Island," *Brown Quarterly*, Vol. IV, No. 1 (Fall 2000).

242 Quoted by Heather Miller in "Emily Greene Balch," *Notable American Unitarians*, www.harvardsquarelibrary.org/unitarians/balch.html.

243 Mercedes M. Randall, *Emily Greene Balch: Improper Bostonian*, p. 423.

244 Parke, "A Wave at Crest," p. 102.

245 Holmes was a founder of the American branch of the pacifist Fellowship of Reconciliation.

246 Parke, "A Wave at Crest," pp. 103–4.

247 Holmes's vision was larger than Christianity, similar to his Universalist colleague at the Community Church of Boston, Clarence Skinner. The theology of most other community churches organized from 1920 on were solidly Christian, if ecumenical. The Community Church of New York returned to the Unitarian fold

in 1949. The International Council of Community Churches continues as a fellowship of about 150 Protestant congregations. See www.icccusa.com.

248 Holmes started writing for the Unitarian *Christian Register* again in 1936; his church rejoined in 1949; he allowed his name to be restored among Unitarian ministers in fellowship in 1960. Balch was given the AUA annual award for distinguished service to liberal religion in 1955, by which time she had both Quaker and renewed Unitarian affiliations.

249 Lamson, *Roger Baldwin,* pp. 73, 111.

250 Parke, "A Wave at Crest," p. 99. See also V. Emil Gudmundson, *The Icelandic Unitarian Connection* (Winnipeg: Wheatfield Press, 1984).

251 Richard Henry, *Norbert Fabian apek: A Spiritual Journey* (Boston: Skinner House, 1999).

252 Louis C. Cornish, *Work and Dreams and the Wide Horizon* (Boston: Beacon Press, 1937), p. 312, as quoted by Parke, "A Wave at Crest," p. 104.

253 Parke, "A Wave at Crest," p. 106.

254 Ibid., pp. 105–6.

255 William L. Sullivan, *Under Orders* (New York: Richard R. Smith, 1944).

256 W.W. Fenn, "War and the Thought of God," in *American Protestant Thought in the Liberal Era,* ed. William R. Hutchison (Lanham, MD: University Press of America, 1968), p. 157.

257 Gary Dorrien, *The Making of American Liberal Theology, Vol. II, Idealism, Realism, and Modernity, 1900–1950* (Louisville, KY: Westminster John Knox, 2003).

258 William F. Schulz, *Making the Manifesto: The Birth of Religious Humanism* (Boston: Skinner House, 2002); Alan Seaburg, "John Dietrich," www25.uua.org/uuhs/duub/articles/johnhasslerdietrich.html; and Alan Seaburg, "Curtis Reese," *Dictionary of Unitarian Universalist Biography*, www25.uua.org/uuhs/duub/articles/curtis-willifordreese.html.

259 Schulz, *Making the Manifesto*, p. 26.

260   www.americanhumanist.org/Who_We_Are/About_Humanism/
      Humanist_Manifesto_I.

261   Alan Seaburg, "Dana Greeley," *Dictionary of Unitarian Universalist Bi-
      ography*, www25.uua.org/uuhs/duub/articles/danamcleangreeley.
      html.

262   Louis Cornish was married to Frances Eliot Foote, daughter of
      Henry Wilder Foote (1838–1889), minister of King's Chapel, and
      Frances Ann Eliot (1836–1896), sister to Charles W. Eliot (1834–
      1926), president of Harvard. His wife's brothers were Arthur Foote,
      the American composer; and Henry Wilder Foote II, a Unitarian
      minister who chaired the joint Unitarian-Universalist commission
      that produced *Hymns of the Spirit.*

263   Parke, "A Wave at Crest," pp. 123–24.

264   Van Eric Fox and Alice Blair Wesley, "James Luther Adams," *Dic-
      tionary of Unitarian Universalist Biography*, www25.uua.org/uuhs/
      duub/articles/jameslutheradams.html.

265   Alan Seaburg, "Frederick May Eliot," *Dictionary of Unitarian Uni-
      versalist Biography*, www25.uua.org/uuhs/duub/articles/frederick-
      mayeliot.html.

Universalism and Modernity

266   Howe, *The Larger Faith*, p. 94.

267   Ibid., p. 98.

268   Josephine Young Case and Everett Needham Case, *Owen D. Young
      and American Enterprise* (Boston: David R. Godine, 1982), pp. 47–
      48.

269   Charles A. Howe, *Clarence R. Skinner: Prophet of a New Universalism*
      (Boston: Skinner House, 1999), pp. 13–14.

270   Ibid., pp. 14–18.

271   Ibid., pp. 20–21.

272   Clarence R. Skinner, *The Social Implications of Universalism* (Boston:
      Universalist Publishing House, 1915), as reprinted in the *Annual
      Journal of the Universalist Historical Society*, Vol. V: 89–122, 1964–
      1965; and by Beacon Press, as Number 4 in the Beacon Reference
      Series, 1966.

273 Howe, *Clarence R. Skinner*, p. 24.

274 Ibid., p. 25, quoting *The Social Implications* as reprinted, pp. 90–91.

275 Ibid., p. 28. Emphasis added.

276 Ibid., p. 29.

277 Howe, *The Larger Faith*, p. 92.

278 Ibid., p. 94.

279 Howe, *Clarence R. Skinner*, p. 35.

280 Howe, *The Larger Faith*, p. 97.

281 Miller, *The Larger Hope,* Vol. II, pp. 481–83.

282 First just for diabetic girls. Meanwhile, Dr. Elliot P. Joslin, also born in Oxford, began to use newly discovered insulin to treat juvenile diabetics. He bought land for a parallel boy's camp in nearby Charlton. Sponsored for many years by Universalist and UU women, the two camps subsequently combined and became an independent, non-sectarian nonprofit. See www.bartoncenter.org/about/history.php.

283 Howe, *The Larger Faith*, p. 96. Emphasis added. Ryder itself had a hard time moving; it combined with Meadville Theological School in Chicago in the 1930s.

284 Ibid., pp. 85–88.

285 Howe, *Clarence R. Skinner*, p. 41.

286 Charles A. Howe, "Clinton Lee Scott," *Dictionary of Unitarian Universalist Biography*, www25.uua.org/uuhs/duub/articles/clinton-leescott.html.

287 Clinton Lee Scott, *Some Things Remembered: A Memoir* (Boston: Church of the Larger Fellowship, Unitarian Universalist, 1976), pp. 41–42.

288 Ida Tarbell, *Owen D. Young: A New Type of Industrialist* (New York: Macmillan, 1932); Josephine Young Case and Everett Needham Case, *Owen D. Young and American Enterprise* (Boston: David R. Godine, 1982).

289 www.time.com/time/subscriber/personoftheyear/archive/stories/1929.html.

290 Josephine Young Case and Everett Needham Case, *Owen D. Young and American Enterprise* (Boston: David R. Godine, 1982), p. 14.

291 Ibid., p. 23.

292 Ibid., p. 40.

293 Ibid., pp. 50–52. At St. Lawrence, Owen later became a trustee, benefactor, and chair of the board. The main library there even now is named in his honor.

294 Ibid., pp. 197–203.

295 Ibid., pp. 209–10, 251–52.

296 Ibid., p. 255.

297 Ibid., pp. 252–53. Emphasis added.

298 Case and Case, *Owen D. Young*, p. 267.

299 Ibid., p. 254.

300 Ibid., p. 369.

301 Ibid., p. 374.

302 Ibid., p. 469.

303 Howe, *The Larger Faith*, p. 101.

304 Ibid., p. 99.

305 Ibid., p. 100.

306 Ibid., p. 102.

307 "The changes from the 1899 declaration are obvious: there is no mention of the Bible, Jesus is no longer referred to as Christ . . . and there is a strong emphasis on the Social Gospel . . . twice calling for the establishment of the Kingdom of God . . . through human effort." Howe, *The Larger Faith*, p. 106.

The Unitarian Renaissance

308 Carol R. Morris, "It Was Noontime Here: Frederick May Eliot and the Unitarian Renaissance, 1934–1961," in *Stream of Light*, p. 125.

309 George F. Baker, founder of First National City Bank (later Citi-Bank), and his son. See Walter Donald Kring, *Safely Onward: The History of the Unitarian Church of All Souls, New York City, Volume 3:*

1882–1978 (New York: The Unitarian Church of All Souls, 1991), pp. 94–95.

310 The term was first used by Carol R. Morris in "Frederick May Eliot, President of the American Unitarian Association (1937–1958)," PhD dissertation, Boston University, 1970. Cf. n. 1.

311 Commission on Appraisal, *Unitarians Face a New Age* (Boston: American Unitarian Association, 1936) online at www.uua.org/documents/coa/36_unitariansfaceanewage.pdf.

312 Ibid., pp. 3–5. Emphasis added.

313 Ibid., pp. 5–8.

314 The most comprehensive recent study is George Kimmich Beach, *Transforming Liberalism: The Theology of James Luther Adams* (Boston: Skinner House, 2005).

315 Van Eric Fox and Alice Blair Wesley, "James Luther Adams," *Dictionary of Unitarian Universalist Biography*, www25.uua.org/uuhs/duub/articles/jameslutheradams.html; and James Luther Adams, *Not Without Dust and Heat: A Memoir* (Chicago: Exploration Press, 1995).

316 Adams, *Not Without Dust and Heat*, p. 60.

317 A gifted pianist, Margaret Young Adams grew up in Salem's First Church. Later she became a social worker. James Luther Adams said she was more of an activist than he was and would hang her towel to the left of his! They had three daughters. Margaret died in 1978.

318 Adams, *Not Without Dust and Heat*, pp. 131–36.

319 I have personally heard Dr. Adams tell variants of this story on more than one occasion.

320 E.g., Gary Dorrien, in his three-volume history, *The Making of American Liberal Theology* (Louisville: Westminster John Knox Press, 2001; 2003; 2006) devotes no section to Adams, since his method seems to have been to consider major books rather than mentoring influence.

321 The JLA Foundation at www.jameslutheradams.org/archives/cat_resources.html lists these. The most accessible is *The Essential James Luther Adams: Selected Essays and Addresses*, edited and introduced by George K. Beach (Boston: Skinner House, 1998).

Notes

322 Playing on Luther's "priesthood of all believers" and Jesus' saying, "by their fruits shall ye know them." Adams also told hyper-rationalists, "People can die from hardening of the categories."

323 Flora Lewis, *Red Pawn: The Story of Noel Field* (Garden City, NY: Doubleday, 1965).

324 Susan Elisabeth Subak, *Rescue & Flight: American Relief Workers Who Defied the Nazis* (Lincoln and London: University of Nebraska Press, 2010). Their recognition can be found at http://isurvived.org/Righteous_Folder/Sharp_REV_and-Martha.html.

325 David B. Parke, "The Historical and Religious Antecedents of the New Beacon Series in Religious Education," PhD dissertation, Boston University, 1985. Publication now pending.

326 Edith F. Hunter, "Sophia Lyon Fahs: Liberal Religious Educator," *Notable American Unitarians,* www.harvardsquarelibrary.org/unitarians/fahs.html.

327 The *Christian Register* had been the leading independent Unitarian journal for more than a century. In 1939 the AUA assumed control and responsibility to keep it from ceasing publication.

328 Elizabeth Gurley Flynn was the admitted Communist Party member expelled by the ACLU, with both ACLU founder, Roger Baldwin, and Holmes voting that supporters of totalitarianism could not consistently and truly support civil liberties.

329 Charles W. Eddis, *The American Unitarians and the Communists*, publication forthcoming.

330 The earlier "defenestrations of Prague" involved the murders of members of the city council by a mob in 1419 and the attempted murder of Catholic leaders by Protestants in 1618, at the start of the Thirty Years' War.

331 The Holmes-Weatherly Award in 1969 and the Distinguished Service Award in 1976.

332 Personal communication from Bobbie Alicen, daughter of Munroe and Martha Husbands.

333 Morris, "It Was Noontime Here," p. 146.

334 Subsidies for this purpose did not become substantial until the 1980s, when grants from the Veatch Program became available.

335 The remarks of the unnamed black member are oral tradition in the church, given to me when I ministered there, 1973–1981. The vote is recorded in Karen Yarbro, *The First Sixty Years of the Tennessee Valley Unitarian Universalist Church*, published by the church in 2009.

Universalist Humanism and Unitarian Universalist Consolidation

336 Howe, "Clinton Lee Scott," *Dictionary of Unitarian Universalist Biography*, www25.uua.org/uuhs/duub/articles/clintonleescott.html.

337 Clinton Lee Scott, *Some Things Remembered* (Boston: Church of the Larger Fellowship, 1976).

338 Ibid., p. 51.

339 Clinton Lee Scott, *Parish Parables* (Boston: The Murray Press, 1946).

340 Mark Harris and Robert Cummins (1897–1982), *Notable American Universalists*, www.harvardsquarelibrary.org/universalists/RobertCummins.php.

341 Howe, *The Larger Faith*, p. 105.

342 Ibid, pp. 107–8.

343 Ibid., p. 108.

344 Mark D. Morrison-Reed, *Black Pioneers in a White Denomination* 3rd Edition, (Boston: Skinner House, 1994), pp. 214–15.

345 Howe, *The Larger Faith*, p. 109.

346 Tracy Pullman, then Minister of the First Universalist Church of Detroit, in 1946, as quoted in Howe, *The Larger Faith*, pp. 111–12.

347 Howe, *The Larger Faith*, p. 112.

348 The first director of the Universalist Service Committee was Carleton Fisher. See www.uusc.org/history; and Ghanda DiFiglia, *Roots and Visions: The First Fifty Years of the Unitarian Universalist Service Committee* (Boston: UUSC, 1990).

349 Melca Quimada Legaje, "The Biography of Rev. Toribio S. Quimada," *Maglipay Universalist: A History of the Unitarian Universalist*

Church of the Philippines, Fredric John Muir (Annapolis, MD: UU Church of Annapolis, 2001), pp. 90–96.

350 International Council of Unitarians and Universalists, http://icuu. net/membergroups/memberpages/philippines.html.

351 Mason McGuinness, then Minister of Grace Universalist in Lowell, MA, as quoted in Howe, *The Larger Faith*, p. 112.

352 Charles A. Howe, "The Humiliati," *Dictionary of Unitarian Universalist Biography,* www25.uua.org/uuhs/duub/articles/humiliati. html.

353 Wayne Arnason and Rebecca Scott, *We Would Be One: A History of Unitarian Universalist Youth Movements* (Boston: Skinner House, 2005).

354 www.ascboston.org/about/history.html.

355 Massachusetts Universalists had built a new building in Boston a few years before, only to see it become what Scott considered "another conservative liberal church." That effort failed, and the building was sold to the Catholics at a loss. Scott, *Some Things Remembered*, p. 58.

356 Maryell Cleary, "Kenneth Leo Patton," *Dictionary of Unitarian Universalist Biography,* www25.uua.org/uuhs/duub/articles/kenneth-patton.html.

357 These symbols now hang in the Hearth Room of the Starr King School for the Ministry in Berkeley, California.

358 Howe, *The Larger Faith*, pp. 115–16. The Charles Street Meeting House did not long survive the 1961 consolidation of the Universalists and the Unitarians, despite the fact that Patton led the creation of a new joint hymnal, *Hymns for the Celebration of Life* (Boston: UUA, 1964). The Universalist Convention of Massachusetts turned its funds over to the UUA, which did not continue subsidies. Patton became minister of the Unitarian Society of Ridgewood, New Jersey. The Meeting House struggled along for a few years, but closed in the 1970s. An architectural firm bought the building and planned its commercial reuse on what is now a chic shopping street. See Maryell Cleary, ed., *A Bold Experiment: The Charles Street Universalist Meeting House* (Chicago: Meadville Lombard Press, 2002).

359 Howe, *The Larger Faith*, p. 119.

360 Conrad Wright, "Parallel Routes to Merger, 1937–1961," in *Congregational Polity: A Historical Survey of Unitarian and Universalist Practice* (Boston: Skinner House, 1997), pp. 170–71.

361 Howe, *The Larger Faith*, p. 123.

362 Ibid.

363 David Parke, paper delivered in Syracuse at the fiftieth anniversary of the joint Unitarian and Universalist assemblies, 2009.

364 Donald Harrington, "We Are That Faith!" *Christian Register*, Mid-Summer, 1960, pp. 3–6.

The Marriage During the First Twenty Years

365 Dana McLean Greeley, *25 Beacon Street and Other Recollections* (Boston: Beacon Press, 1971); Alan Seaburg, "Dana McLean Greeley," *Dictionary of Unitarian Universalist Biography*, www25.uua.org/uuhs/duub/articles/danamcleangreeley.html.

366 Warren R. Ross, *The Premise and the Promise: The Story of the Unitarian Universalist Association* (Boston: Skinner House, 2001), pp. 25–26.

367 Raymond C. Hopkins, "Recollections, 1944–1974: The Creation of the Unitarian Universalist Association and the Administrations of Dana Greeley and Robert West," *Journal of Unitarian Universalist History*, Vol. XXXI (2006–2007), pp. 1–29, esp. p. 21.

368 Ross, *The Premise and the Promise*, p. 38. Universalist state conventions in Rhode Island, Pennsylvania, New York, and the Midwest did not give the UUA their funds. How they used them instead is another topic entirely.

369 When Greeley left office in 1969, he and Homer Jack set about organizing what became Religions for Peace (www.wcrp.org/). Homer Jack became the first secretary general.

370 A Unitarian Universalist congregation in Madison, Wisconsin, is now named for Reeb. See "Who Was James Reeb?" www.jruuc.org.

371 Joanne Giannino, "Viola Liuzzo," *Dictionary of Unitarian Universalist Biography*, www25.uua.org/uuhs/duub/articles/violaliuzzo.html.

372 These included Rabbi Maurice Eisendrath of Reform Judaism, Archbishop Iakovos of the Greek Orthodox Church, Eugene Carson Blake of the National Council of Churches, and John Cardinal Wright of the Roman Catholic Archdiocese of Pittsburgh—all friends of Greeley whom he had known variously and cultivated in 1962 while laying the groundwork for what became Religions for Peace.

373 Ross, *The Premise and the Promise*, p. 49.

374 The UUA later required bylaw changes making it clear that all additions to the budget proposed at the General Assembly must be accompanied by a proposal for what expenditures are to be cut, requiring an annual "contingency" allocation and limiting increases in fundraising expectations.

375 Ross, *The Premise and the Promise*, p. 48.

376 Mark Harris, *Elite: Uncovering Classism in Unitarian Universalist History* (Boston: Skinner House, 2011), p. 119.

377 Ross, *The Premise and the Promise,* p. 49.

378 Quoted in Ross, *The Premise and the Promise,* p. 45. Morrison-Reed rephrased this slightly in his third edition of *Black Pioneers*, p. xiv.

379 Tom Wolfe, "The 'Me' Decade and the Third Great Awakening," *New York*, August 23, 1976; nymag.com/news/features/45938.

380 Robert Nelson West, *Crisis and Change: My Years as President of the Unitarian Universalist Association, 1969–1977* (Boston: Skinner House, 2007).

381 Robert Sunley, assisted by Mary Martin, *We Started with the Children: From Church School to North Shore Unitarian Society, the Early Years, 1941–1955* (Manhasset, NY: The Unitarian Universalist Congregation at Shelter Rock, 1995).

382 Gerald F. Weary, *A Memorial to Caroline E. Veatch and The History of the Veatch Royalties of the New Shore Unitarian Society, Plandome, NY* (published by the congregation, 1983).

383 www.uucsr.org/veatch.asp.

384 www.cdc.gov/nchs/data/mvsr/supp/mv43_09s.pdf.

385 http://finallyfeminism101.wordpress.com/2007/10/19/feminism-friday-the-origins-of-the-word-sexism.

386 West, *Crisis and Change*, pp. 132–33. The Laymen's League was seen, with some justification, as having resisted the advent of women in ministry.

387 West, *Crisis and Change*, p. 128.

388 Arnason and Scott, *We Would Be One*.

389 Kim DeRidder, from the Tennessee Valley UU Church in Knoxville, went on to lead Planned Parenthood International in Thailand, the World Wildlife Fund in Indonesia, and international peacemaking efforts in Sri Lanka. Clearly he should have been a poet.

390 West, *Crisis and Change*, p. 53.

391 The Professional Code of Conduct of the Unitarian Universalist Ministers Association now explicitly says, "If I am married or in a committed partnership I will not engage in sexual contact or sexualized behavior with any person whom I serve professionally except my spouse or partner." This was not always the case. This principle was sometimes shamefully violated. Compared to other religious communities, however, the UUA soon reacted to "the culture of narcissism" by developing quick interventions—often led by women, lay and ordained—for clergy misconduct.

392 West, *Crisis and Change*, pp. 139–43.

393 The UUA Office of International Resources now has a DVD on the Holdeen India Program. See www.uua.org/aboutus/professional-staff/advocacywitness/holdeenindia/index.php.

The UUA Grows Stronger

394 Ross, *The Premise and the Promise*, p. 91.

395 Tom Owen-Towle, *Borne on a Wintry Wind: O. Eugene Pickett, Fourth President of the UUA* (Boston: Skinner House, 1996).

396 Ross, *The Premise and the Promise*, p. 198.

397 Ibid., p. 203.

398 www.americanreligionsurvey-aris.org/.

399 From a 1996 survey of readers of *UU World*; Ross, *The Premise and the Promise* p. 191.

Index

25 Beacon Street and Other Recollections (Greeley 1971), 244

Abbott, Francis Ellingwood, 112, 113, 232
About Your Sexuality (curriculum 1970), 191, 192
Abraham Lincoln Centre for Social Services (All Souls Church, Chicago), 120
Adams, Frank D., 147
Adams, Hannah, xii, 19–22, 26, 27, 33, 217, 218, 221
Adams, James Luther, 136, 152, 154–157, 159, 237, 240, 241
Adams, James Madison, 154
Adams, John, xii, 8, 18, 19, 22, 25, 109, 218
Adams, John G., 219
Adams, Margaret Young, 155, 240
Adams, Thomas (father of Hannah), 19
Addams, Jane, 126, 130, 139
Adler, Felix, 127
Africa, 7, 183, 202, 206
African American Methodist Episcopal Church, 105
Akron, Ohio, 99, 193, 224
Alcott, A. N., 107, 231

Alcott, Abigail, 222
Alcott, Amos Bronson, 37, 53, 60, 86, 222
Alcott, Louisa May, 60, 223
Alicen, Bobbie, 241
Allen, Ethan, 11, 35
Allen, Woody, 19
Alliance of Unitarian and Other Liberal Christian Women, 117
Alphabetical Compendium of the Various Sects, An (Adams 1784), 21
American Almanac and Repository of Useful Knowledge (1849), 225
American Bar Association, 232
American Civil Liberties Union (ACLU), 126, 132, 161, 234, 241
American Congress of Liberal Religious Societies, 107
American Freedom and Catholic Power (Blanshard 1949), 165
American Friends Service Committee, 158
American Heretic: Theodore Parker and Transcendentalism (Grodzins 2002), 223
American Legion, 142
American Moral Tales for Young Persons (Dix 1832), 51

American Originals: Homemade
Varieties of Christianity (Conkin
1997), 215, 219, 220
American Protestant Thought in the
Liberal Era (Hutchison 1968),
236
American Railway Union, 108
American Red Cross, 74
American Reformation: A
Documentary History of
Unitarian Christianity, An,
(Ahlstrom and Carey 1985),
228
"American Scholar, The" (Phi Beta
Kappa address, Emerson 1837),
55, 222
American Social Science
Association, 85, 92
American Union against
Militarism (AUM), 131
American Unitarian Association
(AUA), xi, 19, 48–50, 58, 91,
112–114, 120–122, 129, 131,
132, 135, 136, 143, 151–153,
157, 158, 160–163, 166, 169,
173–175, 181–183, 192, 209,
233, 236, 241
American Unitarian Youth, 161
American Unitarianism (Morse
1815), 25
American Unitarians and the
Communists, The (Eddis 2011),
241
American Universalism (Williams
2002), 226, 228, 229, 248
American Woman Suffrage
Association, 102
Amnesty International, USA, 201
Ancient History of Universalism,
The (Ballou 2d), 39, 98

Andover Newton Theological
School, 157, 218
Andover Theological Seminary, 22
Andrew, John, 91
Angels Revolt, 154
Anglican communion, 132
Anglicans, 17
Ann Arbor, Michigan, 114
Annual Journal of the Universalist
Historical Society, 237
Anthony, Susan B., xii, 85
Anti-Imperialist League, 120
Antioch College, 75, 76, 90, 220,
228
Apostle of Culture: Emerson as
Preacher and Lecturer (Robinson
1982), 221, 222
Appeal in Favor of that Class of
Americans Called Africans, An
(Child 1833), 57
Applegate, Debby, 235
Appleton, Frances E. (Fanny),
223
Appleton, Nathan, 57, 223
Appleton, Thomas Gold, 226
Arius, 18
Arminius, Jacobus, 16
Arnason, Wayne, 243, 246
Arnold, Mel, 161, 165, 166
Association for the Advancement
of Women, 102
Atkins, Chet, 200
Atlanta, Georgia, 128, 197
Atwood, Isaac, 108, 231
Auburn, New York, 69
Austin, John, 69
Austro-Hungarian Empire, 130
Autocrat of the Breakfast Table, The
(Holmes 1858), 234

Babbitt, Irving, 154
Baker, George F., 239
Balch, Emily Greene, 126, 127, 130, 131, 235, 236
Baldwin, Roger, 126, 131, 132, 234, 236, 241
Ballou, Adin, 40, 41, 42, 43, 60, 220
Ballou, Hosea, xii, 10, 11, 12, 31–41, 67, 70, 173, 220, 223
Ballou, Hosea II, 39, 42, 70, 98
Baltimore, Maryland, 49
Bancroft, Aaron, 48
Bangkok, Thailand, 168
Baptists, 7, 8, 15, 20, 23, 34, 43, 52, 104, 144, 154
Barnegat Bay, New Jersey, 4
Barns, Lucy, 74
Barns, Thomas, 74
Barnum, Phineas T., 70, 80, 100, 108, 224, 229
Bartol, Cyrus, 92
Barton, Clara, xii, 73, 225, 229
Barton, David (brother of Clara), 73
Bates, Katherine Lee, 130
"Battle Hymn of the Republic" (Howe), 89, 229
Beach, George Kimmich, 240
Beacon Press, 161, 165, 166, 189, 194
Beecher, Henry Ward, 111, 127, 235
Beginnings of Unitarianism in America, The (Wright 1955), 216, 248
Belknap, Jeremy, 27, 218
Bellows, Henry Whitney, 78, 79, 88–92, 174, 226, 227, 228
Belsham, Thomas, 25

Benevolent Fraternity of Unitarian Churches, 50
Bennington, Vermont, 59
Bentley, William, 21, 25, 26, 218, 220
Berlin, 130
"Beyond Boston" (Weston), 220
Biddle, Francis, 234
"The Biography of Rev. Toribio S. Quimada", 242
Birmingham, England, 17
Bisbee, Herman, 99, 100
Black Affairs Council (BAC), 185, 186, 187, 188
Black and White Action (BAWA), 186
Black Pioneers in a White Denomination (Morrison-Reed 1994), 188, 242, 245, 247
Black Unitarian Universalist Caucus (BUUC), 186, 187, 188
Blackwell, Antoinette Brown, 75, 76, 225
Blackwell, Elizabeth, 89
Blake, Eugene Carson, 245
Blanchard, Paula, 223
Blanshard, Paul, 165
Bleak House, 192
Bold Experiment: The Charles Street Universalist Meeting House, A (Cleary 2002), 243
Bolster, Arthur S. Jr., 223
Book of Common Prayer (American unitarian version), 21, 217
Book of Common Prayer (Anglican unitarian version), 18
Borne on a Wintry Wind: O. Eugene Pickett Fourth President of the UUA (Owen-Towle 1996), 246
Boston Association of Ministers, 24

Boston Athenaeum, 21, 23
Boston Investigator, 36
Boston University Law School, 144
Boston, Massachusetts, 5, 12, 15, 19, 21, 22, 23, 25, 26, 28, 31, 34, 36, 38, 39, 40, 43, 45, 48, 53, 56, 57, 58, 59, 78, 84, 86, 91, 92, 107, 120, 125, 136, 137, 139, 162, 166, 173, 176, 181, 182, 188, 208, 211, 231
Boston, Massachusetts Free Religionists, 99
Boston, Massachusetts Ministers Association, 60
Boston, Massachusetts Ministers Conference (1820), 48
Boston, Massachusetts Vigilance Committee, 86
Bowers, J.D., 217, 247
Boy Scouts of America (BSA), 204
Brahmo Samaj, 119, 233
Braude, Anne, 223
Briant, Lemuel, 25
Brook Farm, 42, 43, 60, 223
Brookline, Massachusetts, 47
Brooklyn *Eagle*, 139
Brooklyn, New York, 127, 139
Brooks, Elbridge Gerry, 98, 229
Brooks, Seth, 170, 175
Broughton, Thomas, 20
Brown Quarterly, 235
Brown University, 52
Brown, John, 88
Brown, Olympia, 75, 76, 107, 108, 225, 231
Brownson, Orestes, 40, 41, 220
Bruner, Edna, 169
Bryant, William Cullen, 89
Bryn Mawr College, 130

Buchtel, John, 99
Buckminster, Joseph Stevens, 21, 26
Buehrens, John A., 201–203, 205, 206
Buescher, John B., 223, 247
Bumbaugh, Beverly, 230
Burns, Anthony, 86, 87, 227
Butler, Grant, 163

Cabot, Eliza Lee. *See* Follen, Eliza Lee Cabot
Calcutta, India, 84, 119
Calderwood, Deryck, 191
Call, Lon Ray, 163
Calvinists, 16, 19, 22, 23, 24, 25, 40, 47, 56, 83
Cambridge Bank, 39
Cambridge, Massachusetts, 39, 40, 61, 218
Cambridgeport, Massachusetts, 39
Camp Hill, Alabama, 168
Campbell, Jeffrey, 169, 170
Campbell, Marguerite, 170
Campbellites, 220
Canadian Unitarian Council, 202, 209, 230
Canton, New York, 76, 103, 140, 146
apek, Norbert, 132, 200, 236
Capetown, South Africa, 188
Carey, Patrick, 220
Carlyle, Thomas, 61, 223
Carnegie, Andrew, 101
Carnegie, Mrs. Andrew, 140
Carnes, Paul, 176, 193, 194, 198
Caron, Sandra Mitchell, 198, 199
Carpenter, Estlin, 233
Carpenter, Mary, 233

Carpenter, Victor, 188
Carroll, John, 21
Case, Everett Needham, 237, 238, 239
Case, Josephine Young, 237, 238, 239
Cassara, Ernest, 219
Cate, George, 107
Cayuga Association of Universalists, 74
Ceausescu, Nicolae, 200
Central Intelligence Agency (CIA), 158
Chadwick, John White, 127
Chamberlain, Neville, 158
Channing, Henry, 27
Channing, Ruth Gibbs, 27
Channing, Walter, 59
Channing, William Ellery, xii, 26–28, 36, 37, 40, 41, 46–53, 56–60, 86, 109, 136, 160, 181, 220, 221, 222, 248
Channing, William Henry, 226
Channing: The Reluctant Radical (Mendelsohn 1971), 218
Chapin, Augusta Jane, 103, 230
Chapin, Edwin H., 98, 229
"Chardon Street and Bible Conventions", 220
Charlotte, North Carolina, 201
Charlottesville, Virginia, 17
Charlton, Massachusetts, 9, 238
Chauncey, Charles, 16, 17, 217
Cheatham, Henry, 216
Cherokee Tribe, 31
Chicago, 90, 155
Chicago World's Fair (1892), 107
Child, Lydia Maria, 51, 57
Christian Ambassador, 69
Christian Connexion, 220
Christian Freeman, 74

Christian Messenger, 224
Christian Non-Resistance (A. Ballou 1846), 42
Christian Register, 111, 161, 236, 241, 244
Christian Scientists, 162
Christian Union, 111
"Christianity and Socialism" (Holmes 1908), 129
"The Church of the Living God", 229
Church of England, 9, 17, 217
Church of Jesus Christ and Latter Day Saints (Mormons), 162
Church of Scotland, 17
Church of the Larger Fellowship, 160, 161, 162, 163, 198
Church, Forrest, 201, 217
Cincinnati, Ohio, 217
"Civil Disobedience" (Thoreau 1849), 85
Clara Barton Homestead, Oxford, Massachusetts, 142
Clarence R. Skinner, Prophet of a New Universalism (Howe 1999), 237, 238
Clark, Charles E., 142
Clarke, Anna Huidekoper, 61
Clarke, James Freeman, 58–62, 89, 91, 92, 112, 115–117, 211, 223, 226
Clay, Henry, 68
Cleary, Maryell, 243
Clements, Charles, 206
Cleveland, Grover, 108
Clinton Liberal Institute (New York), 73
Codman, John, 24, 25
Coffin, William Sloane, 184
Coit, Stanton, 140
Cole, Alfred Storer, 13, 216

Cole, Paula, 222
*The College, the Market, and the
Court: or, Woman's Relation to
Education, Labor, and Law* (Dall
1867), 85
Commission on Appraisal (1934),
136, 151, 155, 157, 240
Commission on Social Service,
143
Communist Party, 161
Complete Works (Channing 1843),
220
Concord, Massachusetts, 26, 54,
56, 81, 85, 227
Confessing Church movement,
155
*Congregational Polity: A Historical
Survey of Unitarian and
Universalist Practice* (Wright
1997), 244
Congregationalists, 9, 15, 23, 39,
79, 97, 111, 146
Conkin, Paul K., 215, 219, 220
Constantia. *See* Murray, Judith
Sargent
Constantine, 18
Constitution League, 128
Continental Army (American
Revolution), 4, 6, 10
Continental Congress, 8
Convention of Friends of
Universal Reform (1840), 43
Conversations on Common Things
(Dix 1824), 51
*Conversations with Children on the
Gospels* (Alcott 1836), 53
Conway, Moncure, 87
Cook, Maria, 74, 225
Cooke, George Willis, 232
Cooper, Peter, 89

Cornish, Louis C., 132, 136, 151,
236, 237
Cottrell, Robert C., 234
Council of Liberal Churches, 172,
174
Courter, Gini, 205
Cousens, John, 141
Craft, Ellen, 86
Crane Theological School, Tufts
University, 140, 172
*Crisis and Change: My
Years as President of the
Unitarian Universalist
Association,1969–1977* (West
2007), 245, 246
*Crisis of the Standing Order:
Clerical Intellectuals and Cultural
Authority in Massachusetts,
1780–1833, The* (Field 1998),
218
Cummins, Robert, 168, 169, 170,
172, 174, 242
Curie, Marie, 146
Curtis, George Ticknor, 86
Curtiss, Elizabeth, 217, 218

Dall, Caroline Wells Healey, xii,
62, 81–85, 92, 119, 226
Dall, Charles Henry Appleton, 62,
81–84, 119, 226
Dallas, Texas, 190
Dalton, Gloster, 4
Darfur, 206
*Darkening the Doorways: Black
Trailblazers and Missed
Opportunities in Unitarian
Universalism* (Morrison-Reed
2011), 233, 247
*Daughter of Boston: The
Extraordinary Diary of a*

Nineteenth-Century Woman, Caroline Healey Dall (Deese 2005), 226
Davidoff, Denise Taft (Denny), 201, 202
Davies, A. Powell, 160, 161, 163, 175, 196
Davis family, xii, 9, 33, 216
"The Davis Family of Oxford, Massachusetts", 216
Davis, Andrew Jackson, 69
Davis, Benjamin, 10
Davis, Deborah, 9
Davis, Ebenezer, 9, 10, 12
Davis, Edith King, 118
Davis, Elijah, 9
Davis, George, 162
Davis, Horace, 118
Davis, Isaac, 9
Davis, Samuel Jr., 9
Day, John, 132
De Benneville, George, 7, 8, 216
Dean, Paul, 33, 42, 219
Debs, Eugene, 108
Declaration of Social Principles, 143
Dedham, Massachusetts, 52
Deese, Helen R., 226
Deism, 17
DeRidder, Kim, 246
DeRoche, Celeste, 226
Detroit, Michigan, 184
Dewey, John, 159
Dexter, Elizabeth, 158
Dexter, Robert, 158
Dial, 59, 60, 61, 62, 220
Dialogues on the Universal Restoration (Winchester), 42
Dickens, Charles, 192
Dickinson, Emily, 75, 227

Dictionary of Religions (Adams 1817), 21
Dictionary of Unitarian Universalist Biography (DUUB), 215, 225, 248
Dietrich, John, 134, 135, 154, 236
DiFiglia, Ghanda, 242
Dimock, Marshall E., 182
Disciples of Christ, 220
Discourse of Matters Pertaining to Religion, A (Parker 1842), 223
"Divinity School Address" (Emerson 1838), 41, 53, 55, 221, 222, 227
Dix, Dorothea Lynde, 51, 52, 62, 73, 90, 221, 222
Dods, John Bovee, 67, 68
Dole, Charles Fletcher, 127
Dorchester, Massachusetts, 6
Dorrien, Gary, 236, 240
Douglass, H. Paul, 151
DuBois, W.E.B., 105, 127, 128, 140, 235
Dumaguete City, Negros, Phillipines, 171
Dunham, Ethel, 232
Dunn, Sally Barns, 74
Durant, Will, 143

Eaton, Walter Pritchard, 152
Eddis, Charles W., 241
Edinburgh, Scotland, 24
Edmonds, Josephine (Jo), 144
Edwards, June, 233
Eisendrath, Maurice, 245
Elgin, Illinois, 107
Eliot family, xii
Eliot Seminary, St. Louis, Missouri, 110

Eliot, Abby Adams, 233
Eliot, Abby May, 118
Eliot, Abigail Adams Cranch,
109–112
Eliot, Charles W., 120, 237
Eliot, Christopher Rhodes, 117
Eliot, Dorothea Dix. *See* Wilbur,
Dorothea Dix Eliot
Eliot, Edward Cranch, 232
Eliot, Frederick May, 118, 136,
137, 152–154, 157, 158, 160,
161, 166, 169, 174, 237
Eliot, Henrietta Robins Mack,
111, 112
Eliot, Henry Ware, 232
Eliot, John, 109
Eliot, Martha, 118
Eliot, Martha May, 232
Eliot, Mary Jackson May, 117
Eliot, Samuel A., 234
Eliot, Samuel Atkins, II, 120–122,
129, 132, 136, 146, 181, 183
Eliot, Thomas Lamb, 110, 111,
117, 121, 228
Eliot, Thomas Stearns (T.S.), 155,
232
Eliot, William Greenleaf, Jr., 111,
113, 135
Eliot, William Greenleaf, Sr., 90,
109, 110, 112, 228
*Elite: Uncovering Classism in
Unitarian Universalist History*
(Harris 2011), 245
Ellery, William, 26, 160
Emergency Conference on
Unitarian Universalist Response
to the Black Rebellion, 185
Emerson in His Journals (Porte
1982), 227
Emerson, Dorothy May, 230, 247
Emerson, Ellen Tucker, 54

Emerson, George B., 226
Emerson, Mary Moody, 54, 222
Emerson, Ralph Waldo, xii, 26, 28,
37, 41, 48, 53, 54, 55, 56, 58,
60, 61, 83, 84, 85, 88, 92, 220,
221, 222, 223, 226, 227, 248
Emerson, William, 54
Emerson, William, 26, 48
Emerson, William, 48
*Emily Greene Balch: Improper
Bostonian* (Randall 1964), 234,
235
*Empire of Liberty: A History of
the Early Republic, 1789–1815*
(Wood 2009), 216
Episcopalians, 210, 223
Essays (Emerson 1842), 220
Essays and Sketches (Dall 1848),
62, 83
*Essential James Luther Adams:
Selected Essays and Addresses,
The*, 240
Ethical Culturists, 119, 140, 231
*Events and Epochs in Religious
History* (Clarke 1881), 115
The Everlasting Gospel (Siegvolk
1753), 7, 8
"The Everlasting Yea", 223
"*The Evil of Sin*" (Channing 1832),
40
Eyes on the Prize, 183

Fahs, Sophia Lyon, 158, 159, 160
Faith that Makes Faithful, The
(Gannett 1886), 114
Falwell, Jerry, 195
Federal Bureau of Investigation
(FBI), 189
Federal Council of Churches, 170
Federal Council of Churches of
Christ, 170

Federal Council of the Churches
of Christ in America, 169
*Fellowship Movement: A Growth
Strategy and Its Legacy, The*
(Ulbrich 2007), 248
Fellowship of Reconciliation, 235
Feminine Mystique, The (Friedan
1963), 190
Fenn, William Wallace, 133, 236
Ferber, Michael, 184
Ferry Beach, Maine, 103
Fetter, Ted, 233
Field, Noel, 158
Field, Peter S., 218
Fifty Affirmations (Abbott), 232
Fifty-fourth Massachusetts
Volunteer Regiment (Civil War),
73, 225
Fillmore, Millard, 85, 227
Fire Island, New York, 62
First National City Bank (later
CitiBank), 239
*The First Sixty Years of the
Tennessee Valley Unitarian
Universalist Church*, 242
First South Carolina Volunteers
(Civil War), 227
Fisher, Carleton, 171, 242
Fisher, Ebenezer, 76
Fisher, Joseph Lyman, 187
Fisher, Lewis, 142
Florence, Italy, 88
Flynn, Elizabeth Gurley, 241
Follen, Charles, 57, 218
Follen, Eliza Lee Cabot, 57
Foote, Arthur, 237
Foote, Frances Eliot, 237
Foote, Henry Wilder, 237
Foote, Henry Wilder II, 237
*For Faith and Freedom: A Short
History of Unitarianism in*

Europe (Howe 1997), 217
For Full Recognition and
Funding of the Black Affairs
Council (FULLBAC), 186
Ford, Henry, 146
Forrest Gump (fictional
character), 19
Fort Wagner, South Carolina, 73
Fox, Kate, 69
Fox, Leah, 69
Fox, Margaret, 69
Fox, Van Eric, 237, 240
Francis, Convers, 57
Frank, Willard, 230
Franklin, Benjamin, 18, 52
Franklin, Massachusetts, 52
Fraser's magazine, 223
"Frederick May Eliot, President
of the American Unitarian
Association (1937–1958)"
(Morris 1970), 240
Free Inquirer, 36
Free Religious Association (FRA),
92, 112
*Freedom Moves West: A History of
the Western Unitarian Conference*
(Lyttle 1952), 231
Freeman, James, 21, 25, 26, 58,
218
Freewill Baptists, 10
Friedan, Betty, 190
Fritchman, Stephen H., 161
Frost, Barzillai, 227
Frothingham, Octavius Brooks,
92, 112
Fruitlands, 60
FULLBAC, 202
Fuller, Margaret, xii, 55, 59, 61,
62, 82–84, 117, 221, 223, 226
Fuller, Timothy, 61

Gage, Frances Dana Barker, 72, 73, 225
Gaines, Renford. *See* Mwalimu Imara
Gandhi, Mohandas, 42, 132
Gannett, Ezra Stiles, 48, 57, 86, 87, 89, 91
Gannett, William Channing, 114
Gardner, Massachusetts, 34
Garrison, William Lloyd, 37, 71, 83, 87
Gay, Ebenezer, 16
General Baptists, 216
General Electric (GE), xii, 144, 145
Georgia Universalist State Convention, 70
German Dunkers (Baptists), 7
Germantown, Pennsylvania, 7
Gettysburg, Pennsylvania, 87
Giannino, Joanne, 244
Gibbons, Brainerd, 172, 175
Gibson, Gordon, 216
Giles, Philip, 175, 182
Gilman, Samuel, 222
Glasgow, Scotland, 103
Gleaner, The (Murray 1798), 5, 215
Glory (film), 225
Gloucester, Massachusetts, 4
Goddard Academy, 167
Goodridge, Hillary, 207
Goodridge, Julie, 207
Goodwin, Joan W., 222, 223, 225, 232
Gordon, Eleanor, 120
Gospel Visitant, 34
Grant, Ulysses S., 100, 118
Gravel, Mike, 189
"The Great Lawsuit: Man *versus* Men, Woman *versus* Women" (Fuller), 62

Greeley, Dana McLean, 136, 166, 181–184, 187, 190, 237, 244, 245
Greeley, Horace, 62, 71, 74, 76, 80, 100, 229
Greene, Nathaniel, 4, 6
Greenfield Group, 155
Greenway, Cornelius, 170
Grodzins, Dean, 223
Gudmundson, V. Emil, 236
Gulbrandsen, Natalie Webber, 199, 200, 201

Hale, Edward Everett, 80, 91
Half a Man: The Status of the Negro in New York (Ovington 1911), 128
Halifax, Nova Scotia, 86
Hall, Frank Oliver, 140
Hallman, Laurel, 208
Hammond, Charles, 69
Hampton Institute, 105, 127
Harper's Ferry, Virginia, 88
Harrington, Donald S., 161, 176, 244
Harris, Mark, 242, 245
Harvard College, 12, 19, 22, 23, 25, 26, 27, 39, 45, 48, 49, 53, 54, 55, 56, 57, 63, 78, 100, 111, 120, 121, 122, 136, 184, 218, 222, 228, 237
Harvard Divinity School, 55, 61, 88, 110, 115, 118, 120, 133, 154, 157
Harvard Law School, 144
Harvard University, 133, 206
Harvard, John, 21, 218
Harvard, Massachusetts, 60
Havana, Cuba, 50
Hawthorne, Nathaniel, 46, 59, 60, 221

Hawthorne, Sophia Peabody, 59
Haydon, E. Eustace, 135
Haynes, John, 235
Hazlitt, William, 17, 217
Healey, Mark (father of Caroline Healey Dall), 81
Hedge, Frederic Henry, 55, 91, 115, 228
Hedge's Club, 55
Heidegger, 155
Heidelberg University, 100
Henry Whitney Bellows (Kring 1979), 226, 228
Henry, Hayward, 187
Henry, Richard, 236
Heralds of a Liberal Faith (Eliot), 234
Herndon, William, 87
Hewett, Phillip, 230
Higginson, Thomas Wentworth, 85, 86, 88, 227
"The Historical and Religious Antecedents of the New Beacon Series in Religious Education", 241
Historical Dictionary of All Religions from the Creation of the World to This Perfect Time, An (Broughton 1742), 20
History of First Parish in Needham, 223
History of the Corruptions of Christianity (Priestley 1783), 18
Hitler, Adolf, 158
Hocking, W. E., 143
Holdeen India Program, 246
Holdeen, Jonathan, 192
Hollywood, California, 162
Holman, Alice, 233
Holmes, Abiel, 222, 234
Holmes, Fanny, 125

Holmes, John Haynes, 128–132, 135, 143, 161, 235, 236, 241
Holmes, Oliver Wendell Jr., 125, 126, 235
Holmes, Oliver Wendell Sr., 126, 222, 234
Holocaust Memorial, Yad Vashem, Israel, 158
Holocaust Museum, Washington DC, 158
Hoover, Mel, 202
Hopedale Community, 43, 61
Hopedale, Massachusetts, 61
Hopkins, Raymond, 183, 244
Hosea Ballou (Cassara 2003), 219
Houston, Sam, 68
Howard University, 105
Howe, Charles A., 216, 217, 222, 224, 225, 229, 230, 231, 237, 238, 239, 242, 243, 244, 247
Howe, Julia Ward, 59, 89, 116, 117, 221, 222, 229, 232
Howe, Samuel Gridley, 52, 59, 88, 89, 116, 221, 222
Hughes, Lynn Gordon, 220
Hughes, Peter, 216, 219, 222, 225, 226, 232
Hull House, Chicago, 139
Humanism (Reese 1926), 134
Humanist Fellowship, 135
Humanist Manifesto (1933), 135, 147, 167
Humanist Sermons (Reese 1927), 134, 137
Humiliati, xiii, 172, 173, 174, 211, 243
Hunter, Edith F., 241
Husbands, Martha, 162, 241
Husbands, Munroe, xiii, 162, 163, 164, 165, 186, 241
Hutchison, William R., 236

Hymns for the Celebration of Life (1964), 235, 243
Hymns of the Spirit (1937), 147, 235, 237

Iakovos, Archbishop, 245
Icelandic Unitarian Connection, The (Gudmundson 1984), 236
Identifying the Image of God: Radical Christians and Nonviolent Power in the Antebellum United States (McKanan 2002), 218
Illinois Universalist Convention, 107
Imara, Mwalimu, 188
In Our Own Best Interest: How Defending Human Rights Benefits Us All (Schulz 2001), 201
Independent Messenge, 42
Indianapolis, Indiana, 205
"The Inestimable Value of Souls" (A. Ballou 1830), 42
Inheritors of the Spirit: Mary White Ovington and the Founding of the NAACP (Wedin 1998), 234, 235
Inman, James, 230
International Association for Religious Freedom (IARF), 132, 198, 231, 233
International Cooperation Administration, US State Department, 172
International Council of Community Churches, 236
International Council of Unitarian and Other Liberal Religious Thinkers and Workers, 121
International Council of Unitarians and Universalists, 202, 209, 231, 243

International Red Cross, 74, 229
International Women's Congress at the Hague (1915), 130
International Workers of the World (IWW), 142
Invention of Air: A Story of Science, Faith, Revolution, and the Birth of America, The (Johnson 2008), 217
Invisible Minority: Homosexuals in Our Society, The (1972 curriculum), 192 Iowa, 37, 103
Iowa Sisterhood, 120
Issue in the West, The (Sunderland 1886), 114
"It Was Noontime Here: Frederick May Eliot and the Unitarian Renaissance, 1934–1961" (Morris), 239, 241

Jack, Homer, 183, 185, 186, 244
Jackson, Andrew, 31
Jackson, Jimmy Lee, 184
Jackson, William, 122
James Freeman Clarke: Disciple to Advancing Truth (Bolster 1954), 223
Jefferson Bible: The Life and Morals of Jesus of Nazareth, The, 217
Jefferson, Thomas, xii, 8, 17, 18, 160, 210, 217, 218
Jenkins, Lydia Ann, 74, 75, 225
Jesus, 3, 11, 12, 18, 23, 27, 47, 54, 55, 56, 58, 112, 114, 116, 119, 129, 148, 175, 176, 223, 239, 241
Jesus Christ and the Social Question (Peabody 1900), 122
Jews, 3, 119, 127, 158, 184, 209, 231
Johnson, Steven B., 217

Joint Interim Commission on Federal Union, Detroit (1955), 174

Joint Merger Commission, 175, 182

Jones, Jenkin Lloyd, 113, 114, 116, 119, 120, 134, 232

Jordan, Joseph, 104, 105, 230

Jordan, Joseph Fletcher, 105, 142, 230

Joseph Priestley and English Unitarianism in America (Bowers 2007), 217, 247

Joslin, Elliot P., 238

Journal of Unitarian Universalist History, 219, 244

Judith Sargent Murray Society, 216

Justice Holmes, Natural Law and the Supreme Court (Biddle 1961), 234

Keats, George, 217

Keats, John, 217

Kelley, Abby, 225

Kennedy, John F., 181

Kent, Ohio, 198

Khasi Hills, North East India, 119

Khasi Unitarians, 119, 227

King, Coretta Scott, 182

King, Martin Luther Jr., 42, 182, 184, 186

King, Thomas Starr, 77, 78, 79, 88, 90, 91, 118, 226

Kirkland, John, 26

Kneeland, Abner, xii, 34–37, 40–42, 44, 219

Kneeland, Eliza Osborne, 35, 37

Kring, Walter Donald, 226, 228, 239

Kron, Keith, 204

Ku Klux Klan, 142, 168

Kuebler, Ernest, 158, 166

"Laboring Classes, The" (Brownson 1840), 41

Lake Winnipesaukee, New Hampshire, 103

Lamson, Peggy, 234, 236

Lanoka Harbor, New Jersey, 215

Larger Faith: A Short History of American Universalism, The (Howe 1993), 224, 229, 230, 231, 237, 238, 239, 242, 243, 244, 247

Larger Hope: The First Century of Universalism in America, 1770–1870, The (Miller 1979), 220, 228, 229, 238

Last Man Jailed for Blasphemy, The (Papa 1998), 34, 219

"The Latest Form of Infidelity" (Norton), 55

Lavan, Spencer, 227, 233

Lawrence, Abbot, 58

Lawrence, Amos A., 86

Learned, John, 112

Legaje, Melca Quimada, 242

Lend-a-Hand Societies, 226

Letters and Sketches of Sermons (Murray 1813), 6

Letters of Elizabeth Palmer Peabody: American Renaissance Woman (Ronda 1984), 220

Lewis, Flora, 241

Lexington, Massachusetts, 56, 81

Lexington, Massachusetts militia (Revolutionary War), 9

Lexington, Massachusetts Minutemen, 56

Liberal Christians, The (Wright 1970), 217

Liberal Church of America, 79
Liberal Religious Youth (LRY),
173, 191, 197, 206
Liberator, 71, 224
*Life and Morals of Jesus of Nazareth,
The* (Jefferson), 18
Life of John Murray, 39
*Life of Reason, Vol. I, Reason in
Common Sense, The* (Santayana
1905), 215
Life of Rev. Hosea Ballou, The, Vol.
II (Whittemore 1855), 219
Life of Theophilus Lindsey
(Belsham), 25
"*Likeness to God*" (Channing 1828),
41, 53
*Lincoln at Gettysburg: The Words
that Remade America* (Willis
1993), 227
Lincoln, Abraham, 78, 85, 87,
89, 101
Lindsey, Theophilus, 17, 18, 21,
25
Liuzzo, Viola, 184, 244
Livermore, Daniel, 71, 229
Livermore, Maine, 100
Livermore, Mary Rice, 71, 80, 90,
99, 101, 229
Living by Heart (curriculum), 208
London, England, 7, 140
Longfellow, Henry Wadsworth,
223, 226
Los Angeles, California, 197
Los Pinos Reservation, Colorado,
118
Louisville, Kentucky, 49, 58
Lowell Forum, 140, 143
Lowell, Massachusetts, 74, 140
Luther, Martin, 241
Lynn, Massachusetts, 107
Lyttle, Charles H., 231

Macaulay, John, 223
Macdonald, JoAnn, 225
MacDonald, Mary Lou, 191
MacLean, Angus, 170
MacLean, Kenneth Torquil, 202,
234
Madison County, New York, 139
*Maglipay Universalist: A History
of the Unitarian Universalist
Church of the Philippines*, 243
Maine, 10, 47, 51, 68, 100
*Making of American Liberal
Theology, The* (Dorrien 2003),
236, 240
*Making the Manifesto: The Birth
of Religious Humanism* (Schulz
2002), 236
Man Without A Country, A (Hale
1863), 80
Mann, Charlotte Messer, 52, 53
Mann, Horace, 39, 46, 51, 52, 53,
59, 75, 76, 90, 221, 222, 227
Mann, Mary Peabody, 59, 222
Mann, Stephen (brother of
Horace), 52
Mannis, Jedediah, 221
*Margaret Fuller: From
Transcendentalism to Revolution*
(Blanchard 1987), 223
Marini, Stephen A., 216, 219
Marshall, George, 198
Marshall, Megan, 221
Martin, Mary, 245
Mary Institute, St. Louis,
Missouri, 110
*Mary Moody Emerson and the
Origins of Transcendentalism*
(Cole 1998), 222
Masaryk, Charlotte Garrigue, 132
Masaryk, Jan, 161

Massachusetts Anti-Slavery
Society, 87
Massachusetts Association of
Universal Restorationists, 42
Massachusetts Association of
Universalist Restorationists
(1831), 33
Massachusetts Legislature, 39, 52,
207
Massachusetts Magazine, 5
Massachusetts Supreme Judicial
Court, 48
Massachusetts Universalist
Convention, 168, 171, 173,
174, 183, 243
Massachusetts Woman's Christian
Temperance Union, 102
May, Abby, 117, 232
May, Abigail, 53
May, Mary Jackson, 117
May, Samuel, 53, 57, 92
Mayhew, Jonathan, 16
McCalla, William, 36
McCarthy, Joseph, 162
McCollester, Lee, 140, 141
McDade, Carolyn, 188
McDougall, Kenneth, 136
McEmrys, Aaron, 223
McGonigle, Gregory, 223
McGuinness, Mason, 243
McKanan, Dan, 218
McKeeman, Gordon, 193, 194
Meadville Lombard Theological
School (and predecessors), 61,
76, 113, 135, 155, 157, 182,
196, 198, 220, 238
Meadville, Pennsylvania, 61, 76
Medfield, Massachusetts, xii, 19,
33
Medford, Massachusetts, 70

Meditations for Private Hours (Dix
1828), 51
Meeting House Press, 173
Melcher, Frederick, 151
Melville, Elizabeth Shaw, 223
Melville, Herman, 223
*Memoirs of Margaret Fuller Ossoli,
The* (Emerson, Channing,
Clarke 1852), 226
*Memorial to Caroline E. Veatch
and The History of the Veatch
Royalties of the New Shore
Unitarian Society, Plandome, NY,
A* (1983), 245
*Men of Mark: The Washburn
Brothers of Maine* (Webb 1985),
229
Mendelsohn, Jack, 184, 193, 218
Merger and Alternatives (1958),
175
Methodists, 21, 97, 142, 196
Miami, Florida, 197
Michigan Universalist
Convention, 103
Milford, Massachusetts, 42, 43
Miller, Diane, 205
Miller, Heather, 235
Miller, Russell E., 220, 238
Miller, William, 43
Mills College, 152
Miner, Alonzo Ames, 97, 98
Ministerial Fellowship
Committee, 202
Minneapolis, Minnesota, 101
Minnesota State Convention of
Universalists, 99
Mississippi Universalist State
Convention, 70
Modern History of Universalism
(Whittemore 1830), 39, 98
Montgomery, Alabama, 184

Montgomery, Kathleen (Kay), 199
Monthly Anthology, 22
Moral Majority, 195
Morales, Peter, 207, 208
Morgan, John C., 216
Morris, Carol R., 239, 240
Morrison-Reed, Mark D., 188,
  233, 242, 245, 247
Morse, Jedediah, 21, 22, 25, 26,
  27, 218
Morse, Samuel F. B., 218
*Most Famous Man in America:
  The Biography of Henry Ward
  Beecher, The*, 235
Mount Holyoke Female Seminary,
  75
Murray Grove, Lanoka Harbor,
  New Jersey, 215
Murray, John, xii, 3–13, 15, 16,
  33, 71, 80, 97, 98, 142, 214,
  216
Murray, Judith Sargent, 5, 6, 9,
  215, 216
Muslims, 7
*Mystery Hid from Ages and
  Generations, The* (Chauncey
  1784), 217

Naidu, Sarujini, 143
Napoleon III, 99
Nashoba, Tennessee, 36
Natchez, Mississippi, 6, 216
National Association for the
  Advancement of Colored
  People (NAACP), 126, 128,
  140, 234, 235
National Broadcasting Company
  (NBC), 144
National Civil Liberties Bureau,
  132

National Council of Churches,
  169, 245
National Council on Family
  Relations, 192
Native Americans, 62, 109
Nature (Emerson 1836), 54
Nazi Party, 155, 161
Needham, Massachusetts, 81, 83,
  85
Neibuhr, Reinhold, 143
*New Beacon Series in Religious
  Education, The* (curriculum),
  159, 160
New England General
  Convention of Universalists, 34
New England General
  Reform Association among
  Universalists, 40
New England Universalist
  Convention, 10
New Humanist, 135
New North Church (Boston), 26
New Orleans, Louisiana, 206
*New Views of Christianity, Society
  and the Church* (Brownson), 41
New York City, 4, 31, 49, 57, 62,
  74, 78, 128, 132, 135
New York Post, 89, 128
New York State Convention of
  Universalists, 244
New York State Universalist
  Convention (1858), 74
New York Tribune, 62, 71, 76
New York University, 191
New Yorker, 245
Newport, Rhode Island, 26, 27
Newton, Isaac, 17
Niagara Movement, 128
Niebuhr, Reinhold, 134, 155, 157
Nixon administration, 189

*No Silent Witness: The Eliot
    Parsonage Women and Their
    Unitarian World* (Tucker 2010),
    xii, 109, 225, 231, 232, 233,
    248
Noble, Laurie Carter, 225
*Norbert Fabian apek: A Spiritual
    Journey* (Henry 1999), 236
Norfolk, Virginia, 104, 105
Northern Pacific Railroad, 154
Norton, Andrews, 53, 55
*Not Without Dust and Heat: A
    Memoir* (Adams 1995), 240

Oberlin College, 198
Ocean View, Virginia, 105
Office of Gay Concerns, 192
Olmsted, Frederick Law, 89, 90
Olsen, Diane, 205
"On the Equality of the Sexes"
    (Murray 1790), 5
"On the Absurdity and Blasphemy
    of Depreciating Moral Virtue."
    (Briant), 25
Ontario Association of
    Universalists, 74
*Orestes A. Brownson: American
    Religious Weathervane* (Carey
    2004), 220
Origen of Alexandria, 98
"The Origins and First Stage of
    the Restorationist Controversy",
    219
Ossoli, Angelo, 62
Ossoli, Giovanni, 62
*Other Side of Salvation: Spiritualism
    and the Nineteenth-Century
    Religious Experience, The*
    (Buescher 2004), 223, 247
Otto, Rudolph, 155

*Our Chosen Faith: An Introduction
    to Unitarian Universalism*
    (Buehrens and Church 1989),
    201
Our Liberal Heritage (Cole 1951),
    216
Our Slavic Fellow Citizens (Balch
    1910), 130
Ovington, Mary White, 126, 127,
    128, 131, 235
*Owen D. Young and American
    Enterprise* (Case and Case
    1982), 237, 238, 239
*Owen D. Young: A New Type of
    Industrialist*, 238
Owen, Robert, 36, 37, 41
Owen-Towle, Carolyn, 201
Owen-Towle, Tom, 201, 246
Oxford, Massachusetts, xii, 8, 9,
    10, 33, 73, 142, 238

Pacific Unitarian School, 121
Paine, Thomas, 35, 69
Palmer , Elizabeth, 45
Palmer, Stephen, 81
Panoplist, 22
Papa, Stephan, 219
*Paradise of Reason: William Bentley
    and Enlightenment Christianity
    in the Early Republic, A* (Ruffin
    2007), 218
"Parallel Routes to Merger, 1937–
    1961", 244
Paris, France, 54
Parish Parables (Scott 1946), 168,
    242
Parke, David B., 176, 233, 237,
    241, 244
Parker, Theodore, xii, 37, 56, 58,
    59, 60, 68, 78, 83, 86, 87, 88,

91, 100, 116, 117, 221, 222,
223, 227, 235, 248
Parker, Sandra, 225
Parliament of the World's
Religions, 103, 107
Patton, Kenneth L., 173, 174,
243
Patton, Kenneth Leo, 243
*Paul Tillich's Philosophy of Culture,
Science, & Religion* (Adams),
157
Peabody Sisters, The (Marshall
2005), 221
Peabody, Elizabeth Palmer, xii,
45–48, 51, 53, 55–60, 62, 85,
220, 221, 227
Peabody, Francis Greenwood,
122, 234
Peabody, Mary, 47, 53, *See* Mann,
Mary Peabody
Peabody, Nathaniel, 45
Peabody, Sophia. *See* Hawthorne,
Sophia Peabody
*People's History of the United States,
A* (Zinn 2003), xi
Pennsylvania Universalist State
Convention, 244
Pentagon Papers, The (1971), 189,
190
Perin, George, 106, 107
Perkins School for the Blind, 221
Persian Zoroastrianism, 21
Philadelphia College of
Physicians, 8
Philadelphia, Pennsylvania, 8, 31,
104
Philanthropist, 41
*Philosophy of Electrical Psychology,
The* (1850 Dods), 68
Pickett, Helen Rice, 197
Pickett, O. Eugene, 193–198

Pierpont, John, 60, 78
Pigeon River, North Carolina, 143
Pittsburgh, Pennsylvania, 198
Plain Guide to Universalism, The
(Whittemore), 104
Planned Parenthood, 132
Planned Parenthood International,
246
Plymouth Brethren, 154
Polytechnic Institute, St. Louis,
Missouri, 110
Pope, the, 62, 133, 222
Porte, Joel, 227
Portland, Oregon, 111, 117, 121,
137
Post Office Mission, 113
Potter, Charles Francis, 4, 135
Potter, Thomas, 4, 6, 7, 215, 216
Potter, William J., 112
Powell, Hannah Adams, 230
Powell, Hannah Jewett, 143
*Practical Christianity: An Epitome
of Practical Christian Socialism*
(A. Ballou 1854), 43
Prague, Czechoslovakia, 132,
158, 161, 241
*Premise and the Promise: The Story
of the Unitarian Universalist
Association, The* (Ross 2001),
244, 245, 246, 248
Presbyterians, 17, 36, 154, 168,
170, 229
President's Commission
on Business Cycles and
Unemployment, 145
Priestley Memorial Chapel
(Northumberland,
Pennsylvania), 217
Priestley, Joseph, xi, 17–19, 21,
26–28, 36, 47, 217
Principia Mathematica, 133

Principles of Nature, Her Divine Revelations, and a Voice to Mankind, The (Davis 1847), 69
Prisoner's Friend, 70
Process and Reality (Whitehead 1929), 134
Prophetic Sisterhood: Liberal Women Ministers of the Frontier, 1880–1930 (Tucker 1990), 109, 120, 231, 233, 248
Pullman, George, 108
Pullman, Illinois, 108
Pullman, J.M., 107
Pullman, Tracy, 242
Puritans, 9

Quakers, 7, 21, 53, 131, 158, 231, 236
Queen Anne, 7
Quimada, Toribio, 171

Radcliffe College, 127, 130, 144
Radical Sects of Revolutionary New England (Marini 1982), 216, 219
Radical Spirits: Spiritualism and Women's Rights in 19th Century America (Braude 2001), 223
Radio Corporation of America (RCA), xii, 144, 145
Randall, Mercedes M., 234, 235
Rauschenbusch, Walter, 139
Reamon, Ellsworth, 170
Reason the Only Oracle of Man (Allen 1784), 11
"Recollections, 1944–1974: The Creation of the Unitarian Universalist Association and the Administrations of Dana Greeley and Robert West\ (Hopkins 2007)", 244

Record of a School, A (Peabody 1835), 53
Red Pawn: The Story of Noel Field (Lewis 1965), 241
Redman, John, 8
Reeb, James, 184, 244
Reed College, Portland, Oregon, 118, 228, 231
Reed, Amanda Wood, 231
Reese, Curtis W., 134, 137, 236
Reinhardt, Aurelia Henry, 152
Religion in the Making (Whitehead 1926), 134
Religions for Peace, 244, 245
Relly, John, 4, 6, 11
Remarkable Mrs. Ripley: The Life of Sarah Alden Bradford Ripley, The (Goodwin 1998), 222
Rescue & Flight: American Relief Workers Who Defied the Nazis (Subak 2010), 241
Restitution of All Things, The (Stonehouse 1761), 8
"Restoration Christianity", 220
Restorationism, 13, 36, 37, 43, 45, 47, 78, 125, 231, 232
Rhode Island Brigade (Continental Army), 4
Rhode Island Universalist State Convention, 244
Rice, William B., 174, 182, 183
Rich, Caleb, 9, 10, 11, 67
Richmond, Virginia, 68, 197
Riley, Meg, 204
Ripley, George, 37, 54
Ripley, Sarah Alden Bradford, 55, 222
Robinson, David, 215, 221, 222, 225, 228, 247
Rochester, New York, 69

Roger Baldwin and the American
    Civil Liberties Union (Cottrell
    2000), 234
Roger Baldwin: Founder of the
    American Civil Liberties Union
    (Lamson 1976), 234, 236
Roman Catholic Archdiocese of
    Pittsburgh, 245
Roman Catholics, 7, 21, 41, 98,
    133, 165, 184, 243
Roman Republic (1848), 62
Romania, 132, 200, 202
Rome, Italy, 62
Ronda, Bruce, 220
Roosevelt, Eleanor, 165
Roosevelt, Franklin Delano, 144
Roosevelt, Theodore, 120
Roots and Visions: The First
    Fifty Years of the Unitarian
    Universalist Service Committee,
    242
Ross, Warren R., 244, 245, 246,
    248
Roy, Ram Mohan, 233
Ruffin, J. Rixey, 218
Rush, Benjamin, 8, 216
Russell, Bertrand, 133, 134, 143
Ryder Divinity School, Tufts
    University, 238
Ryder Divinity School, University
    of Chicago, 142

Sacco and Vanzetti, 143
Safely Onward: The History of
    the Unitarian Church of All
    Souls, New York City, Volume 3:
    1882–1978 (Kring 1991), 240
Safford, Mary Augusta, 120
Saigon, Vietnam, 184
Salem, Massachusetts, 45, 218,
    221

Salt Lake City, Utah, 162
Salubria Community (Iowa), 37
San Antonio, Texas, 208
San Francisco, California, 187
SANE, 183
Sanger, Margaret, 132, 143
Sanitary Commission, 73, 79, 89,
    90
Santayana, George, xi, 215
Sargent, Winthrop (father of
    Judith Sargent Murray), 4
Sartor Resartus (Carlyle 1831),
    223
Sawyer, Thomas Jefferson, 224
Schenectady, New York, 145
Scholefield, Harry, 187
Schouler, Margaret, 107
Schulman, Frank, 221
Schulz, William F., 193, 198, 199,
    200, 201, 236
Schweitzer, Albert, 155
Scott, Clinton Lee, xiii, 143, 147,
    167, 168, 170, 172–174, 238,
    242, 243
Scott, Edith, 167
Scott, Harold, 168
Scott, Mary Slaughter, 168, 172,
    174
Scott, Rebecca, 243, 246
Seaburg, Alan, 230, 236, 237,
    244
Seasonable Thoughts on the State
    of Religion in New England
    (Chauncey 1743), 16
Seiden, Betty Bobo, 186
Self-Discovery: Group Explorations
    in Life Crises (1970 curriculum),
    191
Sellars, Roy Wood, 135
Selma, Alabama, 184
Seneca Falls, New York, 71

Senghas, Catherine, 235
Senghas, Dorothy, 235
Seventh Day Adventists, 43
Seward, William, 89
Seyavedra, Melinda, 233
Shakers, 10, 21
Sharp, Martha, 158
Sharp, Waitstill, 158
Shaw, Lemuel, 37
Shaw, Robert Gould, 73
Shinn, Quillen, 103, 104, 105, 106, 107, 108, 113, 147, 230
Siegvolk, Paul (George Klein-Nicolai), 7
"Signs of the Times", 220
Sims, Thomas, 71, 86
Singh, Hajom Kissor, 119, 226
Singing the Living Tradition (1993), 200, 226, 235
Sinkford, William G., 202, 205, 206, 207, 208
Skinner, Clara, 140
Skinner, Clarence R., 139–143, 170, 172, 214, 235, 237, 238
Skinner, George K., 98
Slavery (Channing 1835), 57
Smith, Bonnie Hurd, 216
Smith, Daniel, 44
Smith, Elias, 44
Smith, Matthew Hale, 43, 220
Smith, Rose Greenleaf Eliot, 232
Social Implications of Universalism, The (Skinner 1915), 140, 237, 238
Social Reform Club, 127
Society for Ethical Culture, 127
Socinus, Faustus, 18
Socrates, 18
Some Things Remembered: A Memoir (Scott 1976), 238, 242, 243

"Sophia Lyon Fahs: Liberal Religious Educator", 241
Sorbonne Institute, 130
Sorenson, Ted, 181
Soule, Caroline Augusta White, 103, 230
Souls of Black Folk, The (DuBois 1903), 127
South Carolina Sea Islands, 73
South Carolina Universalist State Convention, 70
Southbridge, Massachusetts, 144
Sparks, Jared, 28
Spear, Charles, 70, 224
Spellman, [Cardinal], 165
Spiritual Telegraph, 69
Spiritualism, 67, 69, 70, 97
Spock, Benjamin, 184
Spokane, Washington, 154
Sprecher, Paul, 235
Springfield, Illinois, 87, 128
Sreedhar, Kathy, 193
St. Gaudens, Augustus, 225
St. Lawrence College, 76
St. Lawrence University (including the Theological School), 99, 103, 108, 140, 144, 146, 169, 170, 176, 239
St. Louis, Missouri, 49, 72, 90, 109, 117, 131, 137, 232
Standing Before Us: Unitarian Universalist Women and Social Reform, 1776–1936 (Emerson 1999), 247
Standing Order, 9, 13, 22, 24, 39, 218
Stanford University, 118
Stanton, Elizabeth Cady, 85
Starr King School for the Ministry, 121, 194, 208, 243
Starr, Deane, 187

Stebbins, Horatio, 91
Steinmetz, Charles, 145
Stevens, John, 5
Stevens, Judith Sargent, 5, *See* Murray, Judith Sargent
Stiles, Ezra, 27
Stone, Alice Balch, 234
Stone, Lucy, 87, 117, 225
Stonehouse, George, 8
"Story of US Immigration: Ellis Island, The", 235
Stream of Light: A Short History of American Unitarianism, A (Wright 1989), 233, 239, 248
Streeter, Adam, 10
Streeter, Stephen, 10
Subak, Susan Elisabeth, 241
"Succession of Short Term Ministries, A", 223
Suffolk, Virginia, 105, 142
Sufi Islam, 21
Sullivan, William Lawrence, 133, 135, 236
Summer on the [Great] Lakes (Fuller 1843), 62
Sunday School Society, 160
Sunderland, Jabez, 114, 116, 119, 232, 233
Sunley, Robert, 245
"Suspense of Faith, The" (Bellows 1859), 88, 227, 228
Sutherland, Malcolm, 182
Sutro, Ruth, 223
Swedenborg, Emmanuel, 217
Syracuse, New York, 170, 175, 176

Taft, William Howard, 131, 132
Tarbell, Ida, 238
Tauscher, Cathy, 232

Temple School (Boston), 53
Ten Great Religions (Clarke 1871, 1883), 115
Tennessee Valley UU Church (Knoxville, Tennessee), 246
"Things Commonly Believed Today Among Us" (Gannett 1886), 114
This Day in Unitarian Universalist History (Schulman 2004), 221
Thoreau, Henry David, 61, 62, 85, 87, 227
Three Prophets of Religious Liberalism: Channing, Emerson, Parker (Wright 1994), 221, 222, 248
Tillich, Paul, 157
Time magazine, 144
Today's Children and Yesterday's Heritage: A Philosophy of Creative Religious Development (Fahs 1952), 160
Tolstoy, Leo, 42
Transcendental Wild Oats (Alcott 1873), 60, 223
Transforming Liberalism: The Theology of James Luther Adams, 240
"Transient and the Permanent in Christianity, The" (Parker 1841), 56, 100, 221
Transylvania, 132, 200, 215
Trask, Jabez Nelson, 118
Treatise on Atonement (Ballou 1805), 11, 223
Trials of Anthony Burns: Freedom and Slavery in Emerson's Boston, The (von Frank 1998), 227
Trumpet and Universalist Magazine, 39, 74

Index

Truth, Sojourner, 72, 87, 224
Tucker, Cynthia Grant, xii, 109, 120, 213, 225, 231, 232, 248
Tuckerman, Joseph, 41, 49, 50, 52, 118, 221
Tufts University, 70, 97, 107, 141, 167, 172
Tufts, Charles, 70
Tulsa, Oklahoma, 197
Turner, Edward, 33, 34, 219
Turner, Lucy Davis, 33
Tyler, Charles H., 145

Ulbrich, Holley, 248
Ultra-Universalism, 36, 37, 43, 45, 78
Una, 84
"Uncollected Prose", 220
Under Orders (Sullivan 1944), 236
UNICEF, 233
Union Army (Civil War), 73, 79, 89, 90
Union: or a treatise of consanguinity and affinity between Christ and his church (Relly 1759), 4
Unitarian Advance, 160, 161, 175
"Unitarian Christianity" (Channing 1819), 28, 47
Unitarian Controversy: Essays in American Unitarian History, The (Wright 1994), 217
Unitarian Fellowship Movement, 162
Unitarian General Conference, Montreal (1917), 131
Unitarian Laymen's League, 133, 162, 190, 246
Unitarian Register, 183

Unitarian Service Committee, 158, 160
Unitarian Universalist Church of the Philippines, 202
Unitarian Universalist Commission on Religion and Race, 185
Unitarian Universalist Historical Society, 215
Unitarian Universalist Holdeen India Program (UUHP), 193
Unitarian Universalist Ministers Association (UUMA), 201, 246
Unitarian Universalist Service Committee (UUSC), 184, 193, 201, 206, 230
Unitarian Universalist Urban Ministry, Boston, Massachusetts, 50
Unitarian Universalist Women's Federation (UUWF), 190, 191, 199
Unitarian, 114
Unitarianism and Universalism (Cheatham 1961), 216
Unitarianism in America (Cooke 1902), 232
"Unitarianism in India" (Seyavedra and Walker), 233
Unitarianism in the Antebellum South: The Other Invisible Culture (Macaulay 2001), 223
Unitarians and India: A Study in Encounter and Response (Lavan 1977), 227
Unitarians and the Universalists, The (Robinson 1985), 215, 225, 228, 247
"Unitarians and the Utes, The" (Fetter 2010), 233

Unitarians Face a New Age (1936), 152, 240
Unitarians in Canada (Hewett 1978), 230
United Church of Christ, 209, 220
United Nations, 171
Unity magazine, 114, 134
Universal Baptists, 8, 9
Universalism Examined, Renounced, Exposed (Smith 1842), 43, 220
Universalist "Summer Meetings", 103
Universalist Church of America (UCA), xi, 169, 170, 171, 172, 173, 175, 209
Universalist Church of the Philippines, 171
Universalist Commission on Social Service, 139
Universalist Convention, Gloucester, Massachusetts, 10, 80, 97, 99, 100, 102, 103, 142
Universalist Convention, Murray Grove, New Jersey, 142
Universalist Convention, Oxford, Massachusetts, 8, 10
Universalist Convention, Philadelphia, 10
Universalist Convention, Winchester, New Hampshire, 11
Universalist General Convention, 68, 71, 80, 97, 99, 100, 102, 104, 105, 107, 108, 139, 141, 142, 147
Universalist General Reform Association, 70
Universalist Leader, 140, 170, 171, 183

Universalist Magazine, 40, 42
Universalist National Women's Missionary Association, 230
Universalist Service Committee, 171, 242
Universalist Sunday School Association, 168
Universalist Trumpet, 219
Universalists (Dayton, Ohio), 168
Universalists (Gloucester, Massachusetts), 4
Universalists (Oxford, Massachusetts), 5, 9
Universalists (Pigeon River Valley, North Carolina), 105
University of California, Berkeley, 118
University of Chicago, 130, 134, 135, 155, 157
Urban Church Coalition, 202
US Children's Bureau, 232
US Office of Strategic Services, 158
Ute Tribe, Colorado, 118, 119
UU World, 189, 246
UUA Now, 183, 189
UUA Office of International Resources, 246
UUA President's Council, 202, 203, 204

Van Hornesville, New York, 146
Veatch Program, 190, 195, 197, 201, 241
Veatch, Caroline E., 190
Versailles, 130
Vichy, France, 158
Vicksburg, Mississippi, 101
Viney, Wayne, 221
Voelker, David, 220

Voices of the New Feminism
(MacDonald 1970), 191
von Frank, Albert J., 227

Walden; or, Life in the Woods
(Thoreau 1854), 61
Walker, Marilyn, 233
Waltham, Massachusetts, 71
"War and the Thought of God"
(Fenn 1918), 133, 236
Ware, Henry, 22
Ware, Henry Jr., 54
Washburn family, xii, 100
Washburn, Algernon, 100
Washburn, Cadwallader, 101
Washburn, Charles, 101
Washburn, Elihu, 101
Washburn, Israel, 80, 98, 100,
229
Washburn, Samuel, 101
Washburn, William, 101
Washburne, Elihu, 229
Washington DC, 68, 73, 81, 82,
89, 170, 197, 205
Washington University, St. Louis,
Missouri, 110, 118, 131, 228,
232
Washington, Booker T., 105
Washington, George, 6
Washington, Valora, 206
Wausau, Wisconsin, 172
"Wave at Crest, A" (Parke), 233,
235, 236, 237
"We Are That Faith!" (Harrington
1960), 244
*We Started with the Children: From
Church School to North Shore
Unitarian Society, the Early Years,
1941–1955* (Sunley and Martin
1995), 245

*We Would Be One: A History of
Unitarian Universalist Youth
Movements* (Arnason and Scott
2005), 243, 246
Weary, Gerald F., 190, 245
Webb, Theodore A., 229
Webster, Daniel, 68, 85, 227
Wedin, Carolyn, 234
*Week on the Concord and Merrimac
Rivers, A* (Thoreau 1849), 61
Wellesley College, 130
Wellesley Hills, Massachusetts,
136
Wesley, Alice Blair, 237, 240
West Roxbury, Massachusetts, 60
West, Robert Nelson, 187, 189,
190, 192, 193, 198, 244, 245,
246
West, Samuel, 81
Western Messenger, 58
Western Sanitary Commission,
90, 110
Western Unitarian Conference
(WUC), 110, 112, 113, 114,
120, 134, 232
Weston, John, 220
Westwood, Horace, 133
*What Love Jesus Christ Has for
Sinners* (Davis), 9
White, Ellen, 43
Whitehead, Alfred North, 133,
134
Whittemore, Thomas, xii, 38–40,
42, 74, 98, 104, 219
Wieman, Henry Nelson, 134
Wilbur, Earl Morse, 121
Wilder, Frances Ann Eliot, 237
Williams, Fannie Barrier, 119, 233
Williams, George Huntston, 185,
226, 228, 229, 248

Willis, Annie B., 230
Wills, Garry, 227
Wilson, Edwin H., 162
Wilson, Woodrow, 130, 131, 145
Winchester, Elhanan, 8, 9, 10, 11, 33, 34, 42
Winchester, New Hampshire, 11
Wise, Stephen, 143
Wise, Thomas E., 105, 230
Wolfe, Tom, 189, 245
Woman in the Nineteenth Century (Fuller 1845), 62
Woman's Journal, 117
Woman's Ministerial Conference, 117
Women and Religion, 197
Women's Alliance, 151, 197
Women's Centenary Aid Association, 97
Women's Centenary Association (WCA), 102
Women's International League for Peace and Freedom, 126, 130
Women's National Missionary Association, 142
Women's Rights Convention, 71, 84
Wood, Gordon S., 12, 216
Work and Dreams and the Wide Horizon (Cornish 1937), 236
Workingmen's Party, 41
World Federation of Democratic Youth, 161
World Health Organization, 233
World Wildlife Fund, 246
World's Parliament of Religions, Chicago (1893), 119
Worshipping Together with Questioning Minds (Fahs 1965), 160

Wright, Conrad, 216, 221, 244, 248
Wright, Fanny, 37, 41
Wright, Frank Lloyd, 173
Wright, John, 245

Yale University, 22, 23, 27, 152, 165, 184
Yarbro, Karen, 242
Young People's Christian Union, 105
Young Religious Unitarian Universalists (YRUU), 197
Young, Owen D., xii, 144, 145, 146, 239

Zelig (fictional character), 19
Zinn, Howard, xi